Vaseline Glassware

Fascinating Fluorescent Beauty

Barrie W. Skelcher

4880 Lower Valley Road Atglen, Pennsylvania 19310

Acknowledgments

It must be at least two decades since I set out to research the use of uranium in the glass industry. During that time many people have assisted me. Some have advised on glass production, some have assisted me with dating and attribution, some have allowed me to visit their factories or view their records, some have shared their expertise, and some have just talked glass. It is difficult to recall all the names and I fear if I mention some I will leave out others. I will therefore say to them all a *very big thank you.*

Included in the foregoing, but for whom I would add a special mention, are the late Cyril Manley, the late Stan Eveson, Roger Dodsworth, Eric Reynolds and John Westmoreland.

I would like to acknowledge the help in both my research and proofreading of this book, from my daughter Angela. Finally say the biggest thank you all to my wife Shirley who has helped gather our collection, put up with my wanton spending, allowed a large area of our home to be sterilized with large quantities of glass and also helped in the proofreading of this book.

Other Schiffer Books by Barrie Skelcher:
The Big Book of Vaseline Glass

Library of Congress Control Number: 20079310480

Covers and book designed by: Bruce Waters
Type set in Snell Roundhand heading font/text font Korinna
ISBN: 978-0-7643-2699-8
Printed in China

Published by Schiffer Publishing Ltd.
4880 Lower Valley Road
Atglen, PA 19310
Phone: (610) 593-1777; Fax: (610) 593-2002
E-mail: Info@schifferbooks.com

In Europe, Schiffer books are distributed by
Bushwood Books
6 Marksbury Ave.
Kew Gardens
Surrey TW9 4JF England
Phone: 44 (0) 20 8392-8585; Fax: 44 (0) 20 8392-9876
E-mail: info@bushwoodbooks.co.uk
Website: www.bushwoodbooks.co.uk
Free postage in the U.K., Europe; air mail at cost.

Contents

Preface

Five years have passed since I started to prepare the draft for *The Big Book of Vaseline Glass* (*BBVG*). During that time my research has continued. I have collected and examined many more specimens. This book takes up the story where I left off in *BBVG* and reports my latest findings. Within this text there are some three hundred and fifty items, not already covered in *BBVG*, which have been photographed and assessed. I have also compounded data from items in *BBVG* with the items shown here in order to get better statistics in such matters as density and uranium concentration.

When I started my research few people, including glass collectors, realized that the attractive yellow green glass was colored with uranium and was radioactive. I set out to investigate just how widespread was the use of uranium, the period over which it was used and the concentration in the glass. To this end, I have examined something like two thousand different pieces of glass, about three quarters of which had uranium in their melt.

Most collectors specialize in either the product of a particular factory, such as Thomas Webb & Sons, or a particular type of product such as paperweights. This makes for easier attribution and dating. However in this study it was necessary to cover a wide field of both glasshouse and dates, which makes research that more difficult. To this end I have had to develop practices to minimize the risk that I would get these factors wrong and in the following chapters I will describe the criteria I have used. In a number of the books about glass that I have read, I have come across errors in attribution and dating, and I anticipate that this book may not be any exception. I have therefore used a probabilistic approach, which accepts there will be a margin of errors. It is my regret that some authors, when quoting dates and maker do not give the basis for their conclusions and the reader is left to wonder just how it is known that a particular item came from a particular factory. In the chapters where I make attributions, I will explain my reasoning and put a probability on my being correct.

As part of my research, and to help with attribution, I have made extensive use of glass densities and expanded upon the data that I published in *BBVG*. Density is by no means a fingerprint of a particular glasshouse but, as you follow the item-by-item description, you will see it is on occasion a critical measurement.

In order that this book can be read and appreciated on its own, I have, where necessary, summarized some of the information given in *BBVG*. However, the reader is advised that this publication does not replace that book and it is advantageous to have *BBVG* available in conjunction with this publication. I have used a similar layout and conventions but there is some change in chapter numbering.

Giving an opinion on the market value of the items illustrated is fraught with uncertainty. With regard to *BBVG*, some collectors have thought the values I quoted were significantly low, on the other hand one critic thought some absurdly high, supporting his view by claiming some items could be bought from Car Boot Sales for a few pence. This may well be the case, but I do not think Car Boot prices set values. The yardstick I have tried to use, both here and in *BBVG*, is that at which a willing buyer and a willing seller, both of whom know their glass, would settle. The values quoted are only my opinion, usually based upon what I paid, would have been prepared to pay, or what I have seen similar items sold for elsewhere. Notwithstanding this, I make the same reservation as I did on page 10 in *BBVG*, that the values quoted should not be taken as a fair price guide and I do not accept any liability for what may result if any reader uses them as such.

The values quoted are for items in good condition and free from damage, other than what might be expected as fair wear and tear. For many collectors condition is crucial and even a small chip, let alone a crack or a repair, will greatly reduce the amount they are prepared to pay. Personally I am not too bothered about condition, so long as it remains an accurate indication of what was originally made.

I do not claim to be an expert on glass, its chemistry, aesthetic value, or even how it was made. My interest is in the use of uranium and in that aspect I probably do have more knowledge than most. However, as part of my research I have gained an amount of general knowledge of the subject and this I happily pass on in the following pages.

The thing that has surprised me is the vast extent to which uranium has been used in glass and how readily available such items are to the present day collector. My strong advice to anyone now starting to collect is to specialise in either a subject, perhaps candlesticks, wines or plates or in a glasshouse such as Webb, Walsh or Richardson. Perhaps the big advantage of uranium glass is that an interesting collection can be put together at very reasonable cost.

Throughout the script I have used some terms which I understand are common to the glass industry, but maybe a little confusing to new readers. I list them below.

bud – where the top of the glass bowl is cut with a scissor like tool it leaves a thickening of the glass.

cameo - where the decoration is formed by cutting away the surrounding glass

cased – when glass is layered, usually by taking gathers of different glass in succession.

crizzling - glass deteriorating with minute internal cracks, or developing a moist, sticky film on the surface when in contact with air.

cullet - broken recycled glass.

flashed - a very thin layer of surface glass, perhaps no thicker than a sheet of writing paper, usually on the outside.

frigger's piece -_An item made by a glass worker, in his own time during a break period or after his shift, for his own amusement.

gather – molten glass (sorry, metal) on the end of a blow tube.

glory hole – a hole giving access to the heat of the furnace for re-heating a piece that is being worked.

intaglio - where the decoration is cut deep into the surface of the glass.

marver - A flat slab of iron on which glass on the end of a blow pipe is shaped usually by being rolled.

metal – The term used to describe the glass melt with which the glass blower works. It does not mean metal in the sense of iron, copper or uranium.

pontil, punty – an iron rod, which is attached to part of an incomplete item, to enable the worker to continue to shape the rest of it. Typically this takes place on the underside of the foot of a wine glass or the base of a vase. When it is no longer required, it is snapped of at the iron glass join. This leaves a rough spot, which may or may not be polished out. Hence the term "pontil mark."

pucelas – long, tweezers-like tool for working hot glass.

Section 1: Background

Chapter 1

Uranium, Vaseline and Glass

Uranium has been used to color glass for the past two hundred years. In some cases, but by no means all, it can give the "metal," confusingly the technical term used in the glass industry for the glass itself in its un-worked form, a distinctive oily appearance.

Vaseline, as we all know, is the name of a propriety brand of petroleum jelly sold at most chemist shops. It has an oily, greenish yellow appearance when viewed in its container, usually a shallow tin or small jar. Some glass colors, especially those that have been obtained with the use of uranium, have a similar appearance to this greenish yellow color and therefore, over the years, became colloquially known as "Vaseline" glass. I have not found any evidence that this title or description was bestowed by any glasshouse on any of their products.

In recent years, with the increasing popularity of this color amongst collectors, the original meaning of "Vaseline glass" has been grossly distorted, in a number of cases well beyond any reasonable stretch of the imagination. So much so, that I wonder how many years it will be before the origin of the term is lost. Leading the corruption of this description are a number of internet vendors, who seem to think that by using the word Vaseline to describe an item, it will increase its sale potential. I have even seen the terms "pink Vaseline" and "blue Vaseline."

Perhaps because uranium was responsible for the oily, petroleum like appearance of some glass items, some dealers appear to consider that anything with uranium must be "Vaseline," irrespective of its color. Thus occasionally opaque ivory, dark amber, opaque blue, and so on will get the Vaseline tag. Not to be outdone, others will describe anything that is slightly opaque or has a milky appearance as "Vaseline" even if it has no uranium in the mix.

In my view, NONE OF THIS IS CORRECT and only glass which has that oily, greenish yellow translucent color should be called Vaseline and that almost inevitably means it should contain uranium. My preferred term for my collection and research is "uranium glass," because that is definitive. It is only to take account of the views of others who use the term in a wider sense that "vaseline" is used in the title. It is important to recognize, as the contents of this book illustrates, that uranium finds an application in many other colors and shades that do not have that oily, greenish yellow look, but which are equally or even more attractive.

Uranium glass should not be considered as a thing of the past. With the modern vogue for increasing concern over safety and of exposure to radiation, which in some examples is more of a phobia than a rationale, the use of uranium in glass coloring has greatly decreased. As will be seen in the following text, there are still a few glasshouses currently using uranium in their mixes.

Uranium was used, not only to color glass, but also on ceramics and I have included three examples in the concluding pages of this book. One unusual application, which we can reasonably claim to be associated with the glass/ceramics industry, I found when browsing through some old notes that I had previously overlooked.

Amongst the pattern books which were in the Royal Brierley museum before it closed down, was a diary, with the name, not easily read, of John Scrivers and a date of 1843. Amongst the pages was a loose, undated cutting from *Pottery and Glass Trades Gazette*. It explains that "According to the *Moniteur de la Ceramique et de la Verrerie*, uranium was being used in a patented process, together with gold, for the gilding of pottery and glass. It says, "...the method is evidently simple and appears to differ from the ordinary process of making gold paint by the use of uranium oxide..." Why the addition of uranium oxide should improve gold paint is beyond my chemical knowledge, but from now on I will monitor any gold-painted object that I suspect may have come from France, to see if I can find any indication of uranium.

It was not only in gilding that uranium seems to have found a niche, as the June 1885 edition of *Pottery Gazette and Glass Trades Review* reports that a chemist in Bordeaux dissolved metallic salts in water and precipitated colored solids with ammonia. These fine deposits were then washed out and applied with fatty or resinous oil to glass or ceramic ware. Interestingly, in the case of uranium, the actual amounts are quoted.

> "Yellow color, one ounce of nitrate oxide of uranium, [presumably uranyl nitrate with the formula $U0_2(NO_3)_2\,6H_20$, is dissolved in a good deal of water and the precipitation is effected with ammonia. The whole is then filtered to remove the fluid. The coloring powdered is then added under continuous stirring, to the resinous mass of 3 ounces, heated with a sand bath and 7 ounces of lavender oil are then added. Red, Nankin, and Brown-Yellow are obtained by mixing nitrate oxide of uranium with nitrate oxide of iron in different proportions"

Chapter 2

Uranium, Radioactivity, and Radiation Risks

Uranium, in the form of its oxide, was discovered by the German chemist Heinrich Klaproth. He reported his findings to the Royal Prussian Academy of Science in 1789. He had separated the black U_3O_8 oxide from pitchblende. We cannot be sure just when it was first used to color glass. Credit for this is often given to Josef Reidel, who produced in the early 1830s, Annagrun and Annagelb, green and yellow uranium glass, named after his wife. However, there is evidence that uranium was used in glass prior to, and around the same date, elsewhere. A detailed appraisal of when and by whom uranium was first used is given in *BBVG*. I will summarize below.

The earliest claim goes back to Roman times. In 1912, R T Gunther reported on a mosaic he had found while excavating a Roman villa near Naples, which he dated to about 79 AD. Subsequent analysis at Oxford University appears to have identified the presence of uranium, but there are serious doubts about the validity of these findings. Perhaps the main doubt is cast by the absence of any subsequent corroborative evidence. It would be extremely surprising, if uranium really was used by the Romans, that it should turn up in only one sample, despite the large amount of sophisticated archaeological work carried out in the intervening years.

There is a report of a cut glass beaker colored with uranium, which has the date 1825 cut into it. There is evidence of early British involvement, a suggestion that Cornish uranium was used to as early as 1817 to color glass. British scientists such as Thomas Cock, Michael Faraday and William Vernon Harcourt were involved in uranium/glass research early in the 1800s. We know that in 1835 experiments were carried out at Whitefriars Glass Works to produce a topaz uranium color and from the firm's stock books that candlesticks were being made in this metal.

What seems most likely is that, following Klaproth's published discovery, the use of this new material to color glass was developed independently in several places and that it started to come into more widespread use by about 1840. In the absence of strong evidence to the contrary, I would be reluctant to date any uranium bearing glass before that era.

It would seem that the coloring of glass with uranium gained popularity in the ensuing years and probably reached a peak about the turn of the 19th century. Its use continued in the pre-WW2 days, to produce amber and green as well as the yellow/topaz. It is interesting to look at the formulae in use by Webb. Although these are shown on page 119 of *BBVG*, they are relevant to this work and I have included them later in the text. During the latter part of the 19th century it was used in 19 of their mixes, for crysoprase, lemon, ivory, carmine, various greens, topaz, Burmese, and amber. By contrast, by the 1930s only three mixes, namely amber, Bristol green and *eau de nil*, contained uranium.

Some authors have mentioned that the use of uranium ceased after WW2. This is definitely not the case. However its use in the UK is now probably extinct, thanks to constraints applied on its use in the name of Health and Safety. It is still used in the USA and some other parts of the world. An employee of Fenton Art Glass recently assured me that not only is it still in use, but also described the handling techniques. He explained the uranium comes in sealed bags, which are added to the mix unopened. Only a few named employees are allowed to handle these bags, they wear radiation-monitoring film and the work areas are surveyed for radioactivity. To me this seems an awful lot of fuss, after all nature was fairly liberal with her distribution of the element! By comparison in the 1930s, at Thomas Webb, the uranium was supplied in a large bag, kept in the storeroom with other materials and then scooped out and weighed before being charged into the retort[1].

I had always thought of uranium as being used to color glass products such as vases, plates, dishes and wines. However I recently came across a report that indicates it was and maybe still is, used to produce glass-based enamel.[2] It refers to the use of uranium in glass enamels and on ceramics. In the case of glass enamel, it would seem the uranium content is 0.5 - 1% wt. for the color amber. In some ceramics, such as tableware and tiles, uranium oxide (U_3O_8) or Sodium Urinate (Na_2U0_2) is added to the glazes. This produces a "range of colors from Chocolate brown and red through orange and yellow to blue." These glazes may contain up to 14% uranium by wt. Examples of orange and a brown glaze can be seen in Photos 415 to 417).

Throughout this book, I will quote the individual levels of uranium found in the many examples that I have examined. In some cases, I have attempted to group these and draw conclusions. However, generally they vary from a fraction of a percent to 3% in the dark amber. Nevertheless, it appears there are existing examples of glass with a 7% uranium content.[3] I have neither seen nor had the opportunity to examine them.

Glass, in terms of chemistry, may be regarded as a solid solution. That is to say, it behaves something like water would in dissolving other substances. In this way, colors are spread evenly throughout the material. Just as a crystal of permanganate of potash will dissolve and, with a little agitation, give an even mauve color to water, so agents in molten glass will dissolve and spread through the melt. Again, just as with aqueous media, the color that an element may depart will depend upon its chemical oxidation or valency state and the acidity of the solvent. For example, iron in its ferrous state will give a green solution, but in its ferric state, a brown color. A similar situation applies to glass and this is why uranium can give rise to green or yellow. Uranium is one of the "transition" elements and can have several different valancy states.

When added to the melt it is not in the form of uranium metal but one of the uranium compounds. In the early 1800s, as uranium was coming into use in the glass industry, the science of Chemistry as we know it today was in its infancy and this makes for considerable confusion when trying to interpret old formulae. As far as my studies are concerned this occurs with two critical elements, namely lead and uranium. Lead is a major component of "crystal" glass and in the case of best English Crystal, can be in excess of 33% of the total weight of the melt. Sometimes in old recorded recipes, the term "lead" is used, other times "red lead" or even "lead or litharge." The problem, in trying to estimate the density of such mixes, is to know what lead compound was actually used. Litharge(PbO) contains about 93% lead(Pb)."Red Lead"(Pb_3O_4), the commercial variety of which may contain up to 35% PbO_2, could have as little as 90% Pb by wt.

In the same manner, uranium is sometimes described as "uranium" or "uranium oxide" but to which oxide does it refer? In pitchblende U_3O_8 predominates, in becquerelite UO_3 occurs with two molecules of water(H_2O). "Uranium yellow", which is a stage in the processing of pitchblende, is sodium diuranate and has the formula $Na_2U_2O_7,6H_2O$. The percentages of uranium in these varies between 85% and 64% by wt. In the early years, it is probable that the uranium oxide was in the form of U_3O_8 but this was replaced by the diuranate. In post-WW2 years, "depleted uranium" has become readily available as a by- product of the nuclear industry and this is usually sold in the form of UO_2(see *BBVG.*)

It is not uncommon to find uranium glass which does not fit exactly into the yellow or green category, but may be turquoise, blue, ivory or dark amber. This corruption of the pure uranium color is due to the presence of other coloring agents, which act in much the same way as mixing colors on a painter's palette. Of special interest is the presence of arsenic or gold. Both change color when reheated. An article dosed with arsenic in its mix will turn milky white, while one dosed with gold will turn rose red. The technique is such that once the article has been formed and while it is still hot, to re-present it at a glory hole until there is a color change in the part of the article that receives the re-heat. We will see many examples of this technique in the form of Davidson's Pearline and Webb's Burmese.

Before I discuss the properties of, and possible hazards from, the radioactivity of uranium, it is necessary to explain, for those readers who are not familiar with the basic physics, the nature of radioactivity.

A more detailed explanation is given in Chapter 2 of *BBVG*. The type of radiation that we are concerned with here originates from the atom. For the purposes of this book there are only four types that concern us, namely neutron, alpha, beta and gamma.

The neutron is only of passing interest. It is a particle without any electrical charge, but, in nuclear terms, has a substantial mass. Because it has no charge it will easily pass through matter. Its interest to us here is that when, on infrequent occasions, it strikes a uranium atom, it can cause it to split and in doing so liberate a large amount of energy as well as the uranium fragments that are atoms of different elements. These fragments leave tracks, which can be counted and ultimately provides a method of dating glass, which contains uranium (see p16 & 18 *BBVG.*)

Alpha, beta and gamma particles/rays originate when an atom with an energy unstable nucleus, rearranges its structure to become stable. In so doing it will emit one or more of these types of radiation.

The alpha particle is, de facto, a helium nucleus, consisting of two protons and two neutrons. It is heavy and carries two positive charges of electricity. As a result it does a lot of damage local to its strike point. It is easily stopped. A sheet of writing paper will be sufficient to provide a shield from alpha particles. The beta particle is an electron traveling at high speed. It is a small particle with very little mass and a single negative charge of electricity. Its damage is spread over a much longer path than is the case with an alpha particle and is therefore less intense, but requires more shielding. It will pass through paper and may travel up to half a meter in air. Gamma rays are not really particles, but little "packets" of energy in wave form. They are much more penetrating and will usually require several inches of lead to stop them. Their damage is even less intense but spread over a longer track. Uranium spontaneously emits alpha and beta particles and gamma rays. When alpha or beta particles are emitted, the chemical nature of the element changes. For a fuller description the reader is referred to *BBVG* p17-18. Beta rays can be used to estimate the amount of uranium present and gamma rays to identify the radioisotope causing the radiation.

Uranium is not the only naturally occurring element that is radioactive. There are many but as far as glass is concerned, there are two others, which are significant. Potassium has a very small quantity of isotope K40. This is a beta & gamma ray emitter. As some glasses contain large amounts of potassium, this has to be born in mind when very low levels of radioactivity are detected. As I shall describe later, the level of radioactivity in natural potassium is sufficient to calibrate a beta Geiger counter. It always amuses me to see the "health shops" that sell "low sodium salt". What they are offering is potassium chloride instead of sodium chloride. They do not mention the inactive sodium has been replaced with radioactive potassium.

The other radioactive element is thorium. In many ways it is like uranium, except that it does not color glass. It decays, like uranium, in a complex series, where the product of one decay is also radioactive and so is the next. Like uranium, thorium is also a fairly widely distributed element and can occur naturally with some sands. There are even holiday beaches in some parts of the world, which are radioactive due to this element, but no one seems to worry about them. In fact, thorium, often used as a ceramic on gas mantles is so radioactive it would have to be treated as "nuclear waste" if it were on a nuclear power station. Because thorium can be present in some sands, it very occasionally contaminates glass and the collector, wielding his Geiger counter, needs to be aware of this rare possibility (see p 146 *BBVG*.)

So how dangerous is the radiation from uranium glass? A question that I am frequently asked, which I have tried to answer in *BBVG* and which I will again discuss, albeit in an abbreviated form.

Scientists are not agreed on the nature of dangers from nuclear or, to be more precise, ionizing radiation, at low doses and low dose rates. When radiation strikes a living cell, it may kill the cell. (This is why it can be used to treat cancer, as cancer cells are more sensitive to radiation.) In this case, unless very high doses are involved and large numbers of healthy cells are destroyed, there will be no noticeable effect. On the other hand, the radiation may just damage the DNA in the cell. If this happens, the cell may repair the damage, in which case there will be no noticeable effect or it may corrupt the cell, i.e. cause it to mutate. It may then become cancerous, grow and spread to the rest of the body. (As another aside, I will mention that sunlight carries with it a level of ultraviolet radiation. This is a form of ionizing radiation, something like x-rays but much less penetrating (see *BBVG*.) It is the cause of sunburn and skin cancer. The former occurs when skin cells are killed by the radiation, the latter when DNA is damaged.)

The odd thing is that when the DNA is damaged and permanently corrupted, it seems that it does not immediately start growing as a cancer. There is usually a delay of years between radiation exposure and the cancer becoming detectable. The reason for this is not clear but it may well mean that a second insult on a corrupted cell is necessary to trigger the cancer formation. It might be a second strike with radiation or some other agent.

The "official" scientific opinion is that all radiation is potentially harmful and it will cause some DNA damage, although at low doses the risk of an eventual cancer is extremely small. However there is a minority view, that very small doses at low dose rates such as near natural levels could have a stimulating effect on the repair mechanism and lead to less cancer from all causes. It is a sort of homoeopathic effect. These different views are not easily resolved by epidemiological surveys. This is because the cancer risks at these very low doses are so small they cannot easily be distinguished from background cancers.

For example, some studies have shown that people living in areas of high natural radiation levels have a lower cancer risk than average. However this could be because of other factors, such as a cleaner atmosphere. The journal "Nuclear Issues"[4] December 2004, draws attention to a report presented to an international conference on the effects of radiation in Nagasaki. It is reported that in the Indian state of Kerala, an area of high natural radiation, the life expectancy is 74 years compared with 54 years for the whole of India. It also mentions studies of the mortality rates of airline pilots, undertaken after their Union sought compensation for the additional exposure they suffer from cosmic radiation. It showed that mortality rates decreased with increasing radiation dose. As I am drafting this script, a study has just been published in the *British Medical Journal*[5]. This appears to show that there is a correlation between cancer and radiation exposure, even at very low levels. This report is discussed in the Journal of Radiological Protection[6]. The problem with studies of this kind is that the incidence of cancer from other causes is so high that a very large sample population is needed to obtain reliable results. Even then, corrections and assumptions have to be made, such as the effect of smoking, the social status of those in the study group, age distribution and so on. If nothing else, consideration of this report puts the risk in perspective. If there is a risk, it is so low that it is extremely difficult to detect, even when studying the fate of 600,000 radiation workers.

So where does this leave us with respect to collecting uranium glass? There are three risk areas to consider. First is the alpha radiation. As this has very little penetrating power, it is largely absorbed in the glass and the hazard in handling the glass from this type of radiation is virtually nil. However, one of the decay products is a gas called radon and this is also radioactive. It is radon gas, which is thought to account for the higher lung cancer rates observed in early uranium miners. So, could a collection of uranium glass produce a radon hazard? I have not made any measurements but have discussed the matter with other health physicists and our opinion is the same. The radon gas would largely be trapped in the glass and as it only has a short half life it will decay before any quantity could build up. The other possible route for alpha radiation to affect the body is by ingestion. That is, if it is inhaled or swallowed. We can forget the possibility of inhaling uranium glass, however there is a slight risk from ingestion. We generally consider glass is insoluble in water. In fact, small amounts of glass can dissolve in water, which is why we sometimes see water staining. If the glass has been made with lead or colored with uranium, trace amounts of these will also dissolve into the water. This effect has been investigated (as I reported in *BBVG*) and any such leaching is thought to carry a negligible health risk.

Now what about the beta radiation. As the ingestion risk from alpha radiation is negligible, then it is even lower from beta radiation. However, there could be a risk to the skin from handling or wearing uranium glass items. As discussed in *BBVG*, I have made some "snapshot" measurements and concluded that only in exceptional cases, where high uranium glass is worn next to the skin for extended periods, is there likely to be any risk of skin damage.

Finally let us consider the gamma ray risk. As I have explained, these are more penetrating and it is fair to ask what would be the radiation hazard from, say, a cupboard of uranium glass? Snow[7] (see *BBVG*) did such an assessment and concluded that it would be much less than the dose received from background radiation. My own measurement of dose rate, at a foot from a cabinet full of Davidson's Pearline, is below the limit of reading on my Geiger Counter of 0.5 micro-sieverts per hour.

Photo 1. A cabinet of Davidson's Primrose Pearline, the gamma dose rate measured at less than 0.5 micro-Sieverts per hour.

One reviewer of *BBVG* took me to task for not highlighting the "Inverse Square Law." I had not mentioned it because I did not consider it relevant. Now, out of deference to those comments, I will explain.

If we consider a point source of any type of radiation, be it light, gamma rays or sound, then the intensity of that radiation falls off as the observer moves away from the source. This is due to two factors, namely the adsorption of the radiation by the intervening air, or shielding, and the fact that the radiation is expanding in space. If we neglect the adsorption and if the radiation is not in any way focused, then the area over which the radiation is spread is given by the surface area of a sphere, i.e. $4\pi r^2$. Here the variable factor is the radius and it is clear that the surface area expands as the square of the radius. Thus if we have a point source of radiation and at one foot, the radiation intensity is one unit, at 2' it will be 1/4 units, at 3' it will be 1/9 units, at 4' it will be 1/16 units and so on. Thus my critic argues by keeping a modest distance from his uranium glass collection, he can reduce the dose of radiation he receives by a considerable amount. The situation is not that simple. The inverse square law only applies from a point source, if the area of the source is large, say comparable with that of a human body, the fall- off of radiation intensity with distance is much more complex and not so great. So if the glass collection is held in display cabinets, the "inverse square law" will not hold.

Consider Snow's[7] figure of 0.5 mSv per year from his shelves. Then apply an 'occupancy factor', that is, allow for how long a person is likely to spend close to Snow's shelf. If it is assumed a third of a person's time is spent at work, a third in sleep, then of the remaining leisure time, only some of which is spent near a glass collection. Let us say that for an enthusiastic collector it is only a quarter of the leisure time, the occupancy factor is 1/12. Rounding off figures, the additional exposure from the uranium glass would only be 0.05 mSv pa. Something like 1% of natural background radiation. So why worry about the inverse square law?

Now if our concerned collector is still unhappy about this extra radiation dose, he/she must be careful how their other time is spent. If instead of looking at their glass, they decide to watch television, climb mountains, eat "low sodium salt", jet off to sunny shores, bathe in the Dead Sea or just spend their holidays in a granite location, then their radiation dose could be greater than if they had stayed at home with their uranium glass collection. Perhaps the ultimate absurdity of this anti-radiation reasoning is not to sleep with your partner, by doing so you will be receiving a dose of radiation from the natural radioactive materials in his/her body!

PACKAGE IDENTIFICATION No. 1	Approval Ident. Mark N/A
Package Type N/A	Gross Wt.

To
MR B. SKELCHER

UN 2912
RADIOACTIVE MATERIAL, LOW SPECIFIC ACTIVITY (LSA-I) non fissile or fissile excepted

From

Photos 2 and 3. I once loaned part of my collection to a nuclear establishment for public display. I took it in plastic containers in the boot of my car. When it was returned, because it was "radioactive material leaving a nuclear site" bureaucracy had a field day, returning it by special delivery, in special packages with special labels.

Chapter 3.

Measuring Radioactivity and Estimating Uranium Concentrations in Glass

With regard to measuring radioactivity and estimating uranium concentrations, I have little to add to what I have already written in *BBVG*. My practice has not altered. However, because an understanding of the methodology is an essential part of this work, here is reproduced an edited version from *BBVG*, with additional information.

In this context, we are interested in beta particles and gamma rays. The former is measured with a Geiger counter, the latter using gamma spectrometry, which can tell us the type of isotopes present and their relative abundance.

Radioactivity is the process of an atom emitting a pulse (quantum) of energy. By measuring the rate at which these are emitted (known as counting), it is possible to evaluate the intensity of the radiation and from this estimate the amount of radioactive material present. The unit of radioactivity now in use is the "becquerel" (Bq). One becquerel is the activity of a quantity of radioactivity in which 1 nucleus decays per second. When radioactive atoms decay, they do so at a constant rate, unlike many objects in everyday life. For example, think of a hundred bottles of milk. After one or two days, none of the milk will have soured, but after three days, 90 may have soured and after 4 days, all 100 bottles will probably be undrinkable. If those bottles had not been filled with milk but with a radioactive isotope, (which we will say has a half life of 1 day), then after one day half the isotopes in each bottle will have decayed, after two days three quarters, after three days, seven eighths and after four days, fifteen sixteenths and so on. What is important is that the same percentage of isotopes decays in each equal period. The time for half of those present to decay is called its "half life".

If we know the half-life of the radioisotope and we then measure the number of disintegrations taking place in a specified unit of time, we can calculate the amount of isotope present. There are a number of ways of doing this, but for beta radiation, one of the most convenient is the Geiger counter. It works on the principle that when these rays pass through the sensor they trigger a small pulse of electricity, shown on a meter as a "count". Gamma rays will also have a similar effect but, depending on the design of the sensor, their presence can be either neglected or enhanced. Thus there are Geiger counters for measuring beta rays and Geiger counters for measuring gamma rays, and even some which will adapt to either.

For the purpose of detecting and measuring beta rays from a piece of glass in a typical collection, a Geiger counter with a small area sensor, about a square inch, (2.8 cm sq) is required. It also needs to have the necessary sensitivity. The instrument I have used in this study is shown in Photo 4. Geiger counters of this type tend to be expensive, costing several hundred pounds although I understand much cheaper ones can now be bought.

Photo 4. Geiger counter used by the Author for measurements quoted in this book as well as *BBVG*. Size, excluding detector and lead, 15 cm x 10 cm.

The Geiger counter readings are often expressed in "counts per second" abbreviated to "cps". The familiar click of the Geiger counter is the electronic way in which each measured pulse is presented. The instrument indicates what passes through it rather than what is present in the source, thus it does not provide an absolute measurement and needs to be calibrated. This is done by calibrating it against a known source. For this I make use of the "infinite depth" method, which is well suited for measuring beta radioactivity. The principle of which can be explained as follows. Suppose a very thin layer of radioactive material was placed under the end window of our Geiger. The instrument would show a certain reading. If another identical layer was then placed on top of the first we might expect the reading to double because the amount of radioactivity under the window had doubled. In fact, this would not quite happen. Some of the radiation in the lower layer would be absorbed by the material in the upper layer through which it had to pass, before it reached the detector. It would be acting as shielding. If the layers were very thin, then the loss from the lower layer would be very small, but if building layer upon layer continued the "sandwich" would become so thick that most of the radiation from the lower layers was absorbed before it could reach the detector. The stage would eventually be reached when no matter how many more layers we added it would make no noticeable difference to the reading on the meter. From the detectors point of view the radiation depth has become infinite. Never the less, the reading the instrument gave would reflect the concentration of radioactivity in the layers. Thus, if a calibration source at infinite depth is then when compared with a sample at infinite depth, the radioactivity in the sample can be calculated. This is a standard procedure.[1]

Because it is dense, (specific gravity usually between 2.4 and 3.4) beta rays have a short range in glass and a millimetre would approximate to infinite depth. Except in cases of very thin glass, or where the uranium layer has been flashed, presenting a beta sensitive Geiger to a piece of glassware is, de-facto, measuring the radiation at "infinite depth".

The specific radioactivity, (i.e. radioactivity per unit mass), in the glass Rg = (Rs x Cg) / Cs. where Rs is the specific radioactivity of the standard and Cg and Cs are the Geiger counter readings from the glass and standard respectively.

With readily obtainable material, I have used two methods of calibration. The first is to calibrate against an infinite depth of a potassium salt, the other against glass where the uranium concentration is known. Potassium sulphate can be bought from most garden centres and, providing it is reasonably pure, may be used as a standard. Alternatively, potassium chloride may be used. (The specific beta radioactivity of potassium chloride is 14.4 Bq/g, and of potassium sulphate, 12.4 Bq/g).

As it turned out, on my instrument, a reading of 1 cps (count per second) was indicated against an infinite depth of potassium sulphate, which means Cs = 1. Thus the specific radioactivity in a sample (Rg), becomes the Geiger reading x 12.4.

To use the Geiger to estimate the weight of uranium present it is now necessary to know the specific beta radioactivity of uranium. This is not quite straightforward as it may seem. When uranium is mined, it is contaminated with radioactive daughter elements. These are the products of radioactive decay over many thousand years, and will generally be removed in the chemical extraction process. In the early days of using uranium, the understanding of chemistry was much less sophisticated than it is today and it is conceivable that some traces of daughter products may remain. If this did happen then it would mean that I have over estimated the uranium concentrations. I have taken the radioactivity of natural uranium to be 24,800 Bq/g. Thus, 1 cps on the Geiger counter would be equivalent to 12.4/24800 grams of uranium per gram of sample, which equates to 0.05%. Although this may be taken as a good indicative figure, it is probably too low because the energy of the beta radiation from potassium is significantly higher than that from natural uranium, a factor that affects the calibration of the instrument. In my particular case this method has another problem, namely that the reading from the sulphate of potash was at the lower end of the instruments range where there is likely to be a greater margin of error.

Thus a better method of calibration for measuring uranium in glass is to use a glass with a known uranium content as a standard. Without access to an analytical laboratory, this method also presents difficulties, for as with commercial glass, even when the recipe is known, there must be some doubts over its exact composition. For example, I have measured the radioactivity in 12 examples of Webb's "Sunshine Amber" and found an average count rate of 19.4 cps but with a range of 18 to 22 cps. For my calibration sources, I have used four types of uranium glass, where the recipes are already known:

—Sample supplied by Plowden & Thompson of 1960s boro-silicate glass with quoted uranium content
—Samples of Webb's 1930s "Sunshine Amber"
—Samples of "Bristol Green," recipes published by Eveson[2]
—Jobling's Jade recipe, published by Baker & Crowe[3]

From these results, I conclude that 1 cps on my counter indicates a uranium content of 0.062%. (The calibrations range from 0.07% to 0.054%.) This conclusion is quite consistent with what would be expected from the calibration against potassium. All the uranium concentrations quoted in the following text have been estimated by this Geiger counter method.

I have used the 0.062% factor for all my estimates of uranium concentration. If it is in error, it will show a consistent bias. The closeness of the readings for different examples of identical glass items are probably well within the variations that might be expected between batches of glass, and confirms that this is a reasonable method of estimating uranium concentration without resort to chemical analysis which would be cumbersome and involve destructive testing.

On some items, the layer of uranium is too thin to approximate to an infinite depth. In others, the shape or size is such that I cannot present the full face of the Geiger to the glass. In such cases, I have quoted the uranium measurement in cps to give some indication of the level of radioactivity present.

It is a simple procedure to estimate the percentage uranium present in a mix of a known recipe. It has been pointed out that I failed to explain how this is done in *BBVG* so I will now do so. Each element has an "atomic weight." This is in fact is the mass of the atom with respect to that of a hydrogen atom. It is not the actual weight of the atom. Thus, by definition, hydrogen has an atomic mass of 1. Oxygen is 16, so the atomic weight of the water molecule, (H_2O) is 2 + 16 = 18. Atomic weights of all the elements are now known with great accuracy and readily available in publications. Not all elements have a whole number for their atomic weight. This is because they comprise two or more isotopes that have different masses, the resulting atomic weight then becomes fractionalized according to the proportions present.

It is simple arithmetic to estimate the percentage by weight of uranium, (or lead, or any other element) present in a mix of known composition. For example, consider the composition quoted for Webb's Sunshine Amber, (See Chapter 29). The uranium is present as potassium di-uranate, $K_2U_2O_7$,$3H_2O$. The molecular weight of which is (40x2) + (238x2) + (16x7) + 3(2+16) = 722. The atomic weight of uranium in this molecule is 238x2 = 476. Thus the percentage of uranium, by weight, present in potassium di-uranate is (476/722) x100 = 66%. The batch weight of Sunshine Amber is 560+16+10 = 586 lb. The weight of uranium will be 6.6 lb., i.e. 66% of 10 lb. Thus, the percentage of uranium, by weight, in the mix is 6.6/586 x 100 = 1.13%.

The answer is in terms of percentage by weight, not by molecular or atomic ratio and is only approximate because it does not take account of molecules that have volatilized. The most likely are water and carbon dioxide. Water is usually present in the raw minerals, not by dampness but as part of the crystal structure / composition of the compound. For example, potassium di-uranate contains three molecules of water. These will be lost during the melting process. However, the consequential weight loss will be small compared with the weight of the overall melt and the error, through ignoring this effect, is small. Much the same applies if carbonates, nitrates, or hydroxides are used as alkali. In addition, lead is volatile and traces of that will escape in the exhaust gases. I have not attempted to correct for these factors. In many cases, the uncertainty of the exact nature of the substances in the mix probably well exceeds the error introduced by ignoring these volatilize. It must be born in mind that when I quote estimated values they will only be approximate and may vary a little from measurement results.

A word of caution, all that clicks is not necessarily uranium. Some glass may contain thorium, a natural contaminant of some sand[4]. This could be the case where ceria-titania has been used, instead of uranium, to produce the yellow. The cerium being obtained from monazite sands, would have associated thorium. If in doubt the test with a UV light as well, see Chapter 4.

The other method of detecting (and measuring) uranium in glass is by gamma spectrometry. This analyses the gamma rays for energies that are characteristic of the atom from which they originate. The gamma spectrometer is an expensive and sophisticated piece of equipment, the operation of which requires specialized knowledge. It is not generally available to the glass collector and consequently only a few have made use of it. For more description of this technique, see *BBVG*. Notwithstanding I have had a few glass specimens examined by gamma spectrometry and may occasionally refer to this in the script Included in these were six examples of Davidson's Primrose Pearline and I was able to identify one indicator not found in other non-Pearline glass. This I discuss in *BBVG*. Another asset of gamma spectrometry is that it can assess whether potassium is present, this being a constituent of some glasses.

No matter how accurate the measurements, whether by gamma spectrometry or by the beta Geiger, there will be variations in the measured uranium concentrations between items apparently made from the same formulae. This is likely to be less with the more modern, (mid 20th century) mixes than with older ones because of improved quality control. Another factor is the extent to which a homogeneous mix was obtained. The melt is not stirred but has to rely on thermal mixing. When interpreting uranium concentrations for the purpose of attribution or comparison, allowance must be made for variations greater than the accuracy of the method of measurement. The higher the concentration the less significant these considerations become. Thus a level of 0.05% - 0.1% u by wt could well be from the same nominal formula, but such a percentage variation at (say) 5 times that level would certainly indicate different melt formulae.

Chapter 4

Fluorescence

Some substances, when subject to one form of radiation emit visible light of a distinctive color. There are several mechanisms for this. Chemi-luminescence is the process by which a substance absorbs light then emits it later. Radio luminescence is where a radioactive particle strikes a substance and, in the energy exchange that takes place, emits light. Luminised instruments and watches, now going out of fashion, are good examples. Here we are concerned with the third process, specifically with ultraviolet light. Ultraviolet occurs with sunlight but can also be produced artificially. It lives at the "blue" end of the spectrum and has wavelengths in the range 150nm to about 400 nm. It is invisible to the human eye but otherwise is like light. It will react with some elements and molecules in such away that its energy is converted into visible light, this we call fluorescence

For practical purposes, such as buying a UV lamp, the wavelength is considered in three groups. Down to 365 nm is the "near" or long-wave, to 300 Nm is the midrange, and 250 nm the far, or short range. As I mentioned when discussing the risks from uranium radiation, ultraviolet also carries some risk. This is minimal in the near (long range) but significant in the far (short range) radiation and largely accounts for the effect we call sunburn. Generally, nothing more than common sense is required when working with near UV, it is sometimes used for stage effects, but precautions against eye and skin exposure should be take when working with UV in the far region.

Uranium generally responds to UV light by giving of a ghost like greenish glow. It is usually less responsive to UV in the far region than to UV in the near. UV can be used to detect the presence of some other elements, however this is not discussed as I am only concerned with its use in connection uranium. For this it is better, and safer, to work in the near region.

A numbers of collectors now use this fluorescence to confirm the presence of uranium and even estimate the amount of uranium present. This is unwise even to the point of being reckless. As I have pointed out in *BBVG*, and further illustrate below, not all that fluoresces green is uranium. In addition, the intensity is no indication of the uranium concentration in the glass. Much depends upon the form the uranium is in, i.e. its valance state, and the presence of other interfering elements. Some items with the highest concentrations I have in my collection, i.e. the dark amber's, barely fluoresce at all.

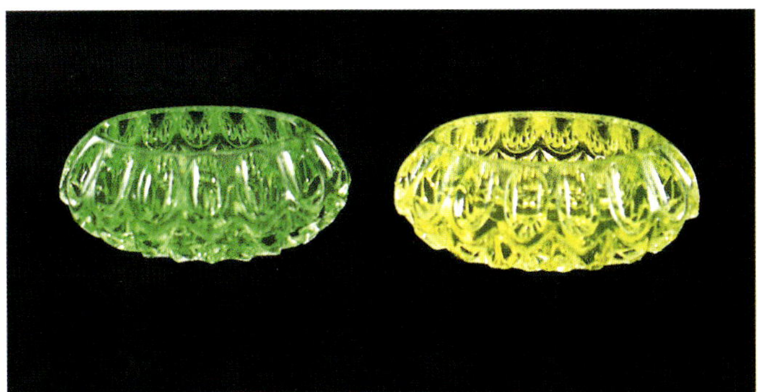

Photo 5. Two pressed glass salts under white light.

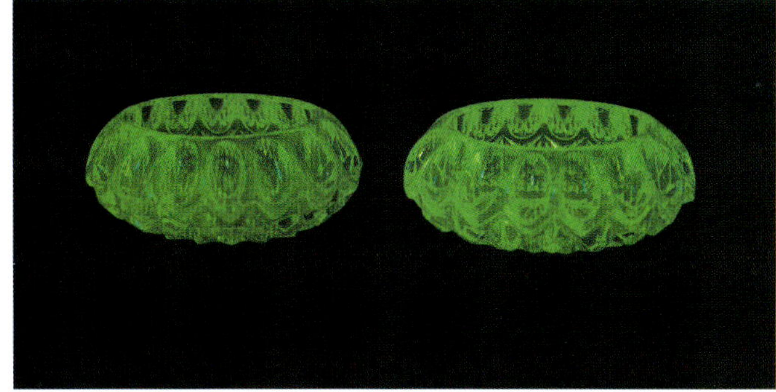

Photo 6. The same pieces as in Photo 5 but under ultra-violet or uv (near) light.

In *BBVG* I mentioned the "small torch like code marker lights" used for reading the "invisible" marking that can be placed on good for security reasons. Since then, I have come across a small key fob that serves much the same purpose. They appear to be imported from the USA and are readily available through eBay. Probably by the time this book is published, they will be in UK shops. An example is shown in Photo 7. While they are generally satisfactory for detecting uranium in glass, they are far from 100% reliable. The ones I have used have a strong visible purple component that, in the case of light colored articles, can overpower a weak uranium response.

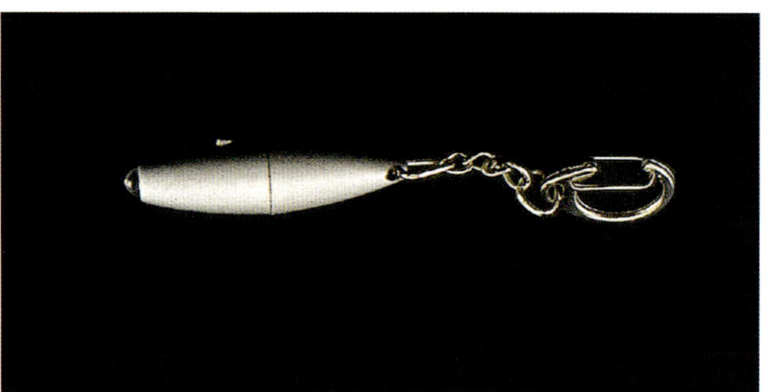

Photo 7. One of the small key fobs that can now be bought with an in-built uv light.

Photo 8. A colored vase, looking like uranium yellow, in white light.

I do emphasize that it is the green glow, and not any other color, which is indicative of uranium. The piece illustrated in Photo 8 looks very much like a uranium yellow in natural light, but under UV light shows an amber like fluorescence, see Photo 9. This lead one dealer to erroneously conclude that there must be uranium present.

Photo 9. The same vase in Photo 8 under uv light. This item does not have uranium and although there is a fluorescence response, it is not that expected from uranium.

Ultra violet light can be used to indicate the extent to which uranium has been used in an item and where a non-uranium melt has been introduced. The dish in Photo 10 shows a white dish with a pink, almost "Burmese", finish on its rim. The Burmese effect is obtained by using a mix which contains gold and then, when the piece has been made, re-heating part of it to produce the pink/red effect. In which case as all the glass in the piece contains uranium it will respond to UV light. Now Photo 11 shows the same piece under UV light. Careful examination shows that the fluorescence does not extend to the edge of the rim. Consequently, I have to conclude the red edging is a different metal to the rest of the item and does not contain uranium.

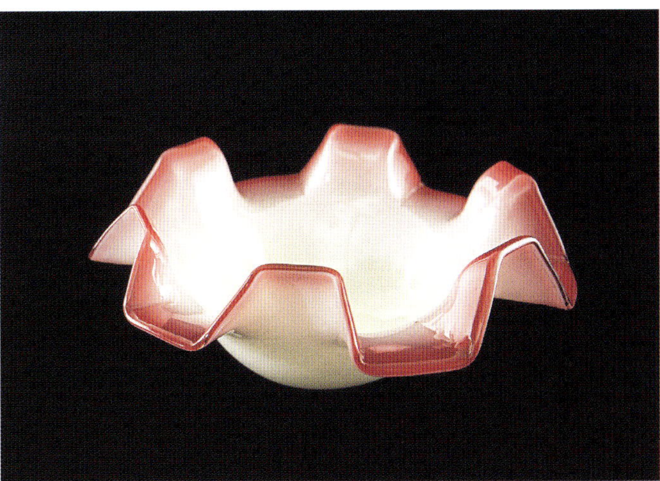

Photo 10. The dish under natural light shows the red merging with the white almost "Burmese" style.

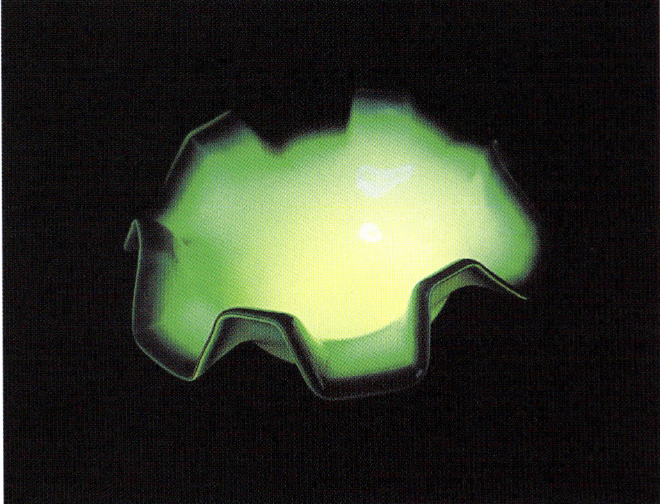

Photo 11. The use of uv light on the item in Photo 10 clearly shows that the uranium does not go to the extremities of the dish.

Generally I regard the Geiger counter as a better way of confirming the presence of uranium. It is the only readily available means of estimating the uranium concentration in the glass. However, in some rare cases, especially when the Geiger response is weak and the color of the item not strong, the fluorescence effect under UV light can be a useful confirmation as thorium, the most likely element to be giving Geiger readings, does not fluoresce.

Not all that glows green under UV light is uranium although the pretenders can usually be identified by simple inspection. It is now not uncommon to color glass with a lacquer that looks like uranium, fluoresces like uranium but is definitely not uranium. Photo 12 shows a sweet dish. Here the lacquer is on the outside and can be removed by scraping. Photo 13 shows it under UV light.

Photo 12. A green dessert dish in white light. It has been coated on the outside.

Photo 13. The dish in Photo 12 under uv light, which glows as if uranium were present yet there is none. In fact, the color is not in the glass but coated on the outside and can be scratched off.

There is scope for more research on the use of UV light to identify characteristics which may help with attribution. However, as the uranium response is so strong it is not an avenue that I have explored.

Chapter 5

Density of Glass

Throughout my research, the density of the glass has played an important part in deciding attribution. It is always surprising that these measurements, which are relatively simple to make, appear to have been neglected by most collectors and dealers, with the exception of Elville[1]. In the following pages, there are examples where density measurement has not just been supportive, but critical to attribution.

The terms "cullet" and "crystal batch" are commonplace in old recipes. Further examination reveals that even when these terms are not used, there is usually little variation in the basic mixes used by an individual glasshouse. When colors are introduced, it is usually done by adding agents to a basic mix. Because of this, the different metals used in a particular glasshouse will have similar densities. Thus, part of my research has been to measure the densities of products where I have a high confidence level in their origin and from this, to establish a pattern of density that I would associate with a particular area or product.

Although density, or weight per unit mass, is not a fingerprint for any manufacturer, it may be an indicator regarding attribution. In my view, it is a crucial measurement for any glass collector or researcher. All that is required is a tub of water at room temperature and suitable weighing scales, preferably with a capacity up to 2 Kg and accurate to at least 0.1 g. The item is weighed normally, then weighed suspended in water. The density is given by the following formula:

$$d = w_a/(w_a - w_t)$$

where d is equal to the density, w_a equals the weight in air and w_t is the weight in water.

Since writing *BBVG*, I have had opportunity to measure the density of several hundred more samples. Many were uranium bearing, but a substantial number were clear glass. Most of the latter items have been identified with a high degree of confidence, as have some of the uranium pieces. This has enabled me to update the information given in *BBVG*.

Figure 1 is a reproduction of Figure 1 in *BBVG*. I still consider it the best general estimate of the relationship between lead content and density. It is only approximate, as it does not take account of factors other than lead. Heat resisting borosilicate glass, used in the manufacture of household Pyrex, has a low density of approx 2.25 g/cc. Barium has a major impact on density, and it can increase densities to those more usually associated with lead.

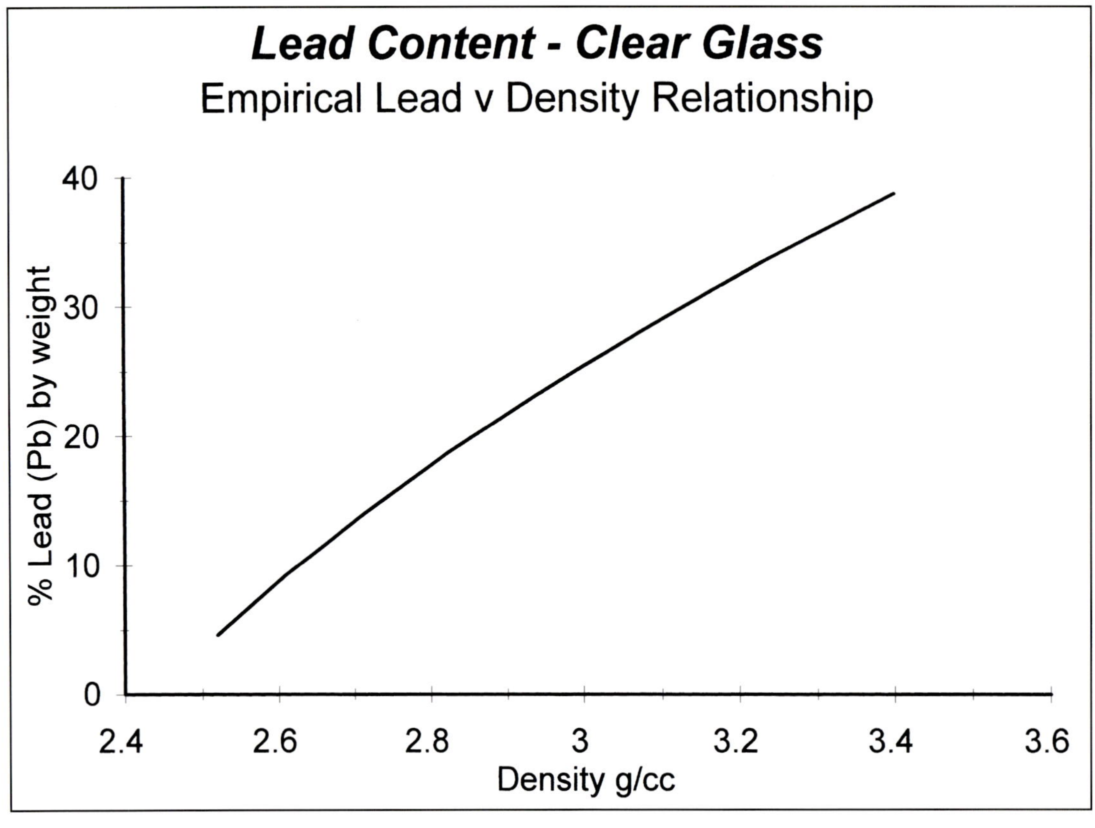

Figure 1

Calculating the density of glass from a known mix is a complex matter, but I have used a simplified approach which gives an approximate answer. It follows the practice for estimating the uranium concentration, but working the example for lead instead of uranium.

By way of example, these are the measurements for Webb's Burmese. The quoted formula is in lb. weight. Sand 500; Litharge 140; Potash 130; Fluorspar 73; Felspar 70; Soda ash 35; Sodium nitrate 30; Uranium oxide 8; Ironstone 3; Gold 7.5 pennyweights. Ignoring the very small quantity of gold, the total weight of the mix equals 989 lb. Note that litharge is PbO. The atomic weight of lead = 207.21 and of oxygen = 16. Thus, the molecular weight of PbO is 223 (neglecting the decimal values.) (The percentage lead in litharge is 207/ 223 x 100 = 92.8% wt.) The weight of lead in the mix is 140 x 207/ 223 = 130 lb., expressed as a percentage as 130/989 x100 = 13% wt. Referring to Figure 1, this would indicate a density of about 2.7 g/cc. Again, as in the case of the uranium estimation, the answer is likely to be a little low because of loss of water and carbon dioxide during the melting reaction. That aside, this answer compares well with the measured results quoted later (see Chapter 29.)

The following tables illustrate graphs and values, updated from *BBVG*. This provides more detail and increases confidence when comparing these values with those of items under research. These densities are for clear glass and most likely represent the basic crystal batch or cullet. The addition of uranium would make a small difference, originally estimated in *BBVG* (p 57) at approx 0.07 g/cc for every 1% of uranium. Other heavy elements may also make a small difference and opacifier may affect the density. This approach is useful in estimating the density of metal prepared from a batch of known composition.

In the following pages, there are a number of examples where knowledge of density has been critical in making an attribution. If nothing else, these indicate the value of not only density measurement, but also of assembling a database of the densities of glass from known producers. Where I have eight or more results, I have displayed them as a scatter diagram, in order to establish if there is a discernible change over time. Generally, there is not, so it seems probable that an individual glasshouse preferred to keep using the same basic mix. The results for those glasshouses for which enough data exists to draw scatter diagrams are illustrated first. The results are restricted to items for which I have a high degree of confidence, (95% see following chapter), in their attribution. Densities of uranium glass are given in the chapter relevant to each piece.

Davidson & Company

Results from measuring the density of 53 items of clear glass from Davidson & Co are illustrated on the scatter diagram. The majority lie between 2.43 g/cc and 2.5 g/cc. The one reading of 2.54 g/cc could be a rogue result, perhaps arising from an out of specification (spec.) batch or even produced by another glasshouse, who had acquired a Davidson mould. The average density is 2.47 g/cc, with a standard deviation of 0.021 g/cc, representing a 95% confidence limit. Results from measurements on colored glass, given to two decimal places, are as follows:

Brown (amber) 5 samples Average 2.51 g/cc Range 2.43 – 2.46 g/cc
Blue 3 samples Average 2.5 g/cc Range 2.42 – 2.47 g/cc
Green 3 samples Average 2.5 g/cc Range 2.5 – 2.48 g/cc
Pink 3 samples Average 2.61 g/cc Range 2.45 – 2.7 g/cc

Undue emphasis should not be given where only a few results are available, as one rogue value may have a disproportionate effect. This is the case with the pink (above), with one reading of 2.45 g/cc and two others at 2.7 g/cc.

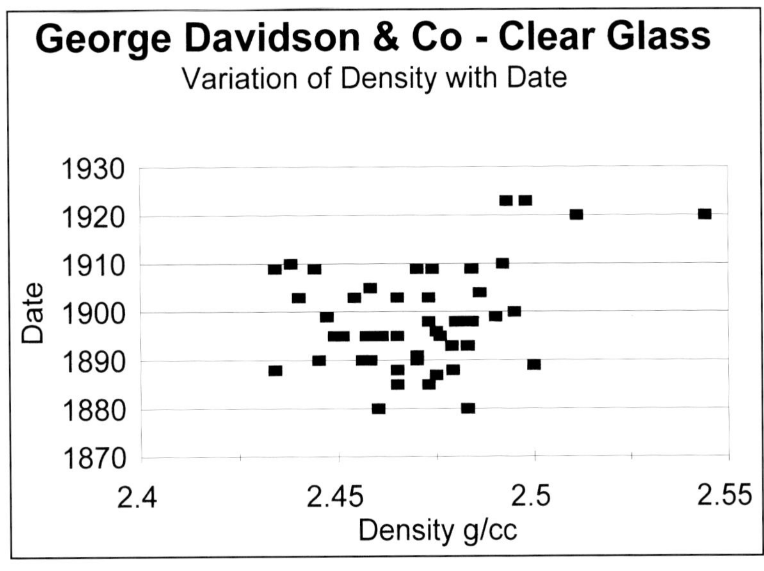

Figure 2

The Derbyshires

This assessment is complicated by the fact that there were three Derbyshire brothers: James, John, and Thomas. From 1873, John went into business on his own for at least four years, but what happened after that is unclear. Therefore, the eight results shown on this scatter diagram, may include items from separate factories. It also possible that some of the moulds may have been acquired by other glasshouses, which could account for the results below 2.6 g/cc.

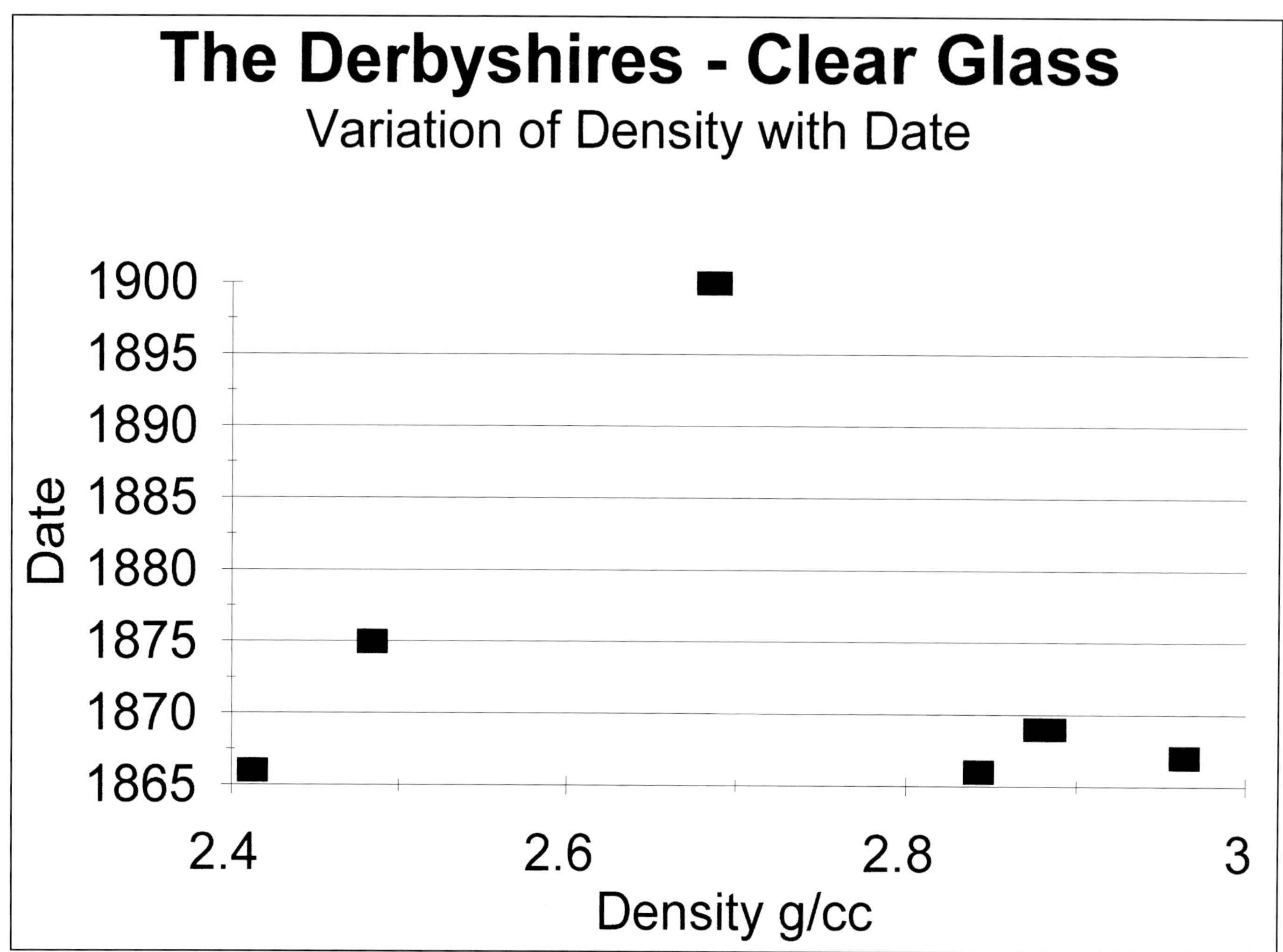

Figure 3

Greener & Company Glass

Greener originally started as Angus and Greener, but in 1886 the company was sold to James Jobling, and continued to trade as Greener & Co until 1921. The densities of differing items produced in the Jobling era are shown in Fig. 5. Forty-six items were measured and the average density is 2.54 g/cc, standard deviation 0.1 g/cc and the range from 2.44 g/cc to 2.88 g/cc. Results appear to indicate that in the firm's early days, their metal contained approx 20% lead. After Angus died, the lead content varied from approx 10% to zero.

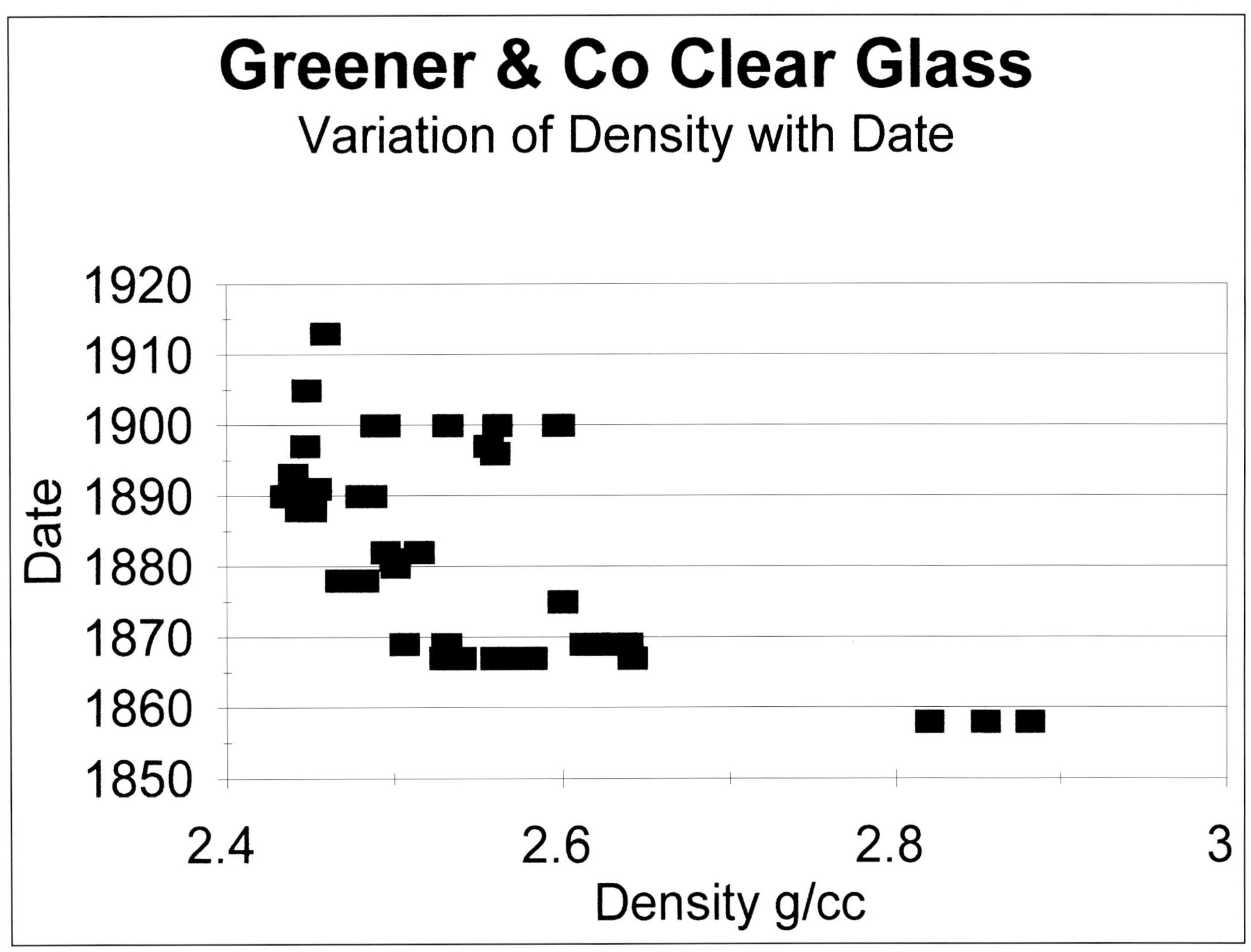

Figure 4

James A Jobling & Co.

The densities of twelve items are shown in Fig 5. The average is 2.48 g/cc with a standard deviation of 0.027 g/cc. The range of those measured is 2.44 g/cc – 2.51 g/cc. (These do not include Pyrex.)

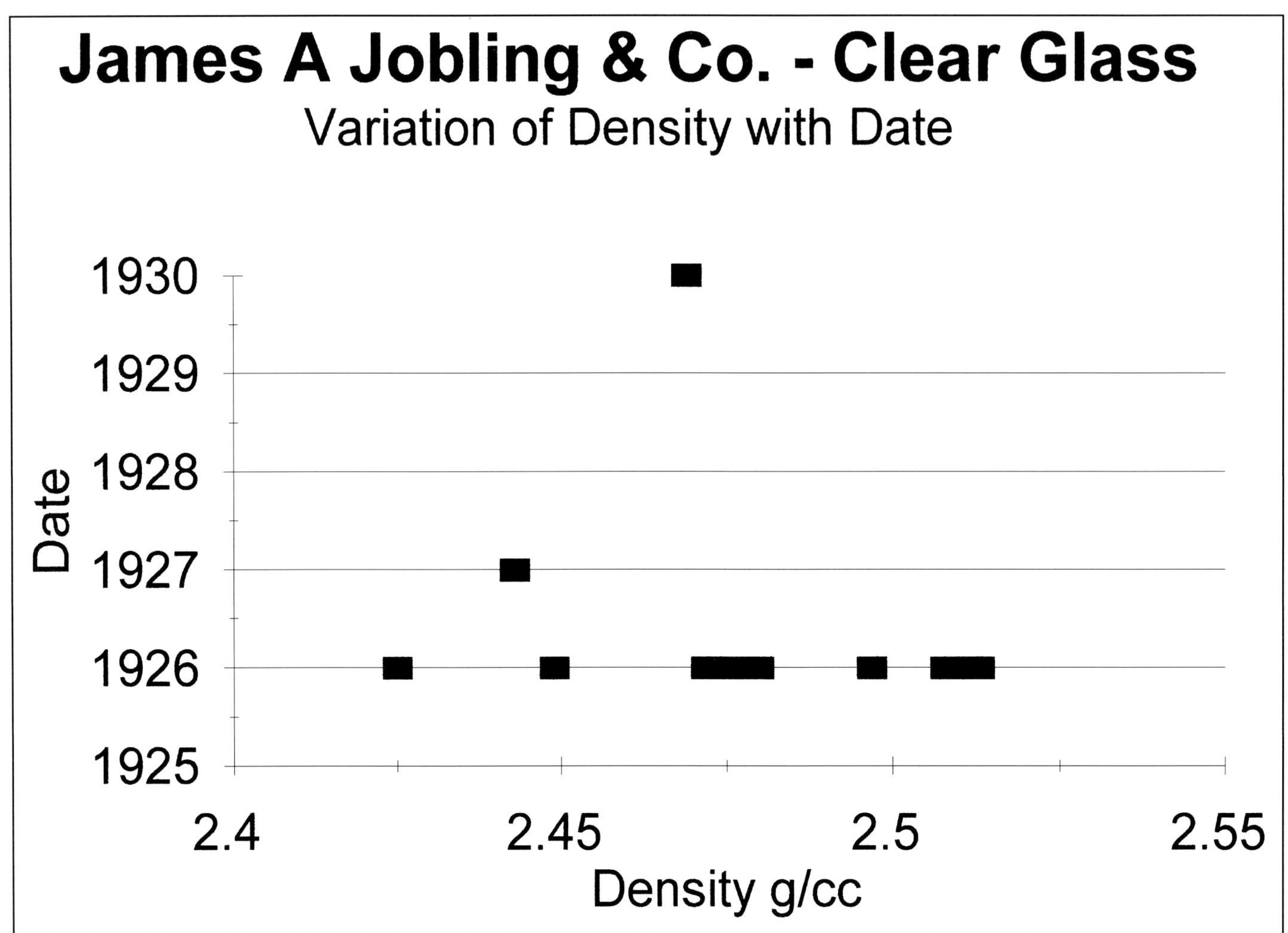

Figure 5

Jules Lang

Nine examples of this firm's items have been examined and the results are shown in Fig 6. They are only of limited value in making attributions. The firm was primarily a glass importer, especially from Belgium, France and Bohemia, although they did have their own glasshouse for a few years in France. They also registered a number of designs, which were presumably put out to contract. On the basis that Lang retained copyright and ownership of the moulds, we might expect identical items to have significantly different densities, if they were not made at the same glasshouse. The average of these nine items is 2.49 g/cc with a standard deviation of 0.02 g/cc and a range of 2.46 g/cc to 2.54 g/cc.

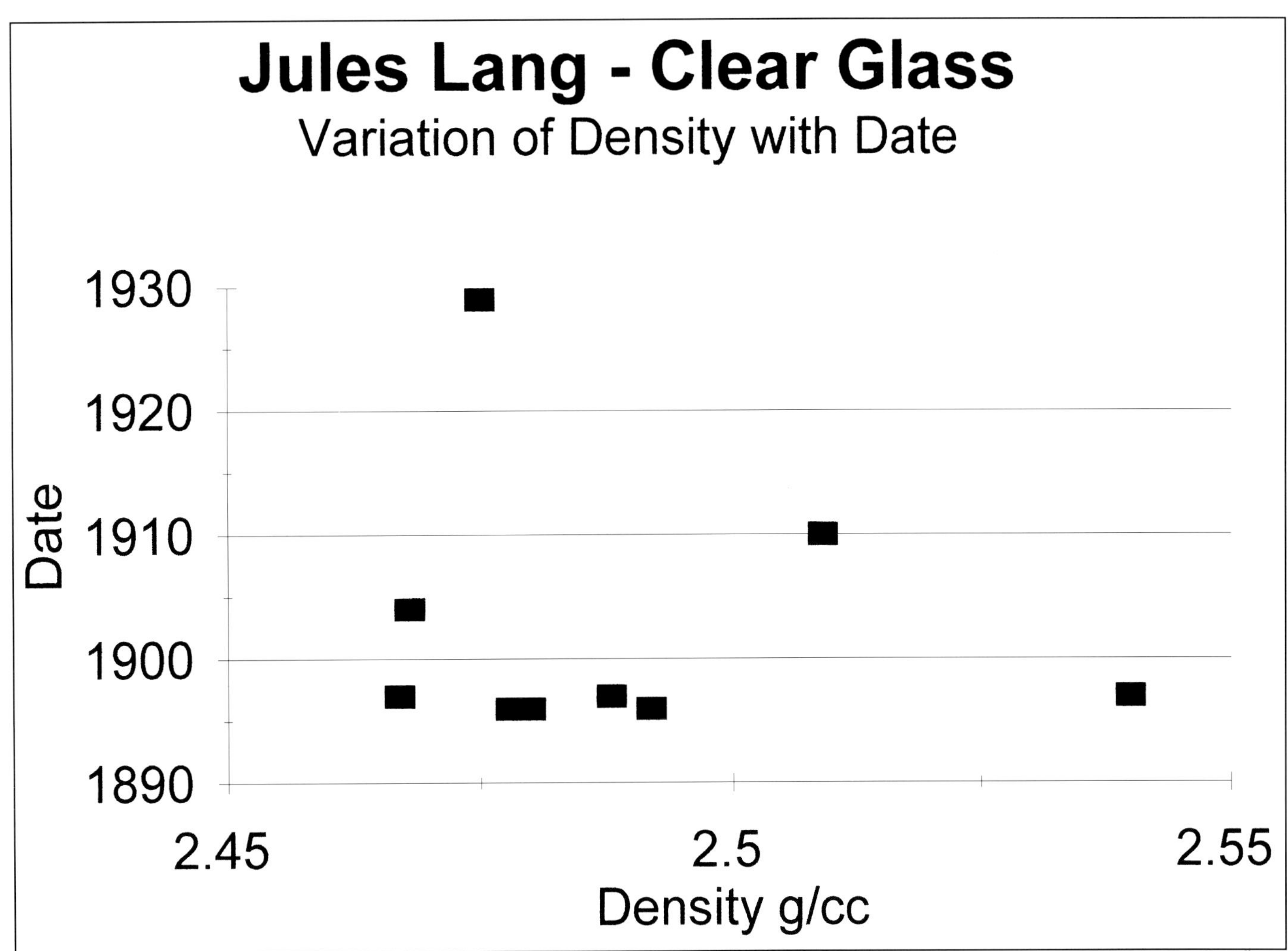

Figure 6

Molineaux, Webb & Company

Fifteen items from this firm were tested, the results are shown in Fig 7. The pattern looks similar to that shown in *BBVG* (Fig 5), but more points reinforce the centre band. The piece with a density of 3.19 g/cc is made from clear glass with a milky appearance. The basic metal would have been doped with an agent, possibly arsenic, to create that effect and this may have affected the density. More likely, the metal was not a standard batch. The item at the other extreme, with a density of 2.55 g/cc might have been made by another firm using an acquired mould. Taking these two results out, the average is 2.88 g/cc with a standard deviation of 0.056 g/cc. On this basis, we would expect 95% of clear glass items from this glasshouse to have a density in the range 2.82 g/cc to 2.94 g/cc.

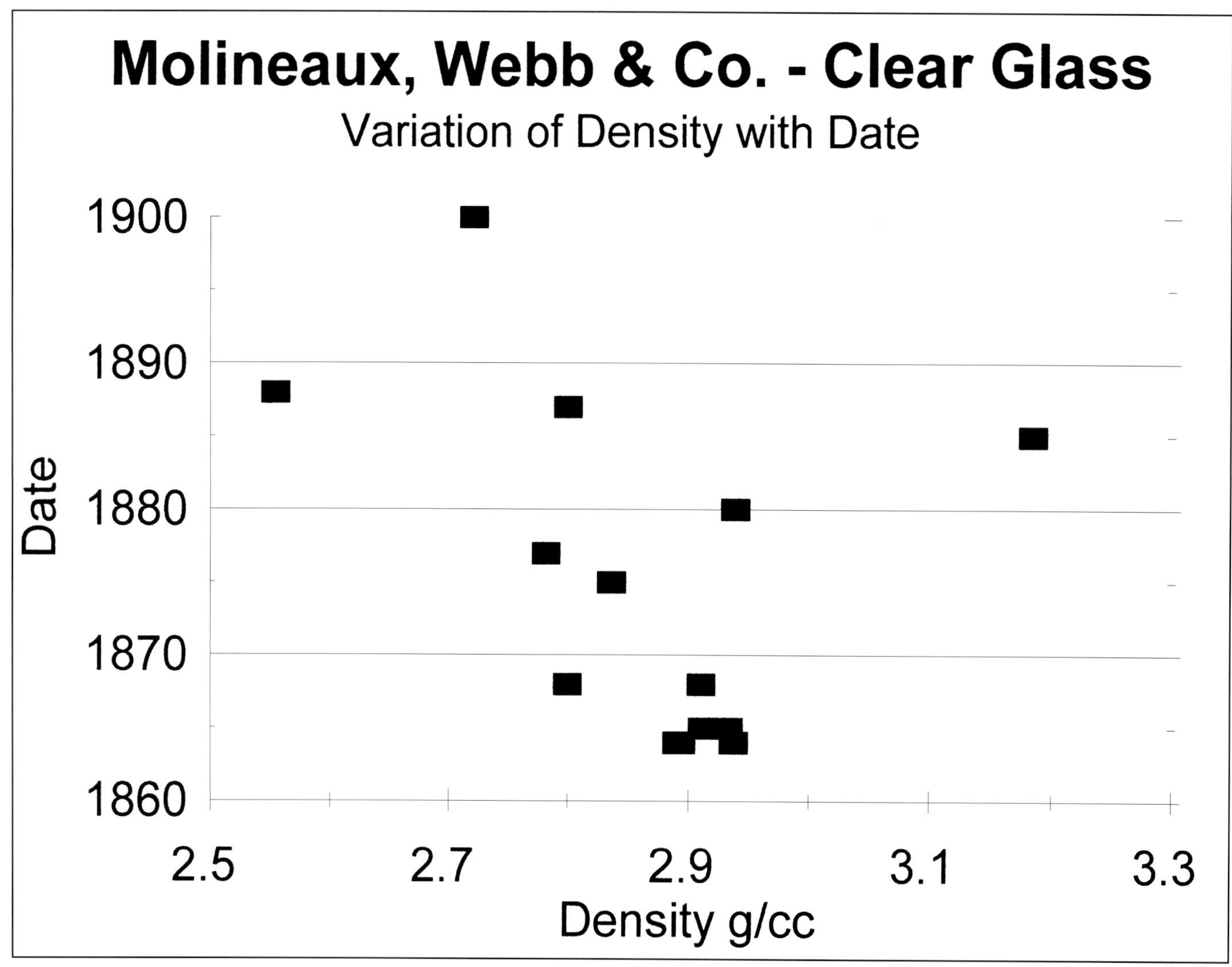

Figure 7

Edward Moore & Company

Apart from one measurement, the densities of this glasshouse are extremely close together, a useful factor when considering attribution. Even the odd one out is not all that far removed from the average, I suspect it is a genuine product of this company. Twenty pieces were considered, the average being 2.45 g/cc with a standard deviation of 0.017 g/cc. The range being 2.42 g/cc – 2.47 g/cc with one result at 2.51 g/cc.

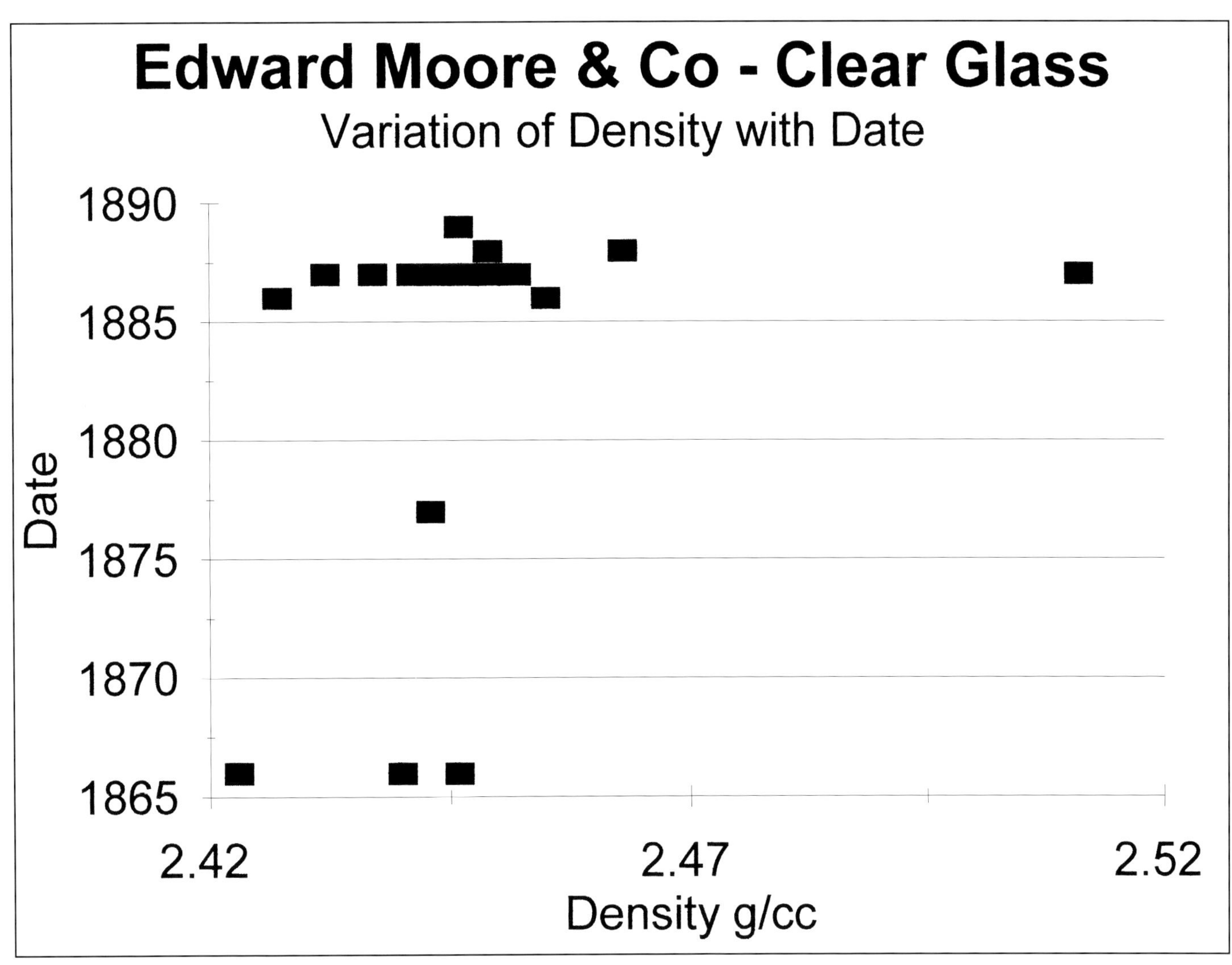

Figure 8

Percival, Vickers & Company

I have added another eight results since those shown in *BBVG*. All these fall within that pattern; again this illustrates the reliability of these density measurements. Number of items measured 22, average 2.82 g/cc, standard deviation 0.1 g/cc. Range 2.63 g/cc to 3.12 g/cc. The spread of densities is wide compared with some glasshouses but the majority, like the other Lancashire glasshouse Molineaux Webb, fall between 2.7 g/cc and 2.9 g/cc. It seems to be a characteristic of glassmakers from this area that they were using metal with lead content of about 15% - 20%. This compares with those in the North East, who were not using leaded glass and those in the Midlands, who had melts with 30% lead.

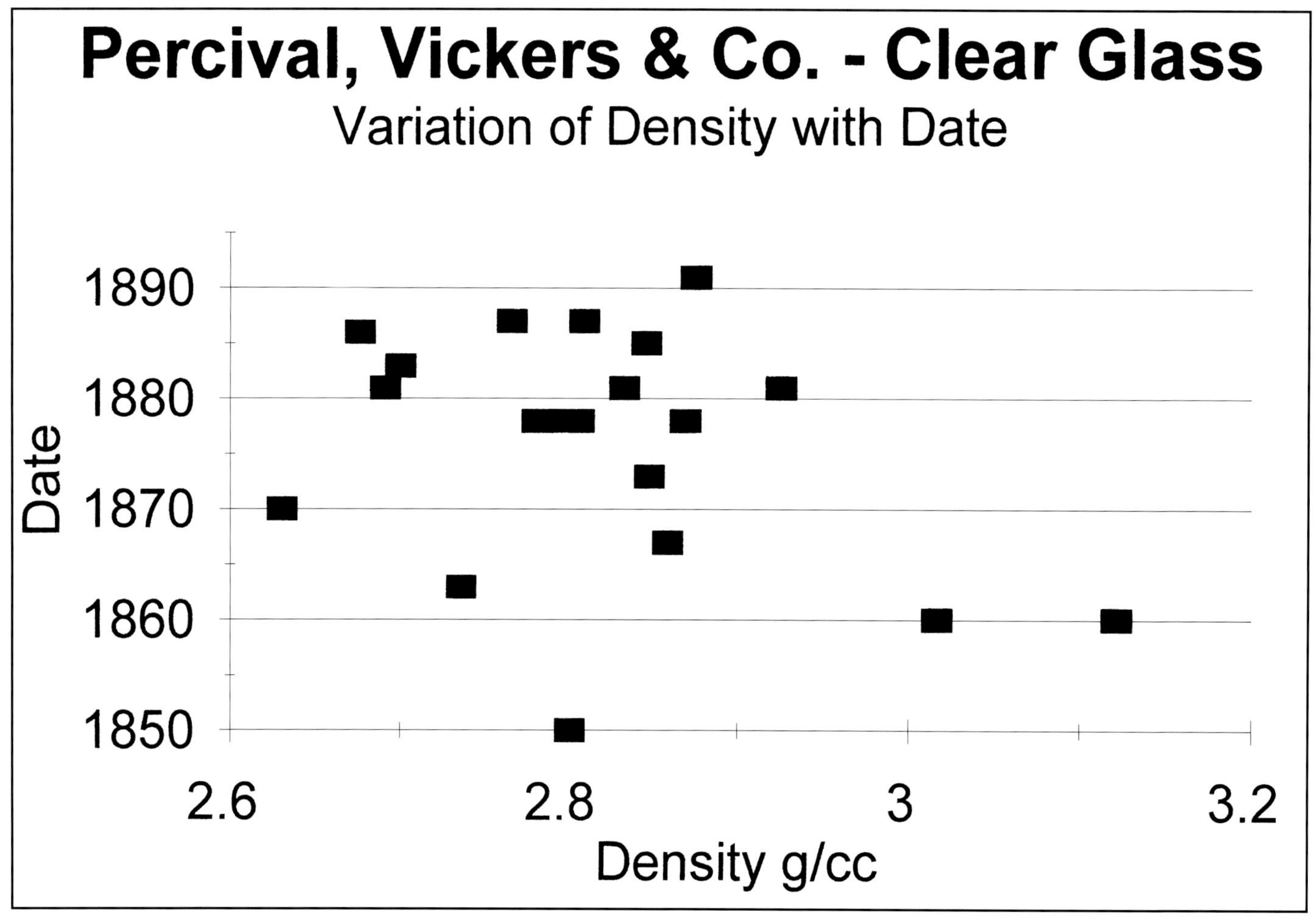

Figure 9

Sowerby of Gateshead

The addition of another seven items to the forty shown in *BBVG* has not altered the shape of the scatter diagram although it does emphasise the pyramid shape. Number of items measured 47, average density 2.5 g/cc, standard deviation 0.04 g/cc. Range 2.43 g/cc to 2.56 g/cc.

I have also made a number of measurements on colored glass:

Black 1 example, about 1900, density 2.652 g/cc

Blue 3 examples, about 1877–1900, density 2.538 g/cc (average)

Brown (slag) 2 examples, about 1877–1900, density 2.548 g/cc (average)

Brown/amber 1 example, about 1930, density 2.473 g/cc.

Dark Green 1 example, about 1877, density 2.59 g/cc.

Green (slag) 1 example, about 1875, density 2.564 g/cc.

Pink 1 example, about 1935, density 2.58 g/cc.

White opaque 3 examples, about 1890, density 2.509 g/cc (average)

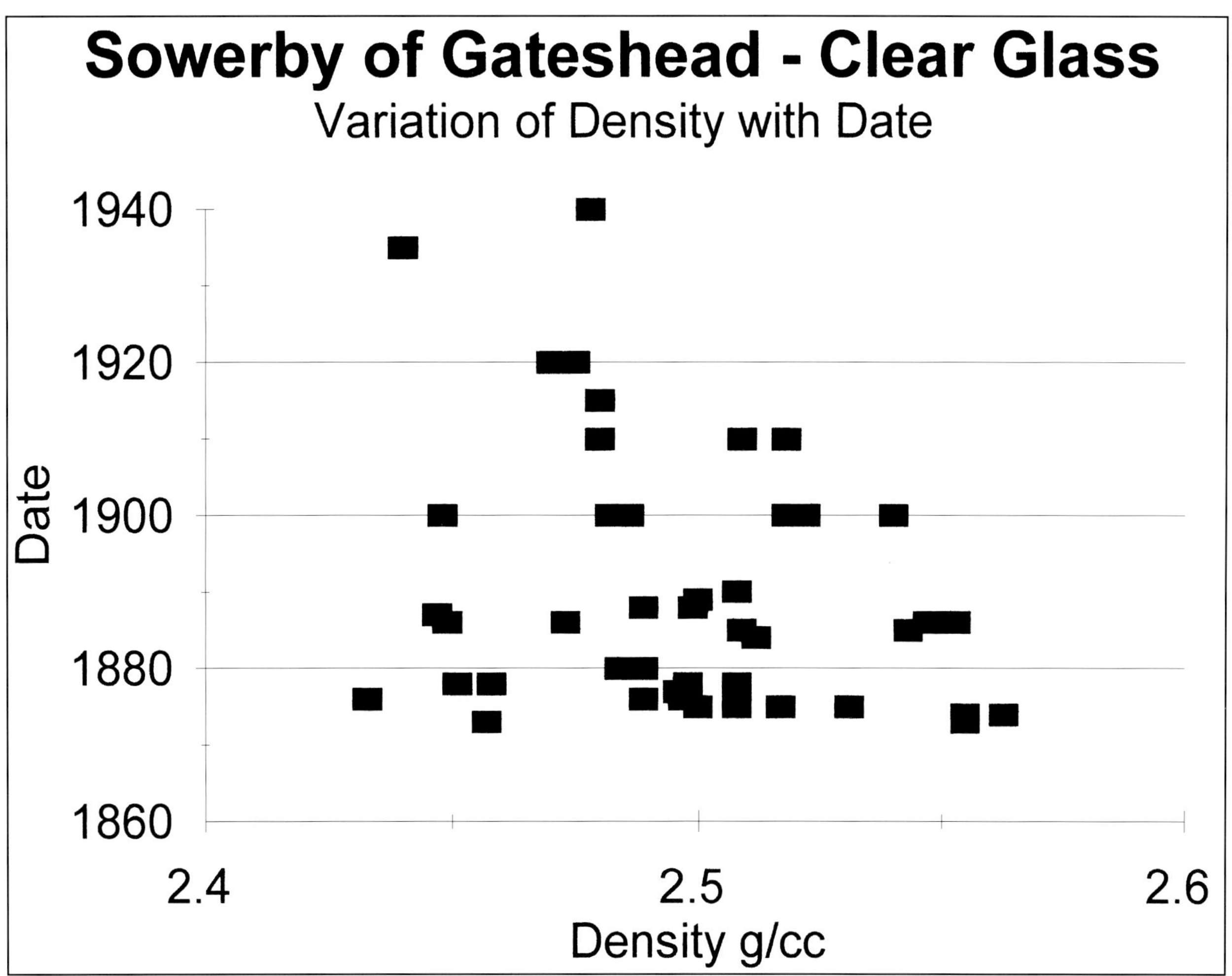

Figure 10

Densities of Glass from Other Glasshouses

I have listed below the results of a number of other density measurements of non-uranium glass. The results, because there are so few for each glasshouse, should be treated with caution as even one rogue result, for whatever reason, could lead to false conclusions.

A Russ & Co; London Glass Importers one item, date density 2.48 g/cc.

Edinburgh Crystal. One vase, date 1970, density 3.27 g/cc.

De Grelle Houdret. One jar, date 1909, density 2.5 g/cc.

Thomas Gray & Co, Gateshead on Tyne; two dishes,

date 1875, density (both) 2.47 g/cc.

M & J Guggenheim, London importers of glass & china; three items 1906, 1924, 1932, densities 2.44 g/cc, 2.48 g/cc, 2.46 g/cc.

W H Hepple & Co, Newcastle Flint & Glass Works, closed down 1884, moulds acquired by Davidson[2]; two clear plates, date 1881, densities each 2.64 g/cc. One white opaque jug, date 1881, density 2.47 g/cc.

International Bottle Company; One bowl, date 1910, density 2.51 g/cc.

Kerr Webb & Co, Prussia Street Glass Works, Manchester; one dish, date 1868, density 2.56 g/cc.

Charles Joseph King, London; One bottle, date 1873, density 2.5 g/cc.

Lalique; One bowl, date 1930, density 2.49 g/cc.

Leerdam glass; Goblet, date 1900, density 2.46 g/cc.

Malta; Sailboat, date 1998, density 2.96 g/cc.

Nazing Glass Works; Ashtrays opaque, one white, one green, date mid 1960s, 2.38 g/cc and 2.47 g/cc respectively.

Richardson's of Wordsley; Two cut glasses, date 1930, densities 3.23 g/cc & 3.26 g/cc.

Robinson & Bolton, Warrington; Five items, date 1856-65, average density 2.909 g/cc, range 2.89 g/cc to 2.94 g/cc.

Stevens & Williams; Two items, date 1876 & 1887, densities 3.06 g/cc & 3.15 g/cc respectively.

Stuart Crystal; Two wines, date 1878, density 3.05 g/Cc. One wine, date 1935, density 3.12 g/cc. Two green wines, date 1921, densities 3.04 g/cc & 3.05 g/cc.

Matthew Turnbull, Sunderland; Four celeries, date 1893, average density 2.53 g/cc, range 2.52 g/cc to 2.55 g/cc. One comport, date 1894, density 2.68 g/cc.

Vassart; two pieces, mauve, date about 1930, density 2.41 g/cc & 2.44 g/cc.

Walsh; One piece, blue cased over white, date 1887, density 3.09 g/cc.

Joseph Webb, Stourbridge; One dish, date 1858, density 2.43 g/cc. It is highly unlikely that a Stourbridge firm would produce a non-leaded glass as early as this. The moulds from this firm were taken over by Edward Moore[3] and the density of this item is exactly what would be expected from that firm. Need I say more?

Whittingham & Percival, Flint Glass Works, Pendleton, Nr Manchester; One dish, date 1876, density 2.75 g/cc.

Whitefriars; One clear lemon bowl, date 1910, density 3.28 g/cc.
One smoke bowl, date 1935, density 3.17 g/cc.
One wine cooler, amber, date 1940, density 3.2.

Val St Lambert; One salt, date about 1920, density 2.5 g/cc.

Data of this kind is only of any use if it is reliable and reproducible. To test the validity of this work, an inter-comparison exercise was organized with two other independent glass collectors who also made density measurements. The results[4] show an extremely close agreement, especially with the heavier samples of the order of 250g.

While density is the best way of testing for the presence of lead, an idea of whether is likely to be present can be obtained by feel and sound. Leaded glass is smooth and almost slippery to the touch. It also gives a distinctive ring when stuck. I usually flip the test piece gently with a fingernail. The amount of ring produced depends upon the shape of the item, for example a wine glass will always give ring when so treated but if it is lead glass it will hold its ring for several seconds. If it is non-lead glass, the ring may be dull and quickly fade. Much the same applies to thick press molded items such as dishes and plates though the effect is not so pronounced. This, I emphasize is only indicative. Don't blame me if you get it wrong or even break the item you are testing!

Chapter 6

Who Made It and When?

Determining who actually made an item and when are the most rewarding aspects of glass collecting. Unlike some collectables, such as postage stamps and coins, glassware is not catalogued in any standard publication, nor is there any readily available price list. Furthermore, unlike coins, glass items do not carry their date of manufacture. When it comes to answering these questions, the collector/ researcher is very much on his/her own. There are a number of books and published research to consult, but they are far from being catalogues akin to Gibbon's on stamps. Like other researchers, I rely upon the findings of others, together with evidence from sources such as trade papers and surviving pattern books. It must always be born in mind that these are only as valuable as the accuracy of the information they contain. Authors of yesteryear were just as prone to making errors as their present day successors.

It is always tempting to take the easy way out and let a casual attribution or date be elevated to the level of certainty. This is of no use to anyone, except perhaps the person wanting to make a dubious and quick sale. It certainly does not help researchers, past, present or future. I dealt with some problems of attribution and dating in Chapters 7 & 8 of *BBVG*. I will summarize those comments and, in the light of experience, add to what I have already written.

Life is full of uncertainties. This appears not to be an accident, but a fundamental aspect of nature. While the Heisenberg Uncertainty Principle means much to the nuclear physicist, it is not relevant here, except, perhaps, to emphasize the point I have just made. In absolute terms, we cannot be certain of anything. For example, you are driving your car and glance at the speedometer; it says 30 mph. You may think that at least you can be certain of your speed. Wrong. There is inaccuracy in the instrument due to a variety of factors of which you are not aware. These may be tire pressure, temperature, maker's calibration error and so on. Furthermore, the instant you looked at the meter was a fraction of a second after your brain issued the instruction. It takes a fraction of a second for the information from the sensors to be transmitted to the dial, for light to travel from the dial to your eye and for your brain to log the data. Ultimately, you cannot claim that at "exactly 12.00 hrs you were traveling at exactly 30 mph." The correct interpretation is that at "approximately 12.00 hrs, you were traveling at about 30 mph." What do we mean by "approximately" or "about"? By various approaches, we can put error limits and probabilities on all this information. We might say, "there is a 90% probability that at 12.00 hrs, + or – 1 second, you were traveling at 30 mph, + or – 1 mph." If the margin of error is widened, then the degree of certainty becomes greater. Thus, we might say that there is a 99% probability that between 12.00 hrs, + or – 5 minutes, you were traveling at between 38 and 42 mph.

When we come to attributing or dating glass, the same principle applies. We cannot be absolutely certain who made an item and when it was made. For this reason, both here and in *BBVG*, I have adopted a probability approach, which is somewhat novel in the field of collecting. It attempts to quantify the uncertainty. It has received a mixed reception[1].

Attribution helps sell items and consequently the serious collector should be wary of a dealer's opinions, unless they are backed by evidence. Whenever a dealer claims an attribution that is not self evident, such as a signature or design registration mark, I always ask how they know. The spectrum of answers can be fascinating. At an antiques fair, a dealer had a decorated Victorian bulbous vase labeled as "Boulton & Mills". In response to my usual question, I was told that it was obviously from that glasshouse, because of the cherry-like decoration. By itself, such a statement is of little value. Any number of glasshouses could have applied a similar decoration and the basis of the attribution needs to be more robust. Does the decoration have any specific and unusual characteristics, or does it appear in any pattern book or design registration?

Another answer that occurs from time to time, is "I showed it to a friend who is an expert on that firm and he says it looks as if it could have come from there, also another dealer has an identical item and he/she has claimed that identity." Again, this is of no real value. If the expert can point to a design registration, advert or other reliable attribution, then that is a different matter.

Perhaps the most astonishing response I have had came from a dealer trading over the Internet. She was selling a piece of Victoriana claiming it to be Webb's. I can do little better than quote verbatim the response I received. *"Being a glass dealer of some 27 years and living here in the middle of the master's home town Stourbridge, it has become quite easy to 'spy' a home-fed piece...it is second nature for me to spot a Webb's or any other piece..."* Strong stuff, but the value as an attribution is zero. She is saying, "I am an expert and if I say its Webb's, then it is." No matter how extensive one's knowledge might be, surely it is the height of conceit to consider oneself infallible. The prospective buyer should shun opinions and just say "gimme the facts". There are examples in this book of items that look alike but that were made by different firms, and it is very difficult to tell them apart.

Unfortunately, the matter does not stop here. The purchaser may treat the dealer's assertion as gospel truth and use a sample to start attributing other pieces, and so perpetuate and enhance the original mistake.

Two preserve/sugar jars are shown in Photo 14. The glass looks identical. The densities, (2.49 g/cc & 2.43 g/cc) and the uranium (each at 0.62% wt), are close enough to suggest that they came from the same factory. Consider the one on the rhs (also shown as photo 256 in *BBVG*.) I quote what I wrote then, "*...this sugar appears identical to one attributed by Glickman to McKee about 1870. Personally I have doubts and would put it much later, perhaps about 1910*." I have no reason to doubt Glickman's attribution and no better idea as to who may have made this glass. So, what is the problem? The lhs bowl has a slightly different lid, which is marked on the underside "Made in England". This does not mean that the glass was made in England. It could have been imported and the lids made locally. It would be quite wrong to jump to the conclusion that glass will always originate from the same country as any associated metal ware. On the other hand, the metal could have been made in England and exported to the USA for McKee. It is worth noting that in 1911, US regulations required imports to have their country of origin marked on them. This would support my dating of "*about* 1910".

Another problem arising with attribution is the straight jacket that constrains thinking. Thanks to the valuable research by other authors, a small number of glasshouses have become household names amongst collectors. You will find them heading the chapters in *BBVG* - there are 17 in the UK. Perhaps add a few more for whom I have not allocated a chapter and inevitably, most collectors and dealers will only be thinking in terms of about 25 glasshouses. Faced with the problem of attribution, the inclination is to think an item must have come from one of these and then go for the best fit.

In order to test my concern, I looked at the Design Registrations for 1873 to 1875. The reason for choosing this period was because it was the last year the "lozenge" was used and this required the registration to be categorized, glass being one of the categories. It was also the start of the era when uranium glass became popular. During this 3-year period, 80 different companies or individuals registered designs. While it is likely that some of these were not glass producers, it still leaves many glasshouses that do not readily come to mind when attempting an attribution. Furthermore, 29 of these were from the English Midlands (compare this with 5 that I included in *BBVG*.) Whilst browsing on e-Bay one day, I came across an advertised piece with the Registration Design No 9807 which dates it 1884. It was registered by Alfred and James Davis of Stourbridge. They had not registered anything in the period 1873-75. If this piece had not carried a design registration , who would have thought of attributing this piece to that otherwise unheard of firm?

In 2003, the Society of Glass Technology[2] published,

Photo 14. The only significant difference between these two items is their lids. One is stamped "Made in England," but that does not necessarily mean the glass came from that country.

in book form, reprints of papers presented by Francis Buckley in the 1920s. These documented his research into English and Welsh glasshouses in the 18th and 19th centuries. While this period is not fully relevant to the uranium period, it does indicate the number of places making glass in one form or another and which are largely forgotten today. The publication tells us that Houghton's List of Glasshouses in England & Wales (May 1696) lists some 90 in total. Twenty-six are in what I would loosely call the London area, 22 in the English Midlands, only 2 in Lancashire, 11 in the North East and 12 in the Bristol-Gloucestershire area. I shall refer to the work of Buckley in more detail under the Regions.

Some pundits may hedge their bets with comments such as "it could be Webb" or "it is probably Davidson". What does this mean? How strong is a "could be" or a "probably", how much reliance can be placed upon it? I maintain when an attribution is made, even with qualifications, the basis of that attribution should be quoted. When I first started my research, I sought to put a mathematical probability on the value of such words but had to settle for a more subjective approach. This has led to the convention that I used throughout *BBVG*. For ease of reference, I have reproduced it at the end of this chapter and now explain the basis for it. When a term is used specifically in this context, especially in the captions to the photographs, it is shown in italics.

In the case of an attribution made based on strong primary evidence and in the absence of contradicting evidence, I do not qualify the attribution, but I assume that error is still possible and assign an error rate of 1 in 100, or a 99% probability. This effectively means that in a hundred such cases I would expect to be wrong, on average, once. An example of such an attribution is in Photo 32 Chapter 8.

I use the term "*Almost Certainly*" where I think my error rate is likely to be 2 in 100, or have a 98% probability of being correct. There is weak primary evidence, but backed by secondary evidence, or there is just very strong secondary evidence on its own. It is a balanced judgment. For example Photo 57 Chapter 9.

I use the term "*Probably*" when I judge the error rate to be about 5 in 100, or 95% probability of being correct. The basis for this is either weak primary evidence, perhaps a similar design found in a pattern book but not exactly the same, or moderately reliable secondary evidence. An example of this is Photo 60 Chapter 9.

"*Could Be*" is a much lower confidence level, with an error rate of about 1 in 5, or 80% probability. This would imply weak primary and weak secondary evidence. A near-matching item might be found in a trade journal illustration or pattern book, but the design is simple and could have been replicated by another glasshouse. Other factors such as density or uranium content support the attribution. An example of this is Photo 76 Chapter 12

"*Best Guess*" means what it says. I don't really know but if I have to make a stab at the attribution, then this is it. I will only venture *Best Guess* when I feel I have a 1 in 2 chance of being correct. You will find a number of examples in the text such as Photo 68, Chapter 11.

The reader may well ask "What is the point of all this?" It is to give some indication of the probability of being correct and is important when taking research a stage further. Suppose we were to investigate a particular characteristic of a product of a glasshouse, perhaps density, design or uranium content. If only unqualified, or *almost certain* attributions were considered, then rogue results would be rare, perhaps as few as 2 in 100. On the other hand, if '*could be*' were included in the survey, rogue results as high as 20 in 100 would not be unreasonable. Unless an approach of this sort is adopted, frequently used expressions such 'probably' lose their meaning.

With all this in mind, let us look at the available aids to attribution. The first is to see the item being made. However, in the case of antiques this is not possible. Even with more recently made items, memory can sometimes play tricks. In the early 1960s, Caithness Glass was just starting production from its new factory in that part of Scotland. As my wife and I were living close by at the time, we bought some of their early pieces, which, we were told, were for training production and only sold locally. They are not marked. Now, 50 years on, while my wife and I agree on some of the pieces that came from that factory, there are a few items on which we do not agree. Memory can play tricks. An attribution based solely on the basis that someone's mother, aunt, cousin, old lady next door, or even Father Christmas "saw it being made" should be treated with caution and regarded as no more than a "*could be*".

In the UK there are comprehensive records of registered designs available in the public domain, held in the Public Records Office at Kew, London. These go back to the Design Act of 1842. From 1842 until 1883, the mark was a diamond shape, with a loop on the top. The figures in the loop indicate the category (111 for Glass) and the letters and figures in the corner of the diamond indicate the date of registration of the design and its "parcel number". With this information, the researcher can identify who registered the design, when it was registered and details of the design itself. After 1883, the registration mark changed to a simple number, usually prefixed by the letters 'Rd'.

The Rd mark is usually shown on the item, either in the form of an engraving, or in the case of pressed glass, included in the pressing process. Having found a mark, there is no need to go rushing off to the PRO, as Slack,[3] Thompson,[4] and the Glass Association[5] have all published the basic registration details. Design registration is strong primary evidence, although even then, you may occasionally come across a piece that you eventually deduce to have an incorrect number. In addition, in the case of pressed glass, moulds may be sold on from one glasshouse to another. This is quite common, in which case the item in your collection may not have been made by the same glasshouse that registered the design. Finally, an individual or company who were *not* glassmakers may have registered the design. They would then get their design produced by a glasshouse of their choice and the problem is to identify which one. It is not uncommon to find near identical pieces, only one of which carries a design registration mark. This does not mean that the one without a mark is a fake or reproduction. Design registration acted only to give protection against copying for a limited period, perhaps as little as 5 years in some cases. If a glasshouse made a new mould or plunger for an out of protection design, it may well not have taken the trouble to include the registration mark, which by then would have had no value.

The patterns deposited as part of the registration process also need to be treated with caution and back up evidence sought where possible. The deposition shown in Photo 15 is for a registration dated 21 July 1851, by George Joseph Green. A plate, shown in Chapter 23 Photo 107, also carries that registration mark, but the only similarity between the two is the small gadroons separated by a circle. Photo 16 is a close up of the edged of the plate in Photo 107. It is not easy to reconcile this with the registration deposition in Photo 15. Photo 17 shows the edge of another plate. Common to these two illustrations, ie Photos 16 & 17, is the gadroons and circle. The conclusion must be that the second plate is also George Joseph Green, but this is doubtful, as it is not marked and the densities are very different.

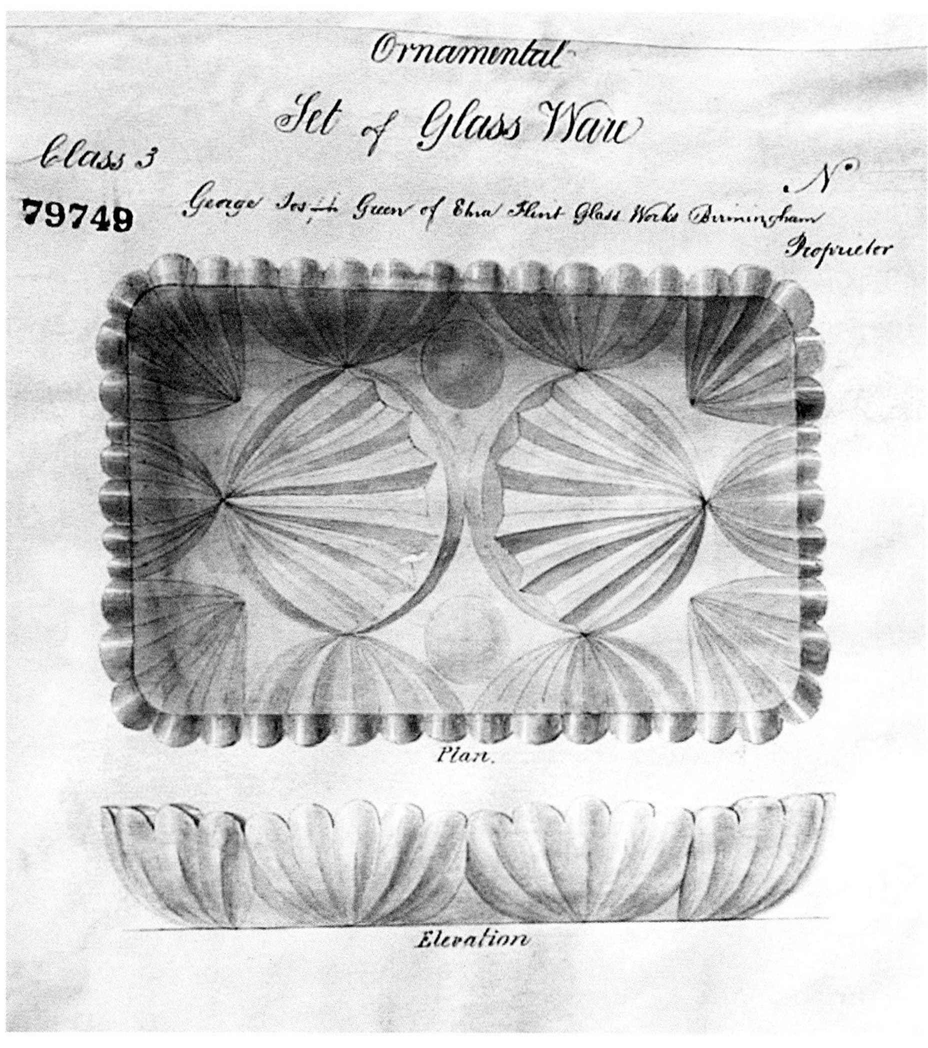

Photo 15. Design Registration deposition by George Joseph Green in 1851.

Photo 16. Edge of plate bearing the Design Registration mark for the deposition shown in Photo 15.

Photo 17. Edge of plate without a design registration mark.

Another example of this type of conundrum is illustrated in Photos 18 & 19. The patterns look much the same: a cruciform separates four circular depressions. The jar in Photo 18 has Design Registration number 764749, for M & J Guggenheim, 2 June 1932. By contrast, the tumbler in Photo 19 is by Percival Vickers, about 1860 (see *BBVG*).

Photo 18. Molded pattern on jar with design Registration Number 764749 for 1932.

Photo 19. Pattern on a tumbler dated about 1860 (see *BBVG* p 86.)

A trademark may be regarded as strong primary evidence. However, even this is not infallible. It may be molded into an item, engraved, sandblasted or acid etched. More recently, from the late 1930s onwards, there was a trend towards using the cheaper adhesive mark. Mold marks are difficult to fake, but they can be removed. I have seen at least two examples of Fenton Burmese Glass, where the trademark has been ground and polished out, in order to pass it off as the more valuable Webb's Queens Burmese. Etched marks can be faked, but this is unlikely on less expensive items. Adhesive paper marks are reliable, but do wear off and are sometimes difficult to read. On one occasion, an adhesive label came away from one piece and was accidentally replaced on another! Perhaps the best publication on glass trademarks, from the point of ease of reference, is Pullin[6].

If finding and reading a registration or trademark is not always easy, photographing it can be even more difficult. A good way of finding a mark on pressed glass is to feel for it with the fingertips on the smooth inside of the item, where it is most likely to be found. However, in some cases it is molded into the pattern, making a fingertip search that much more difficult. Angling an item towards a light source may reveal a hidden mark. Sometimes photographing a mark is not too difficult (as shown in *BBVG* Photo 4) but in the examples in Photos 20 & 21, I had to resort to pencil rubbing, even though I could clearly see the marks with the naked eye.

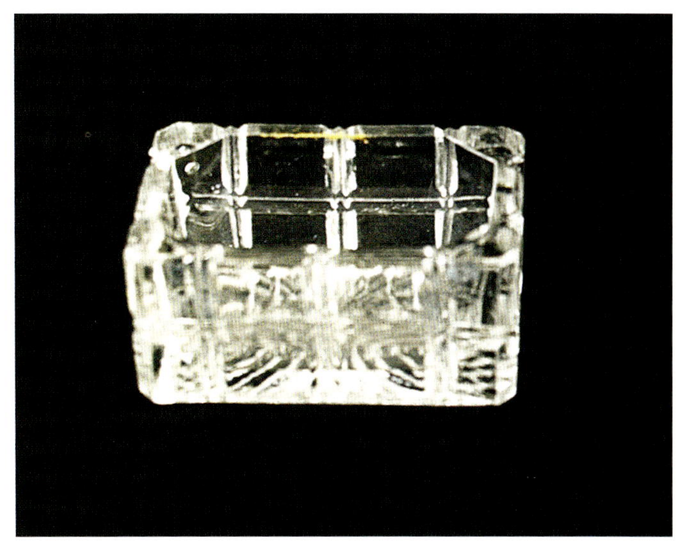

Photos 20 a and b. This small salt has the Design Registration number 409057. It was registered in 1903 by A Riess and Co., London. Importers of Foreign Glass and China. In addition to the Registration number, there is a mark, which I have shown in the pencil rubbing.

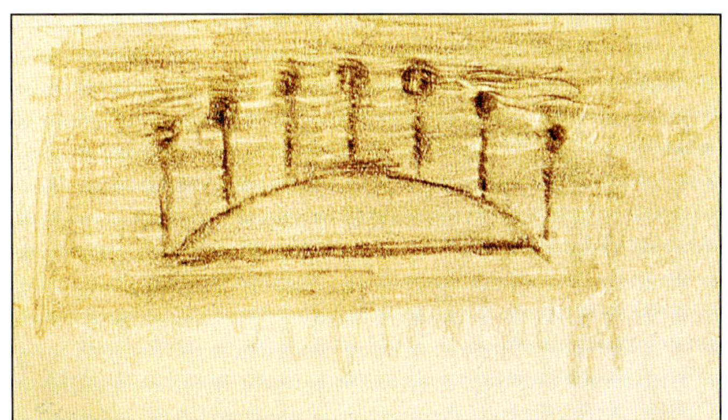

Photos 21 a and b. This bowl carries an unusual mark. The Design Registration number is 626853, which was registered by Greener in 1913. The mark is a four-pointed star on a circle. The circle has the letters "LTD" and between the points of the star are letters "A B A C".

Unfortunately, not many of the old glasshouse pattern books have survived. Where they do exist, they represent a valuable source of primary evidence. Probably the most complete are those from Stevens & Williams, later Royal Brierley, of Stourbridge. The problem that faces the researcher is the sheer number of patterns, in excess of 70,000, that were recorded. In my examination of these, I have only been able to examine and record "snapshot" examples of the items that are most likely to interest me. There are also a number of Thomas Webb's pattern books, but these are incomplete and in some cases badly damaged. Both the Webb and the Stevens & Williams books are held in Dudley Public Records Office[7]. Stuart Crystal books survived the company going out of business and are now in the Wedgwood Museum at Barlaston. A few other pattern books exist and are either with private collectors or held in public museums. Where I have knowledge of these, I will mention it in the appropriate chapter on that glasshouse. A word of caution: Having found your item illustrated in a pattern book does not necessarily mean it was manufactured by that particular glasshouse. Firms were quite adept at copying each other's products, either by design or accident, and it sometimes happens that identical patterns appear in the books of different glasshouses.

Journals such as the "Pottery and Glass Trades Gazette" (usually abbreviated to the "Pottery Gazette"), adverts and trade catalogues are also valuable sources of information, although they may not provide as much information as the original pattern books.

Having exhausted primary sources of evidence we now have to look elsewhere and here we enter a minefield of legend, myth and uncertainty. Secondary evidence is useful to corroborate weak primary evidence or to point the researcher in a particular direction.

Production techniques can be very helpful. Both Manley and Pellatt (see *BBVG* p 40) tell us about continental techniques of production for items such as vases and glasses. Having formed an item, instead of transferring it from blowing tube to Pontil for finishing, a it would continue to be worked on the blow tube. Then, when finished, it would be cracked off from the blow tube. The joint would then be polished flat. It was less time-consuming than the use of a Pontil, shears and reheating. This generally held true until WW2, although examples exist where the cut and grind technique was also used in the UK. We can also study the work of individual glasshouses in order to identify specific characteristics such as crimp work, prunts, patterns and shapes. Again, unless there is a very unusual aspect, this should only be treated as an indicator. I draw attention to some examples in the following chapters

Glasshouses were surprisingly conservative with their basic mixes and coloring agents. Perhaps this was because the composition of their metal was a closely guarded secret. The batch books were guarded with great care, often available only to the principal foreman or proprietor. They would make up the critical part of the mix before it went to the furnace. Because of this, as we shall see in the following chapters, density (reflecting lead content) and uranium concentrations can be good secondary indicators.

It may be helpful if I now run through the procedure I would adopt when attempting an attribution. First, clean the item and make a thorough inspection. If it pressed glass, run fingertips lightly all over, both inside and out searching for a Design Registration or Trade Mark. If it is not a pressed item, then carry out a visual inspection in good light and tilting the item to the light. Design Registrations or trademarks may be etched or engraved and not always easily visible. Any trace of a mark that cannot be resolved with the naked eye should be examined under magnification. In most cases, I find a x5 eyeglass gives good results. If a registration or trademark is found, then verify it by checking with a reference book or the Public Records Office. If all checks are successful and there are no suspicious circumstances, then I would consider it a 99% certain attribution.

If there are no marks, then my next approach is density. As demonstrated in Chapter 5, density can suggest some possible sources. At 3.1– 3.4 g/cc, we are probably looking at the English Midlands, London or Edinburgh Crystal. Of course there are other possibilities, such as Continental Val St. Lambert, but I would start with the most likely. Densities in the range 2.7-2.9 g/cc would suggest Lancashire or the Continent, while those in the range 2.3-2.6 g/cc, the North East. This considerably narrows the field. Then I consider physical characteristics, such as the Pontil mark. Has it been ground out, if so, is it a perfect dimple? This would indicate a top quality glasshouse, such as Webb or Stevens & Williams. I also look at prunts, crimp work and rigoree. Some of these can be common to a number of glasshouses, after all a raspberry prunt is the same the world over, but some are unusual and unlikely to be repeated elsewhere. Having narrowed the field, it is now a question of flogging through pattern books, adverts, trade catalogues and books by other authors. In the latter case, I do not usually accept another author's attribution unless it is backed by a justification.

Finally, it is a question of assessing all the accumulated evidence. This is subjective but I usually follow the adage that "once is happenchance, twice is coincidence, three times is enemy action". Translated into glass attribution, if I have three good secondary indicators, I would be looking at a *probably* or *almost certainly*.

So much for who made it, now let us look at dating it. Following on from my discussion on uncertainty with attribution, much the same applies to dating. It is common in the world of antiques and collecting, to come across the terms "about", "circa" and "period" used without much indication of what they imply or the degree of confidence. I am reminded of the story of the museum assistant, keen to impress a visitor, who pointed to an artifact saying, "That piece is 203 years and 3 months old." The visitor, astounded by such accurate dating, enquired how it had been achieved. The assistant replied, "Well, I was told it was 200 years old when I started work here, and that was 3 years and 3 months ago."

To give a realistic meaning, I define my dating terms as follows: (I repeat this convention at the end of the chapter for ease of reference.)

"**No qualification**" implies the date of a Design Registration, pattern book entry, advertisement, etc.

"**About**" means plus or minus ten years each side of the quoted date.

"**Period**" means plus or minus 20 years of the quoted date.

These groupings are on the basis that I consider them to have a 98% probability of being correct. Where I have more doubt, I would use the term "*probably*" (95% probability) or "*could be*" (80% probability). Thus, if I quote an item as "*probably about* 1900" I am saying that I consider there is a 95% chance the item was made between 1890 & 1910.

Now let us consider how we can arrive at a date estimate. There are a variety of techniques available, all have their weaknesses. The following is a summary of Chapter 8 of *BBVG*, updated.

One of the classic means of dating is by style. I always treat this with the greatest suspicion, although it is standard practice in the world of antiques. I am not saying that dating by style is of no value, it can be very helpful, but it needs backup from other considerations. For example, the plate in Photo 22 is in the style of the deco period and, but for the fact that it carries a Design Registration Lozenge for 1881 (registered by Heppel), could reasonably be attributed to that period. Such examples are not commonplace and the collector is more likely to come up against the repro. syndrom. This is not a matter of faking, but rather that when the piece was made it would have been sold as reproduction. The passing of many years now makes it difficult to distinguish from the real thing.

Photo 22. This design may look deco but the plate has a Lozenge Registration mark for 7th November, 1881, registered by W H Heppell and Co., Newcastle on Tyne.

I have already drawn attention to the presence of "reproduction" items made many years ago being mistaken for the real thing. Another illustration has come to hand. The Pottery Gazette and Glass Trades Review, April 1922, describes a stand taken by John Walsh Walsh and goes on to say "There were special tables of reproductions of glass that was made at the Walsh Walsh over a hundred years ago". This may be a little of an exaggeration, as John Walsh Walsh did not purchase the works until 1850, but perhaps he also took over designs made by the previous owner, Samuel Shakespeare. The same article mentions Stuart & Sons as having "a new engraved pattern with an air twisted stem, designed in the spirit of the antique". The important point to bear in mind is the existence of these items when deciding the date of the piece you are holding in your hand.

Design Registration, pattern books, trade catalogues and advertisements are all good indicators, but they must be used with caution and require some supporting evidence. Design Registration only tells us when the design was first registered. It does not mean that the article was made at that time. Pattern books can sometimes be misleading. A design may appear at several dates within the books, thus indicating the item was not made just during one period. Much the same applies to adverts. When it comes to functional glassware, designs can run for perhaps 20 years or more.

Trademarks are reliable, (providing they are not faked) and will often give a time window. For example, Pullin illustrates 4 trademarks for Thos. Webb & Son, i.e., 1889-1905, 1906-1935, 1936-1949 and 1950-1966. Unfortunately, trademarks on glass are not very common, so yet again we must look for other means.

Perhaps one of the best aids to dating is the method of manufacture. If a glass worker of one hundred and fifty years ago sat down and watched his modern counterpart at work, he might not notice many differences, that is outside the mass produced, machine-made market. The old furnace and cone buildings may be replaced by a modern gas fired plant, but the crucibles with the melts are much the same. The "gaffer" still sits in his armchair, rolling his blow tube and working with the classic tools of his trade. He might even be using a Pontil, but more likely a gadget. The dip moulds and the press moulds would look much the same, except, in the latter case, they may be power, rather than manually operated. Fenton, for example, still use tools and techniques from the 19th century.

Photo 23. A present day glass worker sits at a chair that would not have been out of place a hundred years ago.

Photo 24. A press mold from yesteryear in present day use.

Never the less, down the years a few notable changes have taken place and these are important aids to dating. Although some authors will quote specific dates for the introduction of a new technique, this is really quite unrealistic. The most probable syndrome is that when one glasshouse developed a new technique, not all the others followed immediately. In the first place, we would expect the new development to be kept secret or patented. The natural conservatism of the industry may further delay widespread adoption of the practice. I can well imagine the old boys saying "I don't agree with this new fangled way, my dad always..." Thus when these changes do come about, we must think in terms of perhaps a 10 – 20 year period of introduction.

The Pontil mark on a wine or small item can tell us a lot. Consensus is that up to the start of the nineteenth century, the broken Pontil was left as it was. Then in the mid 1800s, it became common practice to grind out the broken Pontil. I therefore take the presence of a broken Pontil, if the item is not repro., to indicate a date up to the mid-1800s. The ground Pontil was in use from between the early 1800s to near the end of that century.

A device known as the "gadget" succeeded the punty as a means of holding the foot while working another part of the item. It consists of a rod with a clamp on the end to hold the foot. At first, it left identifiable marks but later, by the use of asbestos padding, these were largely eliminated. As explained in *BBVG*, there is considerable doubt when these changes took place. After weighing the evidence, for the purpose of dating, I assume that an article with gadget marks would not be earlier than 1870. The absence of gadget or Pontil marks means it was not made before 1890.

The way the foot of a wine or similar item has been made can tell us a lot about its date. There are three basic ways the foot can be formed. It can be hand-shaped, blown or molded. In the case of hand shaping, the hot metal on the end of the stem is squeezed, flattened and worked into a disk shape. Closer examination will reveal several tell-tail signs. The base is likely to be on the thick side, it will be slightly irregular and flat. In the case of early glassware it may be folded over at the rim, to raise the edge upon which it rests above the remains of the broken Pontil. An alternative, originally used in higher quality glassware, was the blown foot. Pellat[8] (1849) describes how the foot is first blown as a sphere, then opened out with pucelas to form a flat disk. This is then attached to the stem. The trademark signs of a blown foot are that it is usually thin and delicate. Somewhere between the centre and the rim, will be a mark where the pucelas were first applied in the opening out process. The extreme edge of the foot will be its lowest part and therefore will attract most wear. It is also likely to curve over at the top edge. This practice was probably phased out from about 1870, when the molded foot replaced it. What I refer to as a molded foot is one formed with the aid of a footboard. This is a flat piece of wood with a circular recess the size of the desired foot. A hinged top plate, half the width of the base, with a centre hole for the stem of the glass, squeezes excess metal on the end of the stem to form the foot. The two main identifying features of this technique are that the edge of the foot is uniformly rounded or even flat, and that the point of contact when it is standing upright is usually just inside the edge and not on its extremity. For the purpose of dating, I make the following assumptions:

The *hand-formed foot* may have been used up until about 1860.

The *blown foot* was probably used between about 1840 and 1890.

The *moulded foot* was used after 1875.

Another date indicator, applicable to jugs, is the shape of the handle. Originally, the handle was formed by starting at the neck and finishing near the base, in the style of the classic village pump handle. This practice changed over to the present day style, with the handle first being attached at the base and then bent over, to be tucked inside itself at the neck. A variation on this starts with a claw shape, where the first joint is made at the base. As I explained in *BBVG*, there is some scope for debate as to when the changes became commonplace. For the purpose of dating, I assume that the "pump handle" fixing was in use up to about 1880, that the claw handle came in about 1865 and the present day style, about 1870.

Acid polishing of cut glass is an important date indicator. The cutting of a pattern in glass is done by an abrasive wheel, which leaves a matt finish. This then has to be polished until it is as clear as the uncut parts. Polishing was a time consuming finishing process, using wooden wheels with pumice slurry, followed by a brush wheel and finally a cork or wood wheel and putty powder. Cut glass polished in this way has two characteristics, namely the cut edges are sharp and there are striations where the cutting wheel has done its duty. This process was replaced with acid polishing. Although John Northwood had been using acids to dissolve glass from the second half of the nineteenth century, acid polishing probably of cut and molded glass did not come into use until the turn of that century. The item is placed in a bath of mixed hydrofluoric and sulfuric acids. This slowly dissolves the surface of the glass, leaving a good clear finish. (Note that if only hydrofluoric acid is used a matt finish, i.e. acid etching, is obtained). Acid polishing dulls the edge of the cut and also removes the striation marks. Because of the uncertainty over the extent to which acid polishing was adopted, for the purpose of dating I assume that, where there is no evidence of acid polishing, the item must be pre-1900. Where the item is clearly acid polished it will be at least post 1945, perhaps earlier.

Acid polishing was also used on pressed glass. Where the mould had joints, a slight ridge or sharp edge would be left on the item. Originally, this was removed by fire polishing. The item would be taken back to the furnace and the surface heated to melt away the mould marks. In the case of heavy items, such as tazzas and comports, some distortion was likely to occur during this process, such as a slight twisting of the stem.

It is also worth noting that as early as 1867, Northwood developed a process of etching with "white acid". This consisted of a mixture of hydrofluoric acid and an alkali carbonate. It attacks the surface of exposed glass leaving a white etched finish.

Another technique for decorating glass is sandblasting. It tends to leave a coarser finish than acid etching. In *BBVG*, I show a tumbler made for an International Exhibition and dated 1886. The underside reads "Sandblast Patent". Thus for the purpose of dating, I assume any item decorated by sandblasting will be post-1885.

A valuable aid to dating is wear on the item. Unfortunately, there is no method of measuring wear and relating it to age so the process is subjective. Further, the amount of wear will depend upon the lifestyle of the piece involved. Over the years, the glass will probably have been washed repeatedly. In the days before WW2, the modern detergents we use today were not available. Steel wool, hot water and soap may well have been used on some items. When deciding the amount of wear to expect, various factors have to be considered. A heavy item would be expected to show more wear than a lighter one and a piece that was in every day use should show more wear than a display item kept in a cupboard.

There are of course cases where wear is not as apparent as would have been expected, the "my great auntie had it in a box in her attic and never took it out syndrome". This maybe so, but genuine examples have to be rare. Photos 25, 26 and 27 show an undoubtedly old comport with true wear. This type is difficult to fake. The wear on the foot is not only matt in appearance, it also has long scratches in random directions. These are unlikely to be seen on a glass that has been rubbed on a piece of carborundum paper. Other wear, often overlooked by the fakers, would be expected on the body of the glass, where it has been scratched while in use or rubbed against other glass in the washing up bowl.

The absence of genuine wear should arouse suspicion, but nothing more. The presence of simulated wear should set alarm bells ringing.

Photo 25. An old comport dating from *about* 1860. It has had a hard life and the wear is excessive but nevertheless is a good illustration of what to look for.

Photo 26. A closer view of the wear on the base of the comport in Photo 25.

Engrained dirt that has resisted "normal" cleaning is also a good indicator of age. Over the years small particles of dirt, or grease that is hardened and become resistant to washing, will find their way into nooks and crannies. This is especially common where there is overlaid crimp work or decoration. It also occurs in fine cut patterns. This is well illustrated in Photo 28, a close up of the pattern on the edge of the plate in Photo 22. Such dirt engraining is not easy to fake, although I have heard of one unscrupulous dealer who buries glass in his garden to age it.

Photo 27. A closer look at the side of the comport in Photo 25.

Making attributions and dating is fraught with uncertainty. The scientific approach would be to test all the assumptions and assertions that have been made on selected items before applying these assumptions and assertions more generally. As absolute certainty of test items is very unusual, this is not a practical procedure. I therefore look to other indicators to validate the approach I have used.

The cut wine in Photo 29 is also engraved with a date. The foot is hand-formed and has been held in a gadget during the finishing process. The engraving is crude and the letters in older style. There is no reason to doubt its authenticity. The quality of the metal is consistent with that age and the density indicates it is unleaded. Using my parameters, the hand formed foot would suggest not later than 1860, the gadget that it was after 1870. Split the difference and say *about* 1865. In fact, the engraving says "Tom Jones 1870 Blue Bell," see Photo 30.

Photo 28. Close-up of the plate in Photo 22 showing the ingrained dirt.

Photo 29. Cut glass wine with inscription.

Photo 30. Inscription on the wine in Photo 30.

Over the past years I have given a number of talks to local groups where I have asked the audience to bring along items of glass, of whatever age, of which they know the history. I then examine these pieces and give my opinion of their age and likely origin. There have been surprisingly few incidences where I have been wrong and the error rate would be well within the probability values I have assumed.

Look at the wine in Photo 31. The foot has been hand formed and has probably been held in a gadget for finishing. The flutes, which do not show up in the photograph, have sharp edges and the striations are easy to see, obviously it has been hand polished. Therefore, following the above, it might be dated 1865. This is where other factors should be taken into account. The principal give-away is the lack of wear. There are no signs of the expected scratch marks on the foot. The surface of the metal is bright and smooth. This is not what would have been expected from a hundred years of washing up. The glass is slightly grey, whereas, if anything, I would have expected a mauve tint. I bought it in a charity shop for a few pence and since then I have seen others at antique fairs on sale for considerably more. I am confident that this wine was hand made, probably using recycled glass and most likely, it hails from the Third World. I would date it about 1990!

Photo 31. A modern wine with an old fashioned look.

Table 1. Summary of My Attribution and Dating Terminology

No attribution qualification	99% confidence, error rate of 1 in 100
Almost Certainly	98% confidence, error rate of 1 in 50
Possibly	95% confidence, error rate of 1 in 20
Could Be	80% confidence, error rate of 1 in 5
Best Guess	50% confidence, error rate of 1 in 2
No date qualification	Design Registration, Pattern Book or Advertisement date
Could Be	+/- 10 years, with a 98% confidence
Period	+/- 20 years, with a 98% confidence

Section 2: Glass From Known

Chapter 7

North East England

Because uranium use is so widespread across the world, I decided in the early days of my research that I would have to concentrate on a limited area of glass production. Partly because I am an Anglophile and partly for ease of research, I have concentrated upon English glasshouses. Notwithstanding this, I have examined a number of items from other countries and included the results in this book.

This section discusses items for which I have made an attribution, with varying levels of confidence. They are grouped here not according to the nature of the item, but rather to their likely place of manufacture.

Although the illustrations are, with very few exceptions, of different pieces to those illustrated in *BBVG*, I have used data from all the glass I have examined to summarize and reveal trends in density and uranium usage from each separate glasshouse. From the early days of my research, it became apparent that the type of metal used to some extent was determined by the geographical location of the glasshouse. I have therefore grouped the glasshouses according to the following locations: the North East, Lancashire, the Midlands, London and the surrounding area and Scotland.

Items attributed to other countries are discussed in a separate chapter, country by country.

Tyneside Area and Yorkshire

Regrettably, like most of the British glass industry, what remains today is only a fraction of what there used to be. Most collectors associate this area with the production of pressed glass, for functional rather than decorative use. The first glass pressings were of leaded metal, as it tended to flow better in the mould. The process probably started in America and was first used in Britain in the Midlands. As the concept of pressing gathered popularity and its potential for large quantity production became more appreciated, a process was developed in the North East for pressing without the use of the more expensive lead in the melts. Curiously, the process appears to have been confined mainly to that area.

The present day collector will only recognize the names of a handful of glasshouses in the North East, indeed my researches have only extended to eight companies, five of whom were using uranium. I feel sure there must have been more, probably smaller, concerns, whose items are now rare. Because their items were not marked and records have not survived, they are not easily identified. Some were concerned with producing mundane items, such as bottles and jars. The most famous were the Kilner brothers, who established the Providence Glass Works in West Yorkshire, manufacturing the Kilner Preserve jar.[1]

Fig. 11 lists the densities of all the examples of non-uranium glass, plotted against their estimated date and which, with a confidence level of at least 95%, I have attributed to the North East. As many points on the graph overlap, it is not immediately clear that there are 223 items represented. It will be noted that the vast majority lie in the 2.4 g/cc – 2.55 g/cc range. The results for pressed glass of the 1850s appear to confirm that leaded metal was already in use. Of the relatively small number that lie in the 2.6 g/cc – 2.7 g/cc range, most were from Greener who made some glass of higher quality (see *BBVG* p. 66-69.) Excluding 3 items with a density in excess of 2.8 g/cc, the average of the remainder is 2.495 g/cc, with a standard deviation of 0.053 g/cc.

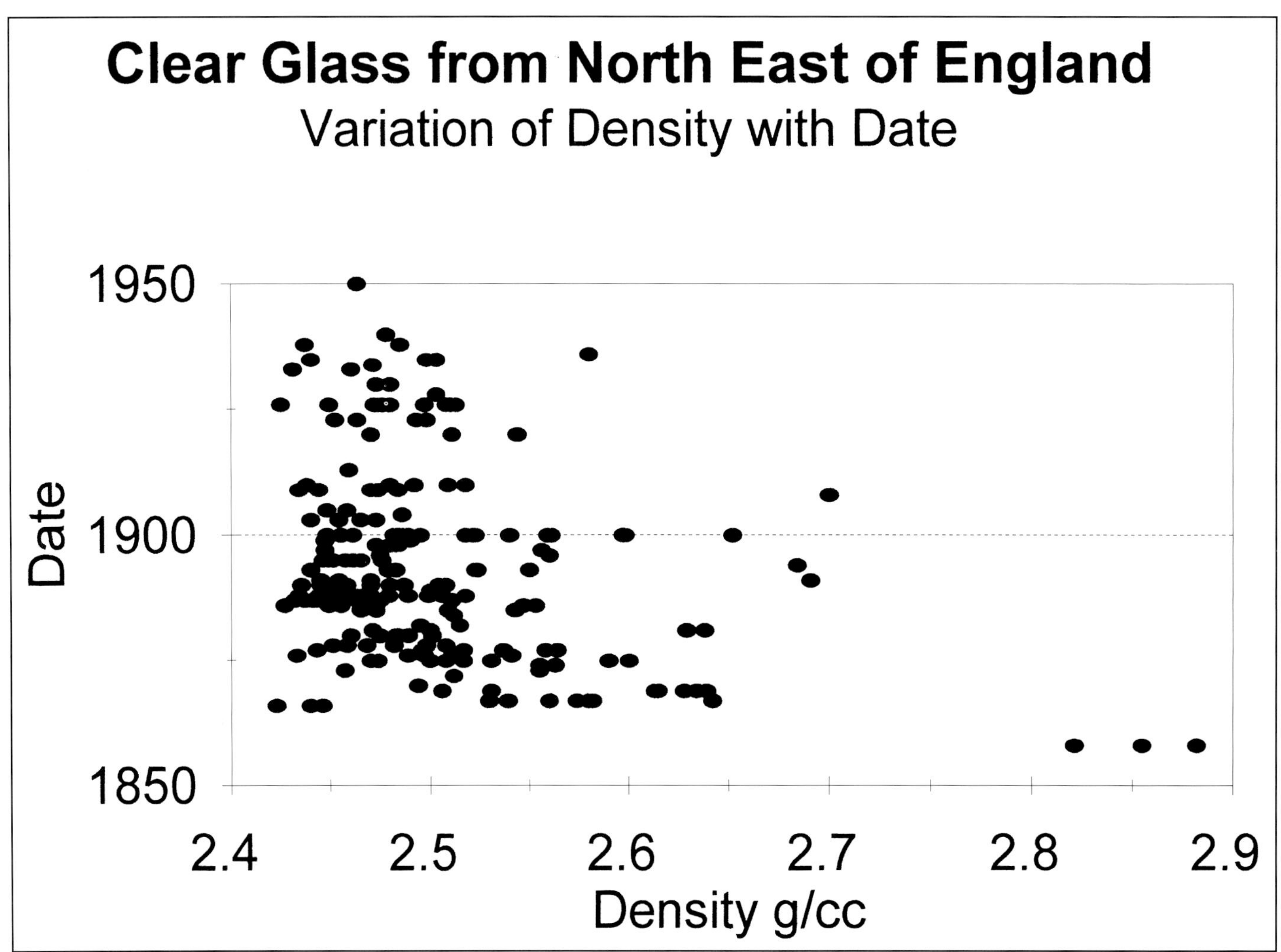

Figure 11

Fig. 12 shows a graph for 175 examples of uranium-containing glass from this area. Again, all results used have a confidence limit of at least 95%. The one extreme density reading greater than 3.2 g/cc is from Sowerby's Giallo (see *BBVG* p 76.) Excluding the Giallo, the average density is 2.51g g/cc, with a standard deviation of 0.035 g/cc.

I am not suggesting that glass with a density in this range therefore comes from the North East. While undeniably a commonly used metal, if you have an item whose density is outside this range, there is a strong probability that it did not come from the North East.

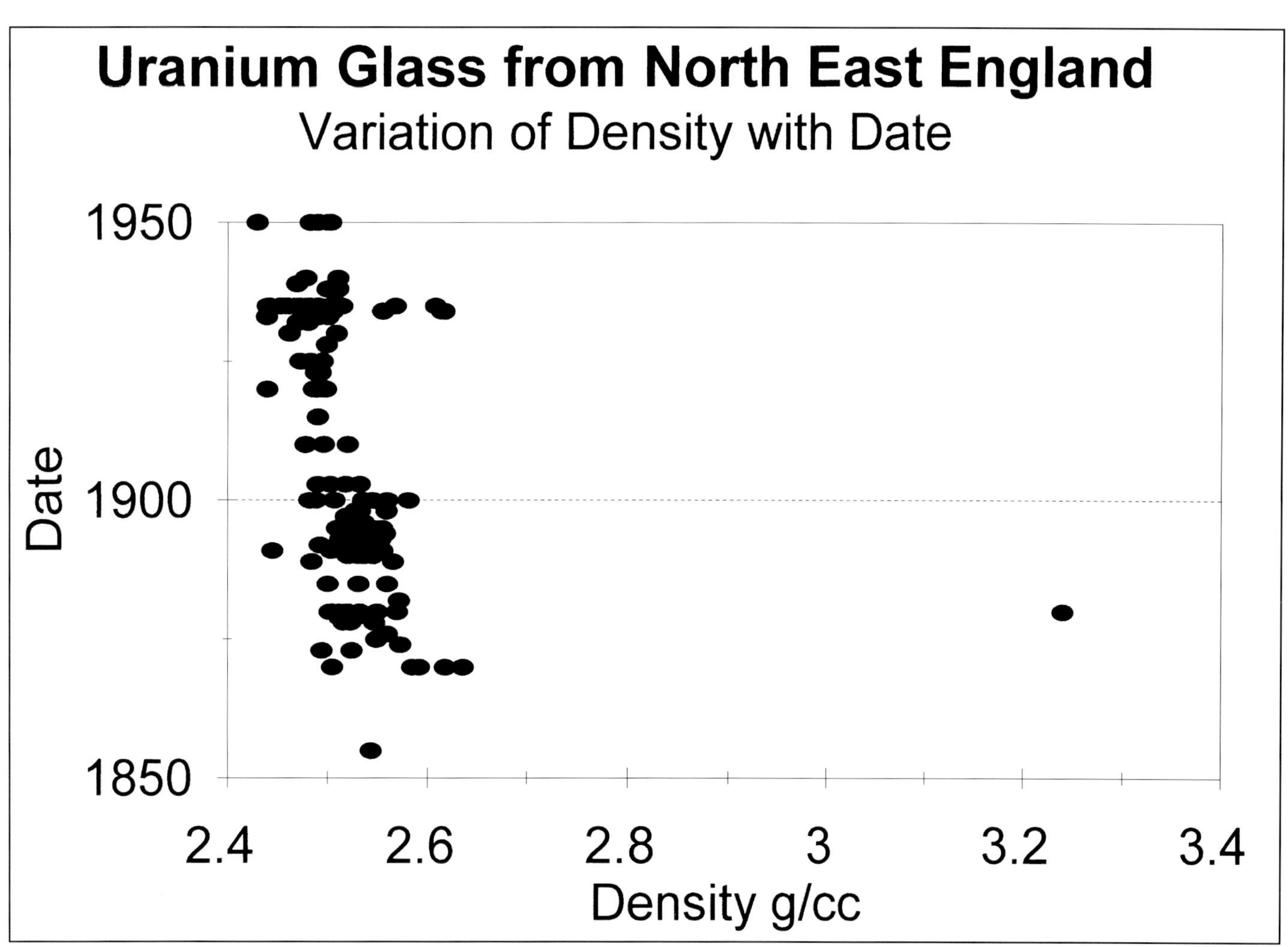

Figure 12

Chapter 8.

Bagley & Company, Yorkshire (Crystal Glass Company)

A history of Bagley & Company and their products is available on CD Rom[1], including a picture gallery and price lists. There appears to have been a glassworks at Ferrybridge, on the outskirts of Knottingly, since the 17th century. However, the cousins J W Bagley and William Bagley founded their factory in 1871. It later came under the control of Stanley and Percy Bagley and following that, the Jackson Group. After the Jackson brothers died, the Rockware Company gained a controlling share, in the late 1960s. The company is now split into Rockware Glass, Headland Works, Knottingly and Stolzle Flaconnage Ltd., Bagley Works, Knottingly. Both firms make bottles.

Bottle manufacture has always been a major part of Bagley & Co., or the Crystal Glass Company, the name under which it traded in the period in which I am interested. During the 1930s and early post war years, it became a prolific producer of tableware and it is this which interests many collectors today.

There is a story that in 1945 their stock of uranium was taken by the Government, to be part of the British weapons program. While I do not dispute this may have happened, I suspect it was a little later. It was not until October 1945 that the Chiefs of Staff recommended the development of a British Atomic Bomb. It would seem that this put only a temporary stop to Bagley's use of uranium. As mentioned in *BBVG*, I have found items with a Design Registration number dated 1950, with uranium in their metal. The illustrations below of Bagley's products add to those reproduced in *BBVG*. Of particular interest is item Photo 34, for while these are identical items, only one is colored with uranium. Was one made before their uranium was confiscated and the other one after, I wonder?

One specialty of Bagley's was the use of leafy metal work to hold the item, see Photo 34. I have not seen this style copied elsewhere and regard it as being equivalent to a signature.

Despite examining a considerable number of Bagley items, I have only found uranium in their green products. While this does not mean they definitively did not use uranium in other colors, it does indicate it may have been a rare occurrence.

Of the total 25 uranium green items measured, the average density is 2.492 g/cc with a standard deviation of 0.021 g/cc. Uranium content had an average of 0.08% wt, with a range of 0.03% wt to 0.13% wt and a standard deviation of 0.03% wt. If a green item has a density outside the range 2.4 g/cc to 2.53 g/cc, it is *probably* not Bagley. If the uranium content is greater than 0.14% wt, it is *probably* not Bagley. If the item is outside both these limits, it is *almost certainly* not Bagley.

Photo 32. Not all the pieces from this dressing table set carry the Design Registration Mark 790482, which is for 20th Feb. 1934. I have only measured the density and uranium concentration on two items, there are slight differences no doubt indicating, as we might expect, that the items were not all made from the same melt. Size of tray, 28 cm x 18 cm. Candle stick, density 2.49 g/cc, uranium 0.9% wt. Small trough, density 2.515 g/cc, uranium 0.12% wt. Value of set $30 - $50.

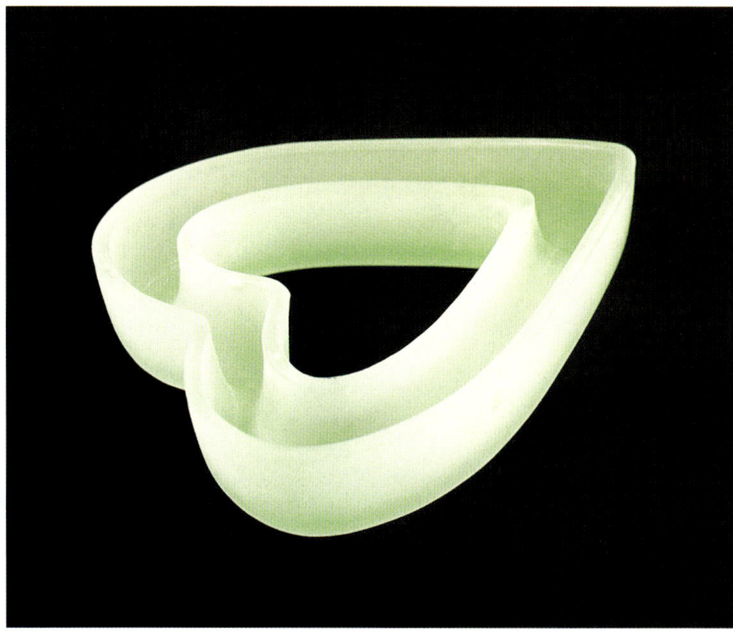

Photo 33. Illustrated in a Bagley Catalogue (late 1930s) as part of the "Bloom Ring" range. Maximum length 17 cm, density 2.49 g/cc, uranium 0.08% wt. Date *about* 1935, value $20 - $30.

Photo 34. Can you spot the difference between this pair of posy vases? They are illustrated in Bagley's catalogues from the 1930s as "Quebec Candlebloom" posy vases. The metal work is typical of the company and is as good as a signature. Of these two, only the one on the left of the Photo contains uranium. Look carefully, it does have a more lively green. So when were they made and why the difference? I can only speculate. It seems highly unlikely they were made in the same era. I suspect the lefthand side was made during the 1930s and the right hand side after the Government impounded all their uranium stocks in the late 1940s. As already mentioned, there is evidence that they resumed the use of uranium in the 1950s, but this was probably only for a limited time, so it is possible that the right hand side vase was made later. 11.25 cm diameter, (4" to be precise), density 2.51 g/cc, uranium 0.16% wt. Value $10 - $30 each.

Consider Photos 35 and 36 together. These show the same design in different modes. Photo 35, a plate, is sometimes seen in a smaller size. Photo 36 is a similar plate with a hole drilled in it and mounted on an aluminum plinth to form a cake stand. I have seen the pattern also produced in pink, blue and amber, but only the green contained uranium. Both glasses have the same diameter of 24 cm, the densities are 2.47 g/cc and 2.49 g/cc. The uranium contents are 0.09% wt. and 0.08% wt. Date about 1935. Value $14 - $24 each.

Consider Photos 37 and 38 together. Clearly these two pieces came from the same glasshouse. They have the same pattern, density, and uranium concentration. The pattern is part of the Bagley Leaf suite, the cocktail dish of that suite is illustrated in BBVG P 55. However unlike that example these are more opaque and have a satin finish. The dish illustrated in Photo 38 is from the Bagley Leaf Fruit Set Cat. No 3055. Dish, height 7.2 cm, density 2.51 g/cc, uranium 0.12% wt. Jug, height 10.5 cm, density 2.51 g/cc, uranium 0.12% wt. Value $20 - $30 each.

Photo 39. This is an example of Bagley's "Elf" posy vase. They were made between 1935 and 1975. It is tempting to assign a pre-war date because of the uranium, but that would be wrong. Although Bagley's stock of uranium was requisitioned for the development of the atomic bomb, there is evidence that Bagley was using uranium after WW2. Diameter 17.7 cm, density 2.50 g/cc, uranium 0.08% wt. Value $20 - $30.

Photo 40. A vase well known to collectors of Bagley glass. Bedford pattern (3057). The interesting point is its very low uranium concentration. It is barely measurable on my Geiger counter, but responds well to uv light. *About* 1935. Height 21.5 cm, density 2.44 g/cc, uranium 0.03% wt. Value $10 - $20.

Photo 41. This bowl, with its lid, is illustrated in the Bagley Catalogue 1938, item 1122; 7" Powder Bowl. It is described as "CRYSTALTYNT", manufactured in four colors, namely green, blue, amber and rose pink. Density 2.5 g/cc, uranium 0.09% wt, (slightly less in the lid). Value $30 - $40.

Chapter 9
Davidson of Gateshead

There has been no diminution in the popularity of collecting the products of George Davidson's companies since I drafted *BBVG*. If anything, interest in the Primrose Pearline may have increased. As I have quoted in my previous book, several authors have written about the history of this Company[1,2,3,4]. Since then, Chris and Val Stewart[5] and the Pressed Glass Collectors Club[6] have also written about this firm. I will not repeat what is in *BBVG* or duplicate these later works, but rather show further examples of Davidson's products and analyse the measurements I have made.

A number of Davidson's catalogues survive. Some are held by the Tyneside Glass Museum. In 2005, the Pressed Glass Collectors Club published data taken from two of Davidson's pattern books, known as Catalogue One and Catalogue Two, together with items shown in catalogues from 1903 & 1910. The authors point out that Davidson acquired the entire moulds and patterns of the Neville Glassworks, W H Heppell and Thomas Gray & Co. and proceeded to produce from some of these moulds. These products, in appearance at least, would be identical to items made from the same moulds by their previous owner.

In *BBVG* I expressed the opinion that, with a few possible exceptions, Davidson used uranium only in their yellow glass. I am still of that opinion and think it likely that there are explanations for these exceptions.

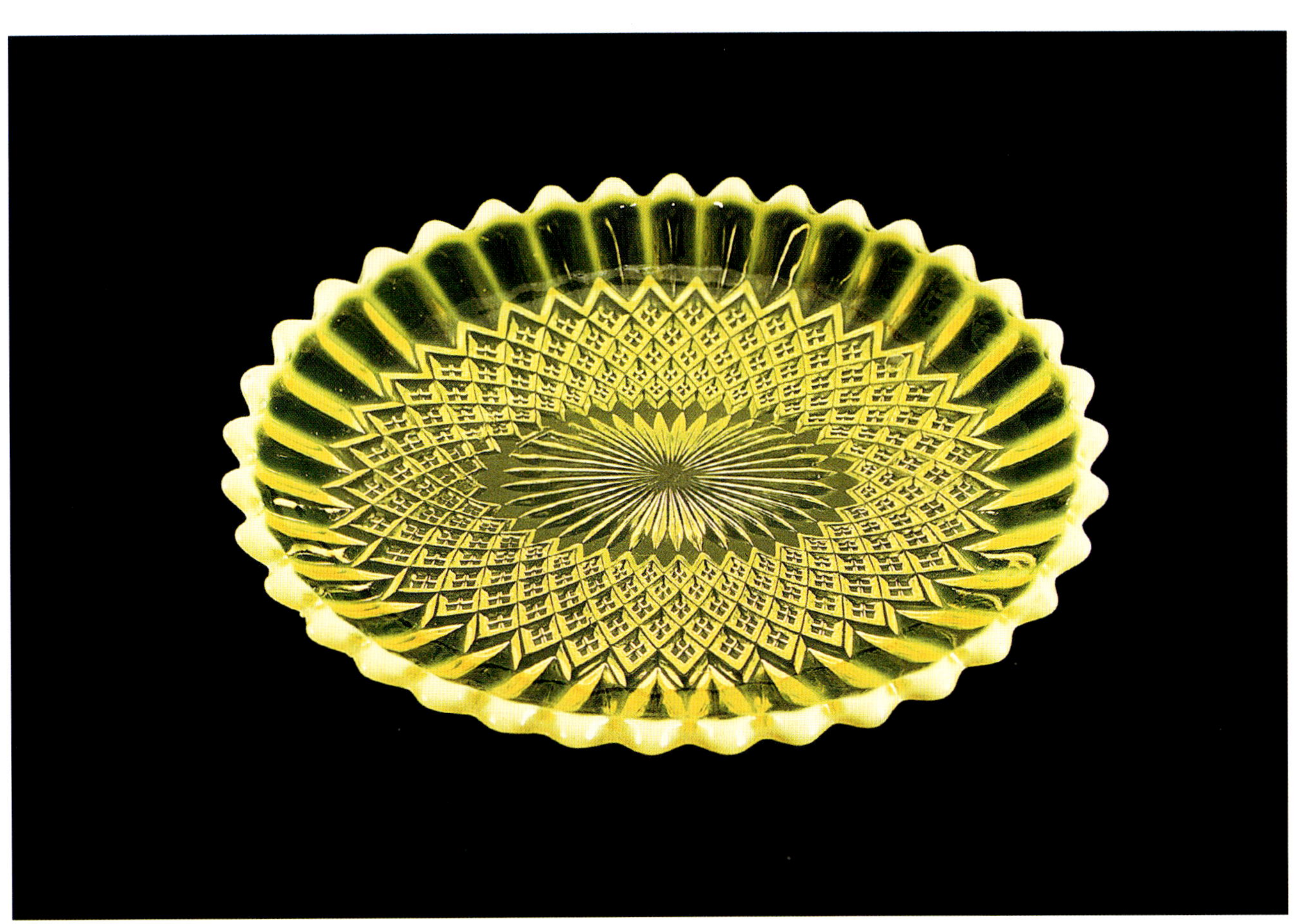

Photo 42. Davidson's Primrose Pearline dish. Design Registration 254027 (1st May, 1895.)
Width 21.5 cm, density 2.54 g/cc, uranium 1.1% wt. Value $100 - $140.

Photo 43. The most exciting example of Primrose Pearline I have yet come across. It carries the Rd 96945, which was a Davidson registration on 31st March, 1888. It also has the word "PATENT" on the inside. As discussed in *BBVG*, Davidson did not take out his patent on Pearline until 1889, although the range was advertised in 1888. That this piece should show the word "Patent" without a patent number suggests it was an early piece in the range, perhaps before the patent had been allocated. It is quite usual to find a Rd Number on Pearline pieces, but this is the first time I have come across the Patent. The dish measures 19 cm x 21 cm, density 2.48 g/cc, uranium 1.12% wt. Value $160 - $240..

Photo 44. This Pearline dish has the Design Registration 217752, which was registered on 6th September, 1893. Width 21 cm, density 2.54 g/cc, uranium 0.99% wt. Value $120 - $160.

Photo 45. This piece of Pearline is low in uranium and weak on color. Where the pattern has been pressed into the plate, the glass appears to be clear. At first I thought the clear layer must have be encapsulated, but I now think this is due to the weak color and the metal being very thin where there are deep indents. It carries the Design Registration number 413701, which is Davidson 14th July, 1903. Diameter 21 cm, density 2.52 g/cc, uranium 0.3% wt. Value $100 - $140.

acid polishing, the item must be pre-1900. Where the item is clearly acid polished it will be at least post 1945, perhaps earlier.

Acid polishing was also used on pressed glass. Where the mould had joints, a slight ridge or sharp edge would be left on the item. Originally, this was removed by fire polishing. The item would be taken back to the furnace and the surface heated to melt away the mould marks. In the case of heavy items, such as tazzas and comports, some distortion was likely to occur during this process, such as a slight twisting of the stem.

It is also worth noting that as early as 1867, Northwood developed a process of etching with "white acid". This consisted of a mixture of hydrofluoric acid and an alkali carbonate. It attacks the surface of exposed glass leaving a white etched finish.

Another technique for decorating glass is sandblasting. It tends to leave a coarser finish than acid etching. In *BBVG*, I show a tumbler made for an International Exhibition and dated 1886. The underside reads "Sandblast Patent". Thus for the purpose of dating, I assume any item decorated by sandblasting will be post-1885.

A valuable aid to dating is wear on the item. Unfortunately, there is no method of measuring wear and relating it to age so the process is subjective. Further, the amount of wear will depend upon the lifestyle of the piece involved. Over the years, the glass will probably have been washed repeatedly. In the days before WW2, the modern detergents we use today were not available. Steel wool, hot water and soap may well have been used on some items. When deciding the amount of wear to expect, various factors have to be considered. A heavy item would be expected to show more wear than a lighter one and a piece that was in every day use should show more wear than a display item kept in a cupboard.

There are of course cases where wear is not as apparent as would have been expected, the "my great auntie had it in a box in her attic and never took it out syndrome". This maybe so, but genuine examples have to be rare. Photos 25, 26 and 27 show an undoubtedly old comport with true wear. This type is difficult to fake. The wear on the foot is not only matt in appearance, it also has long scratches in random directions. These are unlikely to be seen on a glass that has been rubbed on a piece of carborundum paper. Other wear, often overlooked by the fakers, would be expected on the body of the glass, where it has been scratched while in use or rubbed against other glass in the washing up bowl.

The absence of genuine wear should arouse suspicion, but nothing more. The presence of simulated wear should set alarm bells ringing.

Photo 25. An old comport dating from *about* 1860. It has had a hard life and the wear is excessive but nevertheless is a good illustration of what to look for.

Photo 26. A closer view of the wear on the base of the comport in Photo 25.

Engrained dirt that has resisted "normal" cleaning is also a good indicator of age. Over the years small particles of dirt, or grease that is hardened and become resistant to washing, will find their way into nooks and crannies. This is especially common where there is overlaid crimp work or decoration. It also occurs in fine cut patterns. This is well illustrated in Photo 28, a close up of the pattern on the edge of the plate in Photo 22. Such dirt engraining is not easy to fake, although I have heard of one unscrupulous dealer who buries glass in his garden to age it.

Photo 27. A closer look at the side of the comport in Photo 25.

Photo 46 and Photo 47. I will consider these two items together. Neither are marked but they are illustrated in an advert in Pottery and Glass Trades Gazette, 1st April 1893, as examples of Davidson's Pearline. I have seen them described as "Quilted Pillow" pattern. Photo 46 shows a butter dish, length 18 cm, density 2.54 g/cc, uranium 0.5% wt. Value $90 - $110. Photo 47shows a jug, height 10 cm, density 2.52 g/cc, uranium 1.36% wt. Value $70 - $90.

Photo 48. This cute little tumbler is another example of Davidson's Primrose Pearline. The Design Registration Number 217752, 6th September 1893, is clear across the base, possibly indicating the mold was quite young when this item was pressed. Height 7.8 cm, density 2.52 g/cc, uranium 0.62% wt. Value $50 - $80.

Photo 49. There is no Registration mark on this jug but the pattern can be seen in Davidson's catalogues of the turn of the century. Height 13.75 cm, density 2.535 g/cc, uranium 1.1% wt. Date *about* 1900, Value $80 - $120.

Consider the items in Photos 50 and 51. They appear identical in shape and size and are not marked but are illustrated in a Davidson advertisement in *Pottery Gazette* for 1st April, 1893. The densities are so close as to makes no matter, however the uranium levels are different. The piece in Photo 51 has 4 to 5 times more uranium than the item in Photo 50 and consequently is a deeper yellow. It is a good example of similar pieces of Davidson's Pearline having different uranium concentrations. Item in Photo 50, height 10 cm, density 2.51 g/cc, uranium 0.17% wt. Item in Photo 51, height 10 cm, density 2.52 g/cc, uranium 0.74% wt. Date *about* 1895, although Photo 50 may be a little later. Value $80 - $120 each.

Photo 52. This piece is identical to the item shown in *BBVG* p 59, Photo 25. The main difference is that I bought this piece 16 years later, in a different place. There is only the remotest chance that they could have been made from the same batch yet the densities and uranium levels are close, which illustrates the consistency of manufacture. I have shown *BBVG* figures in brackets. Height 8.7 cm; density 2.51 g/cc, (2.52 g/cc); uranium 0.6% wt, (0.56% wt). Date, illustrated in *Pottery Gazette*, April 1893. Value $70 - $90.

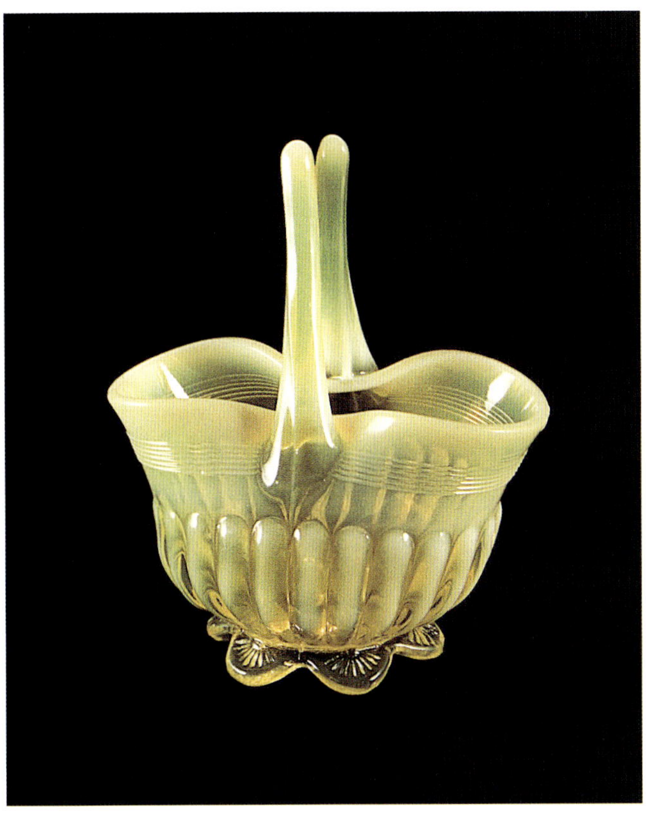

Photo 53. This piece of Pearline is shown in a *Pottery Gazette* advertisement in April 1893. Height 12.5 cm, density 2.53 g/cc, uranium 0.68% wt. Value $60 - $90.

Photo 54. I bought this thinking that it must be Davidson's Pearline. I have included it here to illustrate how easy it is to make a mistake and how valuable density measurements are in making an attribution. The base, with its underside pressed concentric rings, closely resembles that seen on some Davidson pieces. The gadroons and the six rings on the bowl are again to be seen on some Davidson Pearline. When I measured the density I was so surprised that I repeated it to make sure there had been no mistake. Then I took a closer look at the item. The base was slightly different, and the gadroons twist and run into the rings, which they do not on Davidson's items. The metal has several seeds which confirm its age, but who made it? The density suggests a Lancashire glasshouse. Height 6.6 cm, density 2.77 g/cc, uranium 0.34% wt. Date *about* 1890, value $60 - $80.

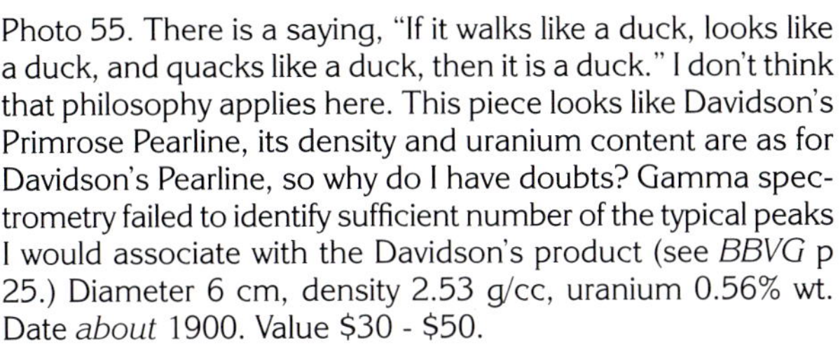

Photo 55. There is a saying, "If it walks like a duck, looks like a duck, and quacks like a duck, then it is a duck." I don't think that philosophy applies here. This piece looks like Davidson's Primrose Pearline, its density and uranium content are as for Davidson's Pearline, so why do I have doubts? Gamma spectrometry failed to identify sufficient number of the typical peaks I would associate with the Davidson's product (see *BBVG* p 25.) Diameter 6 cm, density 2.53 g/cc, uranium 0.56% wt. Date *about* 1900. Value $30 - $50.

Photo 56. This shell dish looks very much like Davidson's Primrose Pearline. At first, I was puzzled by its density, which is a little lower than I would expect for Pearline. I therefore checked the gamma spectrometry (see *BBVG* page 25) but the results were inconclusive, in as much as some, but not all, of the Pearline characteristic peaks were present. However the dish appears in Davidson's pattern books from 1912 onwards as a 5.5" diameter dish. Size 13.7 cm x 10 cm. Density 2.49 g/cc, uranium 0.22% wt. Value $40 - $60.

Photo 57. This Photo will also be seen in Chapter 12 as Photo 75, as it shows both Davidson and Sowerby glass. It illustrates the danger of attribution simply by pattern and demonstrates how designs get copied. The dark amber cucumber dish bears the label of Sowerby, it is identical in size, pattern and density to the green cucumber dish. However this pattern of dish appears in both Bagley and Davidson catalogues, so to whom do I attribute the dish in the middle? As already stated, I do not think Bagley made a Primrose Pearline with uranium and I have seen no evidence that Sowerby did. Furthermore, gamma spectrometry shows a close resemblance to Davidson's Pearline. This, together with its density, justifies an *almost certainly* Davidson, about 1910. Length 24.3 cm, density 2.52 g/cc, uranium 0.1.18% wt. Value $80- $120.

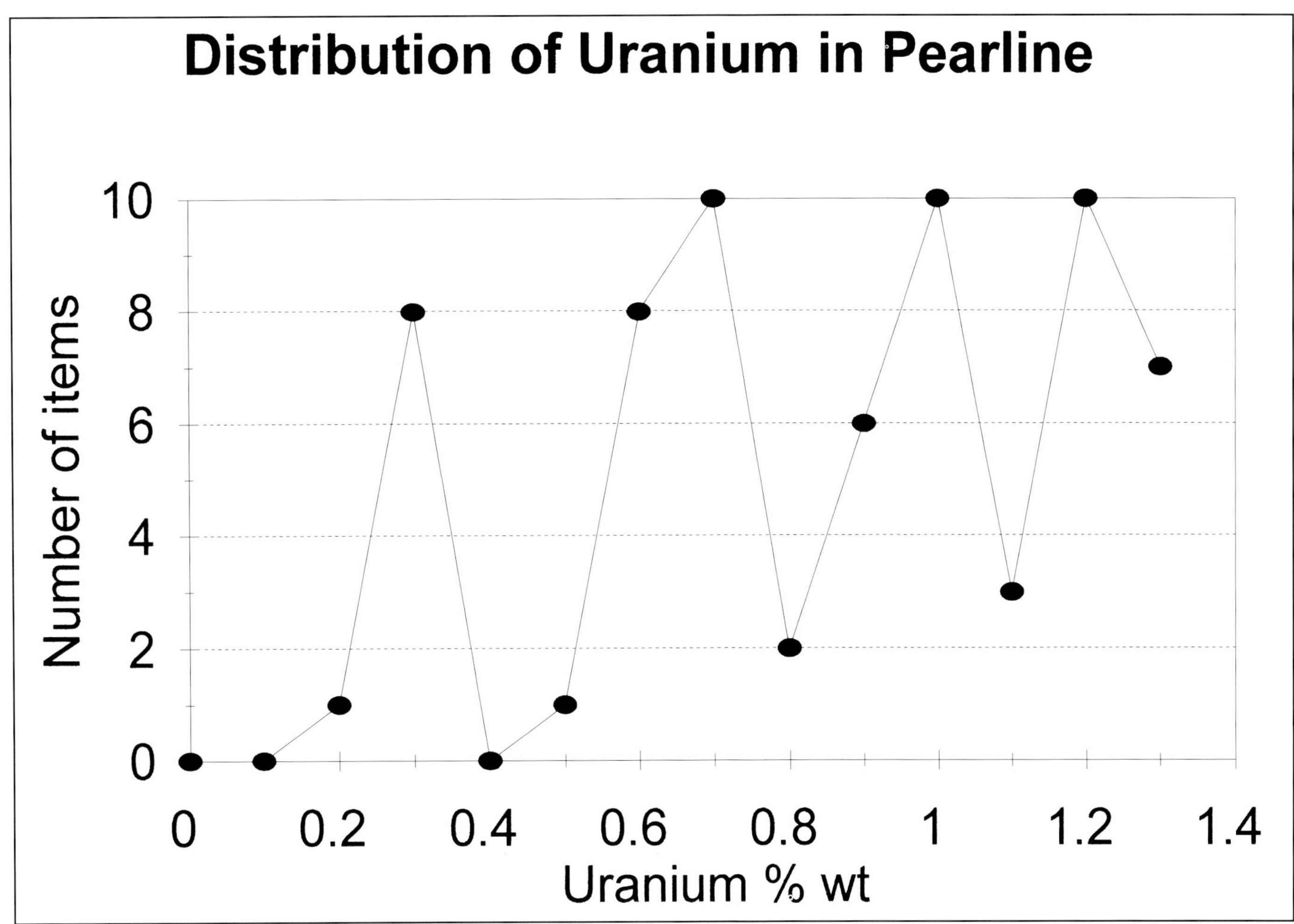

Figure 13

The unusual thing about Davidson's Pearline is that it comes with a range of uranium concentrations. In Fig. 13, I have plotted the frequency of these for 66 examples of this type of glass. It would be incorrect to claim that this was a random sample in the true statistical sense, but they represent my collection for which I have not been biased in selecting by uranium concentration or depth of color. It would seem that there were four concentrations used. One at about 0.28% wt which would give the paler yellow, and others at about 0.6% wt, 0.95% wt, and 1.2% wt. The depth/intensity of the yellow increases with uranium concentration, but after 0.28% the effect is barely noticeable. It is not clear why these different mixes were used, the only theory I can put forward is that as uranium was expensive, after the initial launch of the product, the uranium levels were successively reduced to try to contain production costs.

In contrast to the uranium concentration, the density is very consistent between different items produced at different times. Figure 14 is a bar chart showing the density distribution of the 66 samples quoted above. The statistical mean is 2.531 g/cc, with a standard deviation of 0.017 g/cc. To check whether some of this variation was due to uranium concentration, I have plotted in Figure 15 the density against uranium concentration. The result is not conclusive but indicates a trend, which is overpowered by density variation for other causes, of about 0.03 g/cc increase in density for every 1% wt. increase in uranium concentration. This just under half that I estimated in *BBVG* from a much smaller sample.

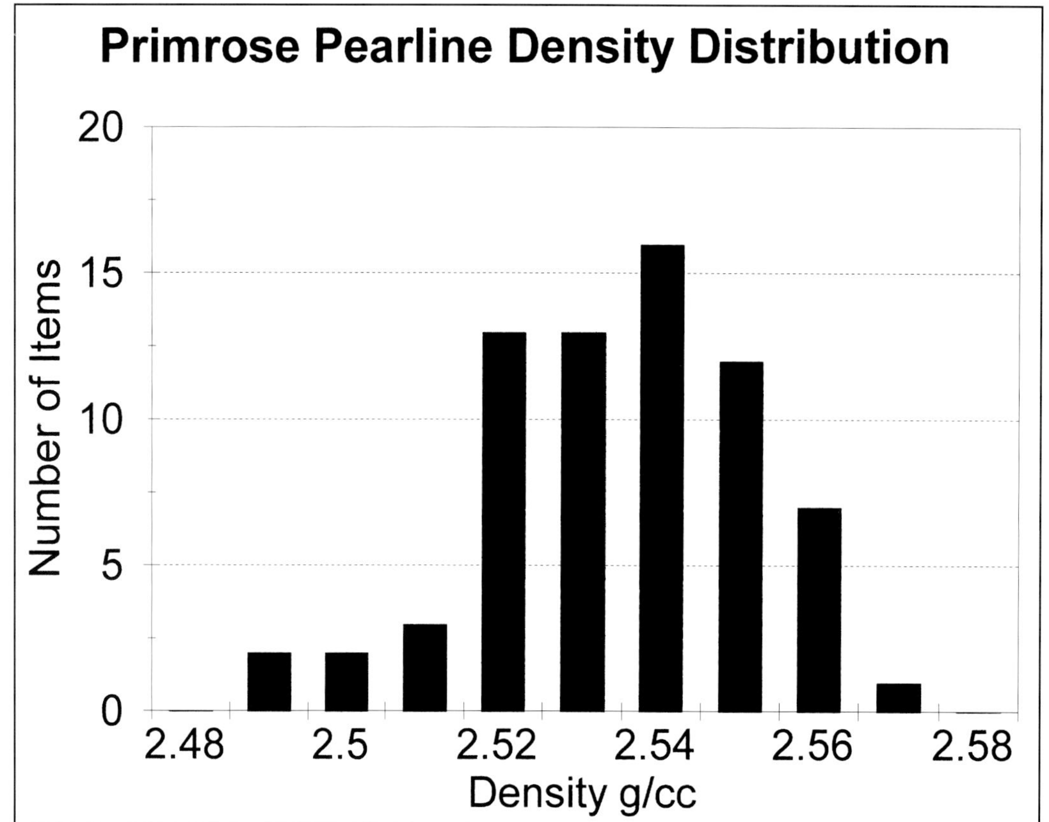

Figure 14

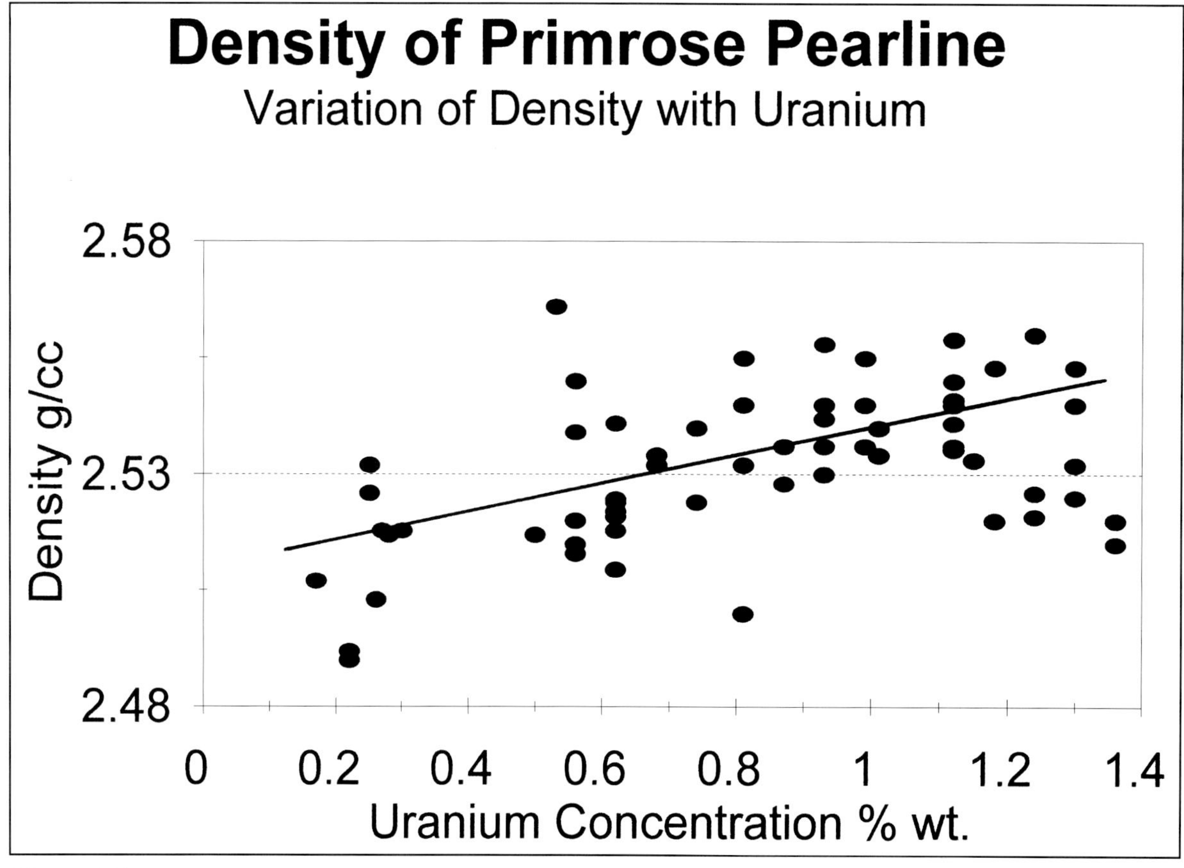

Figure 15

Although Davidson continued production until 1987, then combined with Abrahams and was known as the Brama Teams Glass Works, I have seen no evidence that they used uranium after the end of WW2. My feeling, based upon the Davidson's items I have identified, is that it is probable they had stopped using uranium by the end of the 1920s. It seems likely that they used uranium extensively during the heyday of their Primrose Pearline, but as that lost popularity in the early 1900s, they phased out their production of yellow primrose glass and with it their use of uranium.

Photo 59. Like the examples shown in Photo 34 *BBVG* this piece is not marked but it has all the features associated with Davidson they are the feet, the gadroons, the rings near the rim. An identical piece in Davidson's Blue Pearline is shown in *Pottery Gazette*, 1st July 1891. Diameter 9.3 cm, density 2.48 g/cc, uranium 0.59% wt. Date *period* 1915. Value $40 - $60.

Photo 58. Surely an example of Davidson at their best? Arguably more attractive than the Pearline version of this design. It carries the Design Registration number 176566, registered on 15th August, 1896. The number is sharp and clear, indicating that this was an early piece to emerge from its mold. Width 26.5 cm, density 2.5 g/cc, uranium 0.56% wt. Value $100 - $140.

Photo 60. This is a popular shape of tumbler and could have been made by a number of firms. The style has been in production from the late 1800s to the present day. Close examination shows the following. The top has been hand-finished and is slightly uneven. It has been heavily acid polished. There is a moderate amount of wear. All this suggests a date of the 1920-30 era. The uranium content and density matches very closely what would be expected compared with the celery in *BBVG* Photo 35 and the Grapefruit Dishes in *BBVG* Photos 37 and 38. Height 10 cm, density 2.5 g/cc, uranium 0.68% wt. *Probably* Davidson. Value $40 - $60.

Photo 61. I have not found an exact match to this salt in any of Davidson's patterns but it is extremely close to some. I will therefore give it a *could be, period* 1910. Width 8.8 cm, density 2.51 g/cc, uranium 0.17% wt. Value $40 - $60.

Photo 62. I was reluctant to include this salt under the Davidson chapter, even though a near identical illustration appears in one of their catalogues. Its density is a tad high for that firm. Also it is green and as I have pointed out, there are strong doubts that Davidson ever made green uranium metal. Two possible explanations come to mind. Perhaps another glasshouse was in production of salts that resembled those of Davidson's. Copying of a rival's product was not uncommon. It is also possible that this item was made by a glasshouse that went out of business. Davidson then acquired the mold and included the pattern in their catalogue. Diameter 9 cm, density 2.54 g/cc, uranium 0.17% wt. Date *about* 1890. Value $40 - $60.

Photo 63. This fan vase carries the Design Registration number 831080, which was registered by George Davidson and Co, in 1938. I bought it on eBay because the seller claimed it responded to uv light and therefore contained uranium. I thought it was about to dash my theory that Davidson did not use uranium in their greens. It did respond weakly to uv but not to the Geiger counter. Examination by gamma spectrometry indicated the absence of uranium, so my theory remains intact. Unfortunately the uv response was too weak to photograph, but it compared with the response of a plain glass. The green glow it gave under uv light was probably due to sodium in the metal and serves as another example of how uv testing can mislead. Height 13.7 cm, density 2.44 g/cc, uranium zero. Value $20 - $30.

Chapter 10

Edward Moore & Co.

Although finding clear colorless items from this Tyneside firm is not uncommon, examples colored with uranium are by no means so readily available. During the time I have been researching uranium in glass, I have found, with at least 95% confidence, some 20 examples of the former, but only 8 of the latter. Furthermore, this has been when I have concentrated my efforts on finding uranium glass. This strongly suggests that colored glass, especially that colored with uranium, was not a mainstream product of the glasshouse. Since drafting *BBVG* I have only added two uranium glass items from Ed Moore to my collection. From such a small sample, it is not possible to reach any reasonably firm conclusions about the nature of their uranium products.

Notwithstanding considering these eight, three of which were green, their average density is 2.525 g/cc, with a range of 2.5 g/cc to 2.57 g/cc. Of the 5 yellow items the uranium ranged from 0.14% wt, to 0.25% wt. For the 3 green items the uranium ranged between 0.12% wt and 0.2% wt.

However I have had opportunity to study a document held by Broadfield House Glass Museum. It is titled "Extracts from Reports on Her Majesty's Secretaries of Embassy & Legation on the Manufacture, Commerce, etc., on the countries in which they reside" This document was presented to Parliament in May 1870. It is about an exhibition in the Netherlands in 1869 of domestic economy and reports on the wares of Ed. Moore. Quote "This firm was established in 1860; has a very large home demand for its manufactures which are distinguished for cheapness, durability, and beauty of design and exports very largely to every part of the world. Its collection of glass at Amsterdam was much admired by the Dutch..." The paper gives a number of illustrations of Ed Moore products amongst which are some salts. Not only do the three shown in Photo 41 of *BBVG*, but also the salt shown below in Photo 64 are illustrated. All this makes me revise my confidence limits on those previous attributions from *probably* to an unqualified Edward Moore about 1870.

Photo 64. The style of this salt is very similar to that of the salts illustrated in Photo 41 of *BBVG*. It is clearly illustrated in the document mentioned above. Length 11 cm, density 2.51 g/cc, uranium 0.14% wt. Date *about* 1870. Value $30 - $40

Photo 65. The evidence for this coming from the Ed Moore factory is quite strong. The base and stem are near identical to a candlestick shown in a 1870 catalogue, while the top is identical to an Ed Moore piece shown in a publication by the Pressed Glass Association.[1] I am usually cautious in making attributions based upon additions of this sort, however the pattern is so unusual that there has to be a high probability in this case. Height 22.5 cm, density 2.55 g/cc, uranium 0.25% wt. *Almost certainly* Ed Moore, *about* 1875. Value $60 - $80.

Chapter 11

Greener and Jobling

The business was founded by Henry Greener and James Angus in the 1850s and is now colloquially known to glass collectors as Angus Greener. Angus died in 1869 but Greener carried on trading as Henry Greener. He died in 1882 but the business continued to trade. It was taken over by James Jobling a few years later. He allowed the Company to continue trading under the Greener name until 1921 when it became James A Jobling & Co. Although there is a definite change in product style between the early Greener and the later Jobling years, there appears no clear date when this took place. For that reason I will cover both periods in the same chapter. From the late 1920s through to WW2 the firm concentrated mainly on domestic ware such as jugs, bowls, dressing table sets, vases and so on. Later they also produced, under licence, the heat resistant "Pyrex" boro-silicate glass. However I have found no examples of uranium being used in this glass.

It would seem that while in the early years, Greener period, uranium was used to produce both green and yellow glass, I have found no evidence that uranium was used to produce yellow glass in the later years. There is no doubt that Greener did produce its own version of Davidson's Primrose Pearline, the products being so similar I have been unable to find any simple way of distinguishing their different metal. A fuller account of this glasshouse and some of its products is given in *BBVG*.

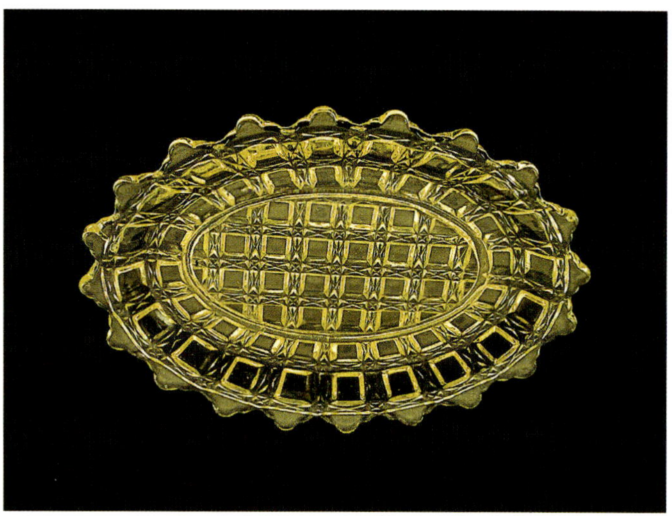

Photo 66. The pattern on this plate is the same as on the jar in Photo 45 in *BBVG*, which has the Design Registration Number 182002, date 1891. However the uranium appears to only be in the square of the design. The in-fill, with its intricate criss-cross patterned roadways, looks as if it is non-colored metal, see Photo 67. It may be an optical illusion but if not, I am mystified how this was achieved. Did it, I wonder, involve a two-stage pressing? The measured uranium level is low, probably because of the presence of this non-uranium glass. The concentration in the squares is likely to be half as much again as that measured. This item does not carry a Design Registration mark, which suggests it may have been molded later than the registration date would imply. I will date it *about* 1900. Even so the Design Registration date is well after the death of Henry Greener and contemporary with James Jobling's ownership. This may explain why the density and uranium concentrations are different from those quoted for earlier examples in *BBVG*. Width 22.5 cm, density 2.48 g/cc, uranium 0.28% wt. Value $40 - $60.

Photo 67. A close-up of the pattern of the dish in Photo 66, showing the apparent presence of non-uranium metal.

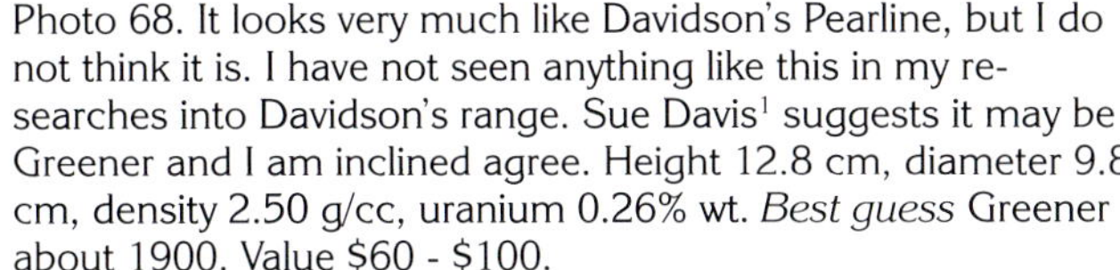

Photo 68. It looks very much like Davidson's Pearline, but I do not think it is. I have not seen anything like this in my researches into Davidson's range. Sue Davis[1] suggests it may be Greener and I am inclined agree. Height 12.8 cm, diameter 9.8 cm, density 2.50 g/cc, uranium 0.26% wt. *Best guess* Greener about 1900. Value $60 - $100.

Photo 69. This plate carries the Design Registration Number 780719 which, unusually, is on the underside of the plate. It is for the Jobling Tudor Rose pattern dated 1933, catalogue No 8000. Diameter 26 cm. Density 2.44 g/cc, uranium 0.16% wt. Value $30 - $50.

Photo 70. Three-footed bowl, bears the Design Registration Number 800443, registered by Jobling on 19th February, 1935. I suspect this piece was made several years later. Diameter 14.5 cm, density 2.47 g/cc, uranium 0.12% wt. Value $20 - $30.

Photo 71. This little jar has not only become separated from the complete trinket set, it has also lost its lid. It carries the Rd 795794 and is shown in the Jobling 1934 catalogue as Jade Trinket Set 12500. The complete set would then have cost 11/6d; the jar or "small puff" as it is called, (5p in today's money). Height 6.3 cm, density 2.64 g/cc, uranium 0.25%. It is interesting to note that both the density and uranium are what I expected from my assessment of the Jobling Jade formula. (See *BBVG* p69). Value $10 - $14.

Photo 72. This flower holder, or as some would call it a frog, is quite different from the hollow ones patented by Davidson at the start of the 20th Century. It is solid and has 19 holes. The evidence favors Jobling as the maker. That firm did make this type of holder, it also bears the words "British Make" (see *BBVG*, p 69), the uranium and density are also close to the estimated values from the Jobling Jade formula. Diameter 9 cm, density 2.57 g/cc, uranium 0.22% wt. *Probably* Jobling about 1935. Value nominal.

Colored Greener glass is not common and I have only examined a handful of examples. With regard to the yellow glass, five examples had an average density of 2.565 g/cc, with a range of 2.45 g/cc to 2.64 g/cc. The uranium content averaged 0.27% wt, with a range 0.19% to 0.37%. The figures exclude a "Pearline style" example, which had a density of 2.53 g/cc and a uranium concentration of 0.62% wt., which makes it indistinguishable from the Davidson product.

With respect to the Jobling era I have only found green glass to contain uranium. Examples of these are more readily available and I show the density distribution for the clear green glass in Fig 16. The uranium content is remarkably constant with eleven examples at 0.12% wt, and one at 0.15% wt. Jobling also made an opaque green, (jade) metal. I have examined five examples, their average density was 2.59 g/cc with a range of 2.56 g/cc to 2.62 g/cc and an average uranium content of 0.26% wt. with a range of 0.22% to 0.37%.

Jobling Clear Green
Density Distribution
Number of Items
0
1
2
3
2.42
2.44
2.46
2.48
2.5
Density g/cc

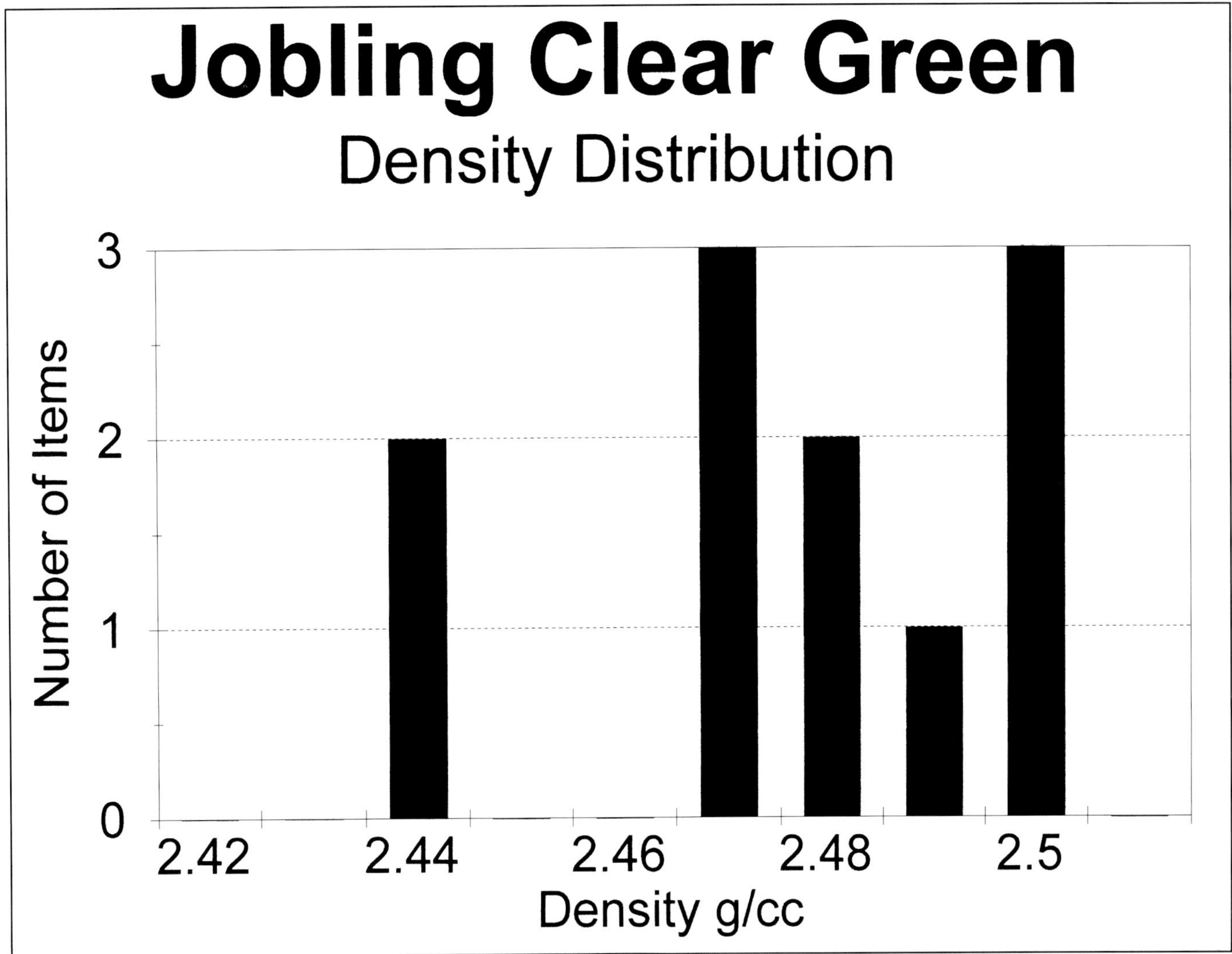

Figure 16

Chapter 12

Sowerby of Gateshead

The history of this Tyneside firm has been well covered by other authors, and I have summarized it in *BBVG*. My research has not added to this aspect, but I have studied more examples of their products and the results are described below. Of particular interest is Photo 75. It is yet another example of the difficulty of attribution by style or design!

Photo 73. An exquisite example of Sowerby Queens Ivory, (see *BBVG* p71), it has the peacock trademark as well as a Registration Lozenge for 6th June 1879. Height, including handles, 3.8 cm, density 2.51 g/cc, uranium 1.12% wt. Value $80 - $120.

Photo 74. Comparing this basket with that shown in *BBVG* page 73, Photo 57 would appear to confirm its origin as Sowerby. But is it, or is it a Sowerby look-alike? The rim and the general shape for the two items look the same. However the handle has different ridging. The bases are similar but not the same and of course the pattern is different. Density would suit a Sowerby attribution but I cannot match the uranium content. I will give it a cautious *could be* and a *period* date of 1910. Width 18 cm, density 2.49 g/cc. Uranium 0.16% wt. Value $40 - $60.

Photo 75. I make no apology for showing this picture twice; it has appeared as Photo 57 in Chapter 9, Davidson's of Gateshead. It illustrates the danger of attribution simply by pattern and demonstrates how designs get copied. The dark amber cucumber dish bears the label of Sowerby, it is identical in size, pattern and density to the green cucumber dish. On this basis I must say Sowerby without reservation. The date is likely to be just before WW2, so let us say *about* 1938. Without that label the problem would have been that this pattern of dish appears in both Bagley and Davidson catalogues. See Chapter 9 for further discussion. Length 32 cm, density 2.47 g/cc, uranium 0.05% wt. Value $10- $20.

Photo 76. I have not been able to find this pattern in any books, but the striking aspect of this candlestick is its color. Green is common with uranium glass, but the effect of the uranium usually gives the color some "life." This green, identical to the candlestick shown in Photo 56 of *BBVG*, is dull and a shade I have only seen in that Sowerby candlestick. Furthermore the density and uranium concentrations are effectively the same. Adding all this evidence together I have resisted the temptation to say "*probably*" and will settle for a "*could be*" Sowerby, *about* 1890. Height 15.5 cm, density 2.56 g/cc, uranium 0.23 % wt. Value $40 - $50.

Photo 77. Its very close resemblance to Photo 76 is the only reason I have included this Victorian candlestick in this chapter, and then only as a "*best guess*." Height 14.4 cm, density 2.58 g/cc, uranium 0.81% wt. Date *about* 1890. Value $40 - $50.

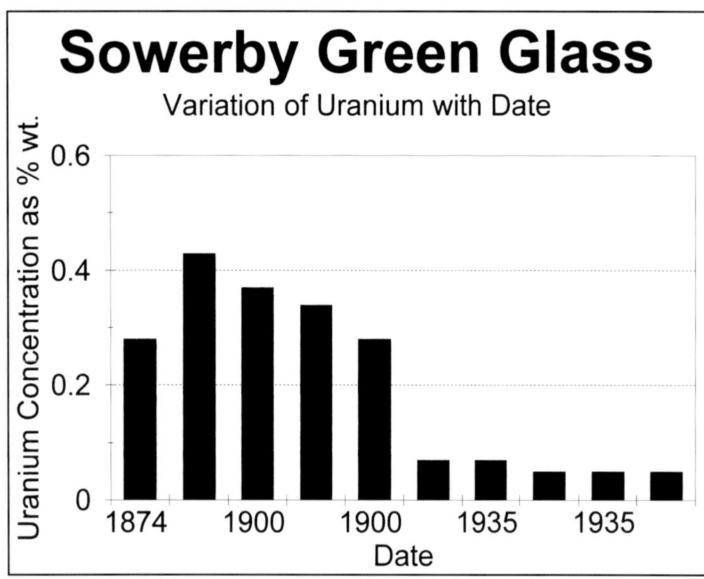

Figure 17

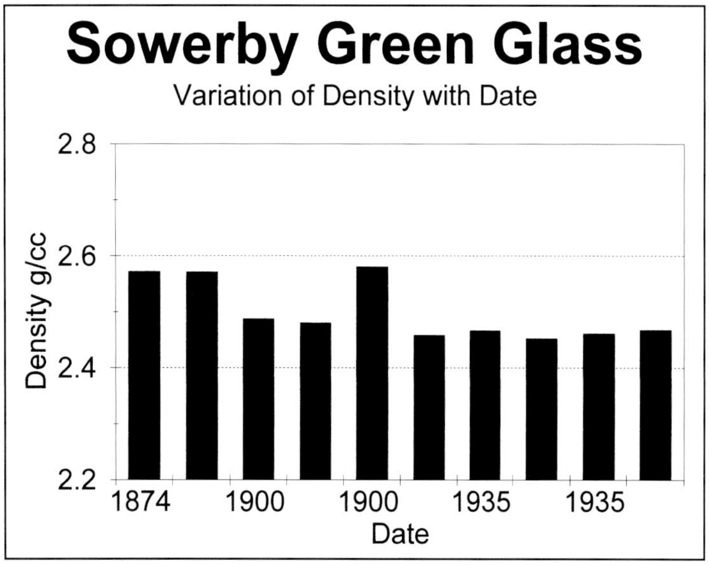

Sowerby Green Glass

Variation of Density with Date

Density g/cc

2.8

2.6

2.4

2.2

1874 1900 1900 1935 1935

Date

Figure 18

To close this chapter I will consider all the high confidence data that I have on this firm with respect to the nature of their metal.

Their yellow uranium glass appears to be confined to the pre 1900 period and then it was not prolific. I have only had four such items in my collection. Their uranium content ranged from 0.25% wt to 0.5% wt. The densities from 2.54 g/cc to 2.56 g/cc. In addition, I have only one piece of Giallo and, surprisingly, its density is 3.24 g/cc and uranium content is 1.05% wt.

Their green uranium glass is more common and appears to extend from the early 1870s to WW2 or even later. Fig 17 shows how the uranium concentrations appear to have changed over time. It strongly suggests that uranium concentrations were kept very much lower after the turn of the century. This may well be due to efforts to contain production costs during the depression years. Fig 18 shows the variation of density of their glass with date. It is not inconsistent with the results for non-colored glass shown in Fig 10 and suggests the higher densities came from the earlier years.

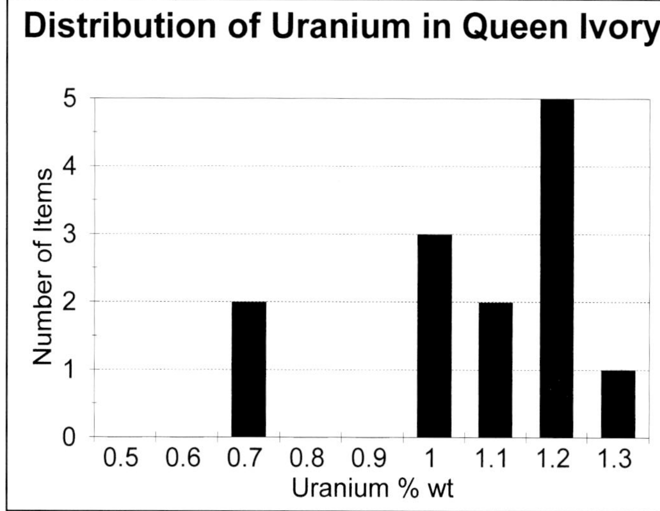

Figure 19

Sowerby also found a use for uranium in their Queen's Ivory range, quite popular with present day collectors. Fig 19 shows the distribution of uranium in the Queen's Ivory items that I have examined. The majority lie in the 1% wt to 1.3% wt range, although it would seem that a few had little over half that amount of uranium. Again, perhaps this was a cost cutting exercise. In contrast the density, see Fig 20 appears to be much more consistent, the majority being about 2.53 g/cc and all within the range 2.5 to 2.55 g/cc.

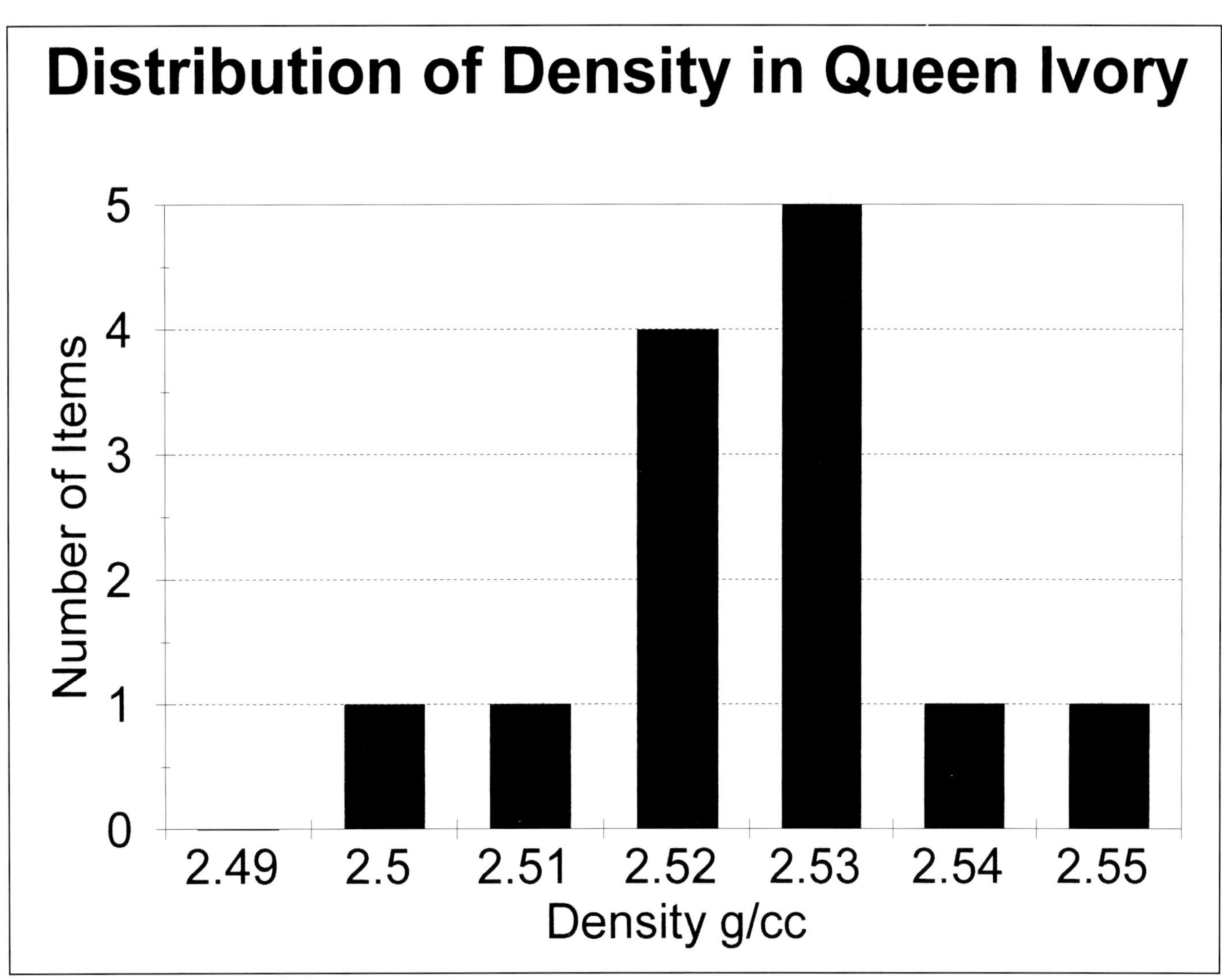

Figure 20

Chapter 13

North West England.

In *BBVG*, I correctly referred to this area as the "The Lancashire Glasshouses." However, with the reorganizations that took place in local government, it is now probably more accurate to refer to the North West of England.

The present day collector will associate firms like Percival, Vickers; Molineaux, Webb; Burtles, Tate; James Derbyshire; Kerr, Webb; Edward Bolton; and Pilkington. There were many more glasshouses in the area but most of them disappeared from the scene around the turn of the nineteenth century. Manchester glass goes back to at least 1605. In the early 1800s other names appear such as Thomas Holt, James Holt & Co., Thomas and George Hawkes (of Dudley, English Midlands), Vauxhall Glass Bottle Works, Orford and Foster's Glass Works, Crown Glassworks, Thomas Robinson & Co., Maginnis Molineaux & Co., Daniel Watson & Co. and Frederick Farham[1].

In contrast, the list of Glass Design Registrations for the years 1873-5 shows that only seven from this area registered designs. Arguably, the dominant firms for this area, by the late 1800s and early 1900s were Percival, Vickers & Co., and Molineaux Webb & Co. As described in *BBVG*, some catalogues from these firms survive and illustrate a very large range of both pressed and blown glass.

During my researches I have examined 53 pieces of clear non-uranium glass and 62 pieces of uranium glass, for which I have high confidence levels, (>98%), as being from this part of England. The density characteristics are shown in Figs 21 – 23.

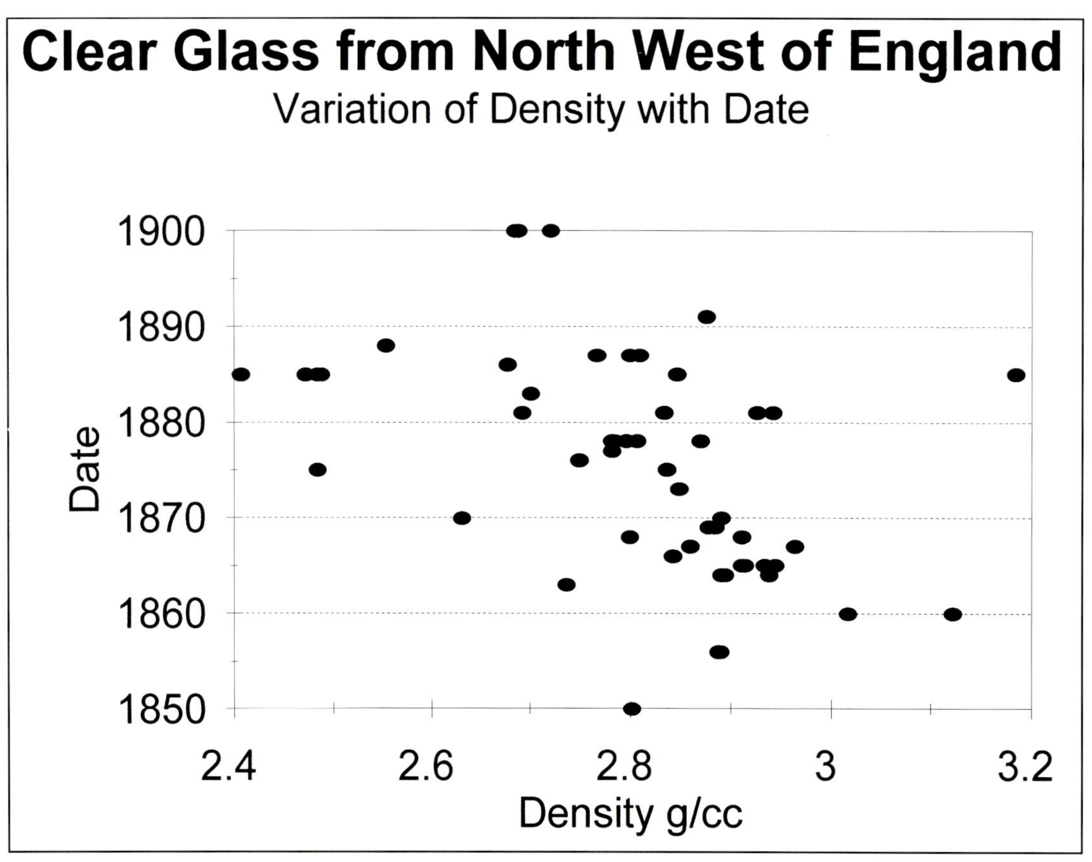

Figure 21

Fig. 21 shows how the densities varied with date for clear non-uranium glass. It is seen that most densities are greater than 2.6 g/cc. The few that are not could well have been made from old moulds acquired by another glasshouse, perhaps in the North East of England. Generally there is a trend for the higher densities to be associated with the earlier dates.

Fig 22 shows how the densities of uranium glass vary with date. The general trend is much the same as for the non-uranium glass, but with a few more examples of densities less than 2.6 g/cc. and three as high as 3.4 g/cc.

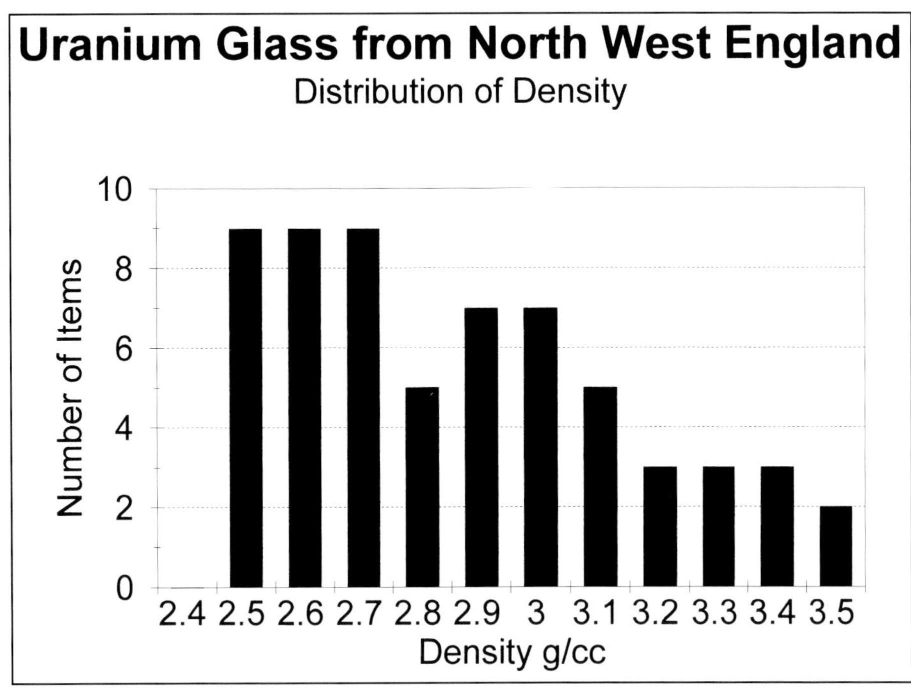

Figure 22

Fig 23 shows how the density of the uranium glass is distributed and again we see the bulk is above 2.6 g/cc. and less than 3.1 g/cc.

As with the North East of England glass, we see the area appears to produce glass within a significant and identifiable range. However, in this case there is a greater spread and a clear indication of lead in the mix, but as we shall see, not as much as that associated with the English Midlands.

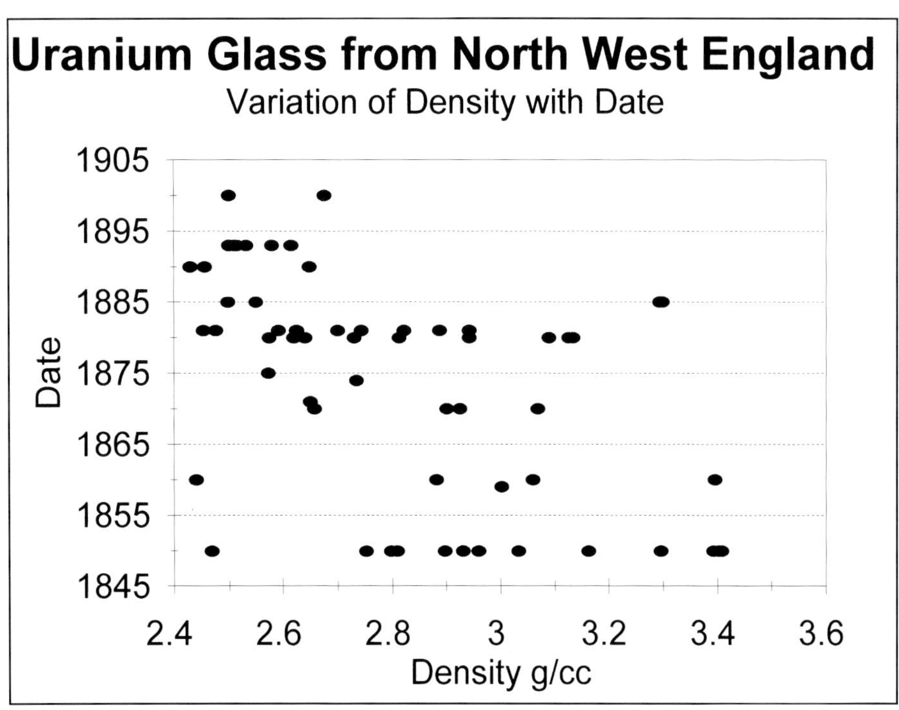

Figure 23

Chapter 14

Edward Bolton, Orford Lane Glassworks

I have included this company under Lancashire because that is where the British 1881 census places Warrington. Modern maps show it as being in Cheshire.

Lancashire Bolton should not be confused with Boulton (note the different spelling), associated with the English Midlands. Little is known about Edward Bolton and most of what I have read appears to have its origins in the work of Lattimore.[1] It would seem the Orford Lane Glassworks dates back to 1797, when Thomas Robinson set it up, to be joined later by his nephew Peter Robinson. Edward Bolton, (who was born in 1823 in Warrington), joined after the founder's death. According to Lattimore, they separated by mutual consent in 1869 when Edward Bolton stayed on to run the Orford Lane Glassworks. Indeed, a design was registered by "Peter Robinson and Bolton of Warrington" on 18th October 1867, but on 5th July 1869, less than two years later, a design was registered by "Edward Bolton, Orford Lane Glassworks, Warrington."

According to Lattimore, Bolton took his two sons into the business. Charles eventually immigrated to Australia but George remained. The 1881 census shows a George Y Bolton, aged 29, glass manufacturer, living at 11 Museum Street, Warrington. This would put his birth date about 1852, and is quite consistent with his father's birth date of 1823. In 1877 a design was registered in the name of Bolton, Son & Wood, again at Orford Lane Glass Works, Warrington. It is not clear who Wood was or how long he/she stayed with Edward & Son, but in December 1885 the "Grace Darling" boat design was registered in the name of Edward Bolton. Finally, on 11th August 1888, Design No 105464 was registered in the name of "Edward Bolton & Sons, Orford Lane Glass Works, Warrington, Glass Maker." We do not know who these sons were for Edward appears to have had five in all. Best guess is that one of them would have been Walter S Bolton, who would then have been aged 25.

Edward Bolton died on 26th December 1889, but what happened to his glassworks? I have not been able to find any further design registrations in the name of Bolton or Orford Street Glass Works.

Consider the glass "Grace Darling" boat shown in Photo 78. This is an example in yellow Pearline style glass. The more common version is in clear glass and comes in several sizes. Generally they are the same pattern and those I have seen have the design registration numbers 39414 & 23527. The former, registered by Edward Bolton on 11th December 1885, is for the boat. Some collectors have told me the latter refers to the Grace Darling name. I have tried to trace the Design Registration number 23527, but found it only applies to a pattern on a piece of cloth and has nothing to do with Grace Darling. So clearly on the basis of the Registration Number 39414, we should attribute the boat in Photo 78 to Bolton, or should we? There are two anomalies, one of which demonstrates the value of density measurements. As stated on p 77 of *BBVG* and confirmed in the analysis here in Chapter 13, I have generally found that the Lancashire Glasshouses were using a metal with a density in the range 2.7 - 2.9 g/cc. Robinson & Bolton followed in this tradition, their glass densities being about 2.9 g/cc. However the density of the boat in Photo 78 is 2.5 g/cc, only slightly higher than the densities of several clear glass boats I have examined. So did Bolton go to a lower density metal after he split from Peter Robinson? It is quite possible but not likely.

Now consider the color. It is clearly in the style of Davidson's Pearline, however the Pearline Patent was not registered until December 1889, which was when Edward Bolton died and four years after the Grace Darling boat design was registered. It seems highly unlikely that Bolton was producing Pearline four years before Davidson. Thus I think the boat in Photo 78 was made by Davidson from either the Bolton design or mould. This being the case, it would seem probable that all the clear glass Grace Darling boats, having a density about 2.5 g/cc, also came from Davidson and not Bolton's glasshouse.

Photo 78. This "Pearline" type boat flower trough has several marks. On the inside of the floor of the boat, in circular format in raised letters is "Grace Darling Boat." In the middle of this circle is the Design Registration "23527". On the stern of the boat all these are repeated but in straight lines. The impressions are so indistinct I cannot say whether the Rd 39414 is also present. Probably indicating that this item was pressed from a much-used mold. Although this design is without doubt linked to Ed Bolton, the foregoing explains why I do not think the item was made by that firm, but rather by Davidson about 1900 or later. Length 28 cm, density 2.5 g/cc, uranium 0.17% wt. Value $200 - $300.

Chapter 15

Burtles, Tate & Company, Manchester

Not a lot has been written about this Lancashire firm and I have given a brief outline in *BBVG*. Suffice to say here that they were founded in Manchester in 1858. At this time pressed glass was coming to the fore but mainly using leaded metal. The use of uranium would also have been gathering popularity. The firm was taken over by Butterworth in 1924. Compared with others they do not appear to have been prolific with Design Registrations. Their first was on 24th Feb 1870 and from then until 1900 I have only found 31 registrations in their name. There is a cluster in the years 1884/5.

Examples of this firm's uranium glass are few and far between and it is unwise to draw conclusions from the three pieces I have examined. I have not seen any of their wares in uranium green, only in yellow with a Pearline effect.

Because of the rarity of marked items from this firm, in Photo 79 I show another Swan, similar to the one shown in *BBVG*, Photo 71. However, as the caption explains, it has much less milk in the color. It is interesting to note the closeness of the uranium and density of these two items. (The value for the swans in *BBVG* are shown in brackets for comparison.)

Photo 79. Although this is similar to the swan shown in Photo 71 *BBVG*, it has far less of the milky effect and illustrates the variations between pieces. It carries the Rd No 20086, for 1885. These pieces were bought at different times from different dealers, but their characteristics are similar and I give the equivalent measurement for the item in *BBVG* in brackets. Height 8 cm (8 cm), density 3.28 g/cc (3.29 g/cc), uranium 0.22% wt (0.25% wt.) Date *about* 1885. Value $80 - $120.

Photo 80. Although this swan has no uranium in its makeup, I have included it because of its close resemblance to the one in Photo 79. It is a little smaller and has no Design Registration mark. It would be easy to attribute it to same glasshouse. Closer examination should raise doubts, it is crudely molded, the pattern work on the neck of the swan is sparse, and the animals head is not so well formed. However the density has the final word in saying this is probably not a genuine Burtles piece. Unfortunately I haven't a clue who did make it. I would have suspected its birth of being nearer 2000 than 1900 but the density makes me wonder. Was it another Lancashire glasshouse in from the Continent? Height 5.6 cm, density 2.75 g/cc, uranium nil. Value nominal.

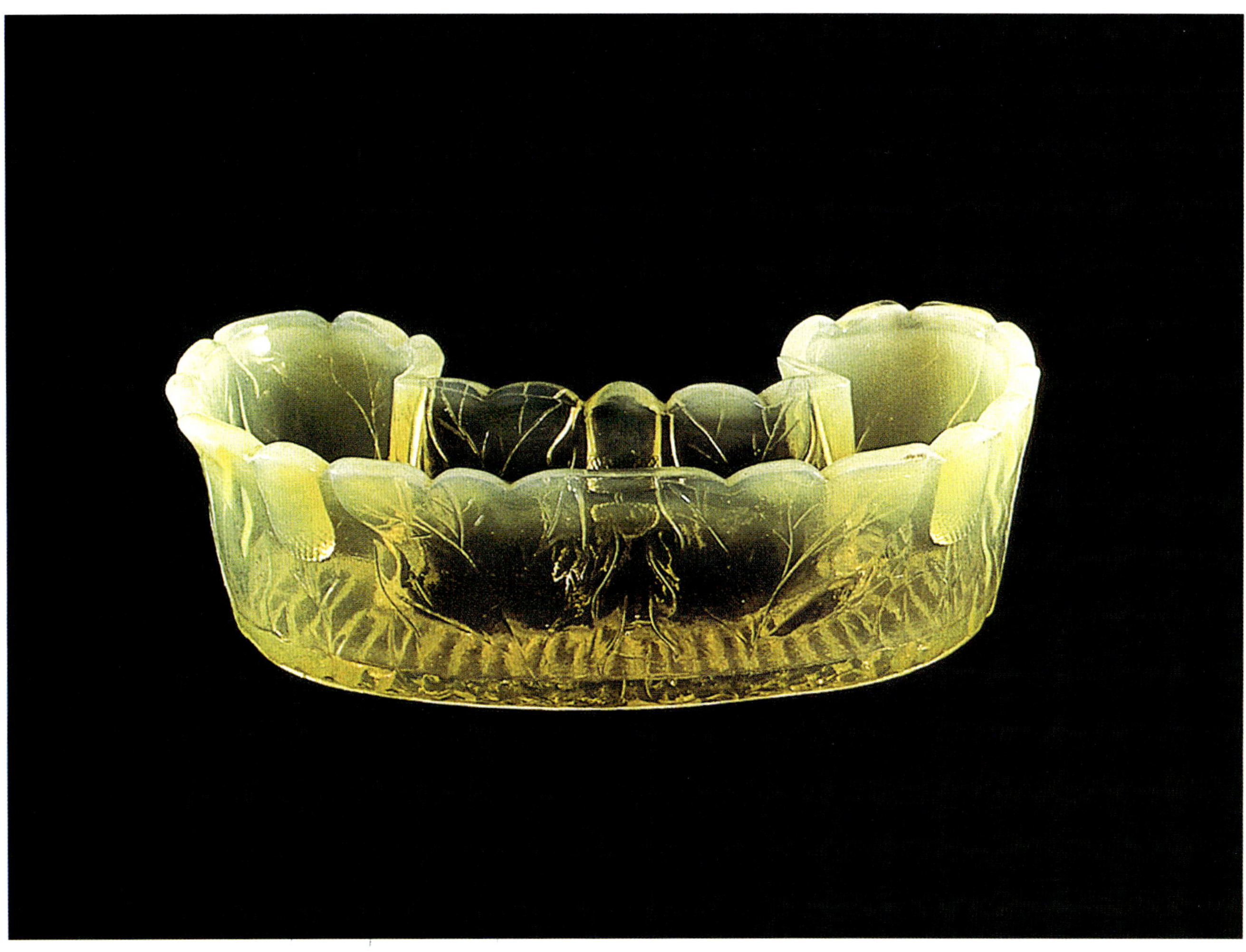

Photo 81. This flower trough carries the Design Registration 29106, which was from Burtles, Tate and Co. 29th June 1885. This is some 4 years before Davidson patented their Pearline. However it is quite possible that when Burtles made this piece they were using an old mold. However, like the other examples of Burtles, the density is far to high for it to be confused with any of Davidson's products. Length 15.2 cm, density 3.3 g/cc, uranium 0.19% wt. Value $100 - $145.

Chapter 16

The Derbyshire Brothers

What is loosely referred to as Derbyshire Glass does not indicate that it originated from that English county, but came from the one of the glassworks of the Derbyshire brothers. As explained in *BBVG*, they were James, John and Thomas and they started up business in 1858. In 1873 John left the partnership and set up on his own. This business only lasted four years, but John did adopt a characteristic trademark of an anchor blended with a back-to-back JD, (see *BBVG* Photo 72). The Derbyshire brothers appear to disappear from glass-making after 1881 and it is not known what happened to their molds. The three photos below are all I have to add to the entry in *BBVG*.

Photo 82. This vase carries a clear Design Registration lozenge for 15th March 1871, parcel No 9. Registered by J J and T Derbyshire. Height 21.25 cm, density 2.75 g/cc, uranium 0.19% wt. Value $140 - $180.

Photo 83. I have included this piece under Derbyshire with some hesitation. It is unmarked but the very unusual double knop on the stem is similar to Photo 82. Moreover, the density is consistent with what I associate with this firm. I will give it a *probably*. Height 19 cm, density 2.77 g/cc, uranium 0.28% wt. Date *about* 1880, value $30 - $40.

Photo 84. The similarities between this vase and the ones in Photos 82 and 83 are striking. The base is the same size and shape with the same number of serrations as in Photo 83. The top of the vase is similar to that in Photo 82. It seems very unlikely that these could have come about by accident. The problem is with the density, which is much lower than that of most other pieces of Derbyshire glass. While I will give this a *could be* Derbyshire, I would make the reservation that it may have been produced elsewhere from a Derbyshire mold, which, as I indicated in *BBVG*, is quite likely. For that reason I date it 1890 *period*. I have examined two of these vases and both densities and uranium concentrations are nominally the same. Height 20.5 cm, density 2.46 g/cc, uranium 0.37% wt. Value $40 - $60.

Chapter 17

Molineaux Webb & Company

There is little I can add to what I have already written in *BBVG* about this Lancashire glasshouse, which dates back to 1827. Identification of their products is difficult due to the absence of catalogues and design books in the public domain.

I have examined some sixteen pieces for which I have high confidence levels that they originated from this firm. Unfortunately this is too few to draw firm conclusions and they should be regarded as indicative rather than confirmed.

With regard to 10 yellow (topaz) pieces, 8 had uranium concentrations in the range 0.45% wt to 0.56% wt. With regard to 6 green pieces, with 1 exception, their uranium concentrations lay between 0.25% wt and 0.37 % wt.

In Fig. 24 I have plotted the variation of density with date for 16 of these pieces. Two results show a density of just over 2.4 g/cc. Almost certainly these were not made by Molineaux, Webb & Co. but from their moulds after they had been acquired by another glasshouse. The remainder all have densities greater than 2.7 g/cc and there is evidence to say that the earlier pieces were made from a full lead mix.

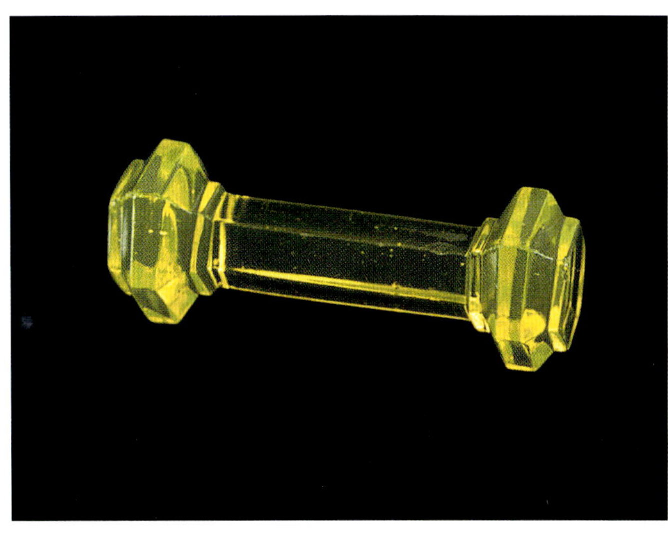

Photo 85. This knife rest is virtually an exact copy of the pair shown in *BBVG* Photo 79, except, whereas that one was green, this is golden yellow. Although the density is a tad lower than I would have expected, it is within the range of other Molineaux items and I can raise the confidence level from *could be* to *probably*. Length 8.8 cm, density 2.73 g/cc, uranium 0.46% wt. Date (possibly later than the green ones) *about* 1880. Value for a pair, $40 - $60.

Photo 86. There are nine large flats on the lower part of the bowl and a 27-point starburst on the base. Close examination shows the presence of striations, which indicates these have been cut and hand polished, not molded or acid polished. While the base does not show heavy wear, the marks and scratches on the body of the glass is a true indication of genuine use over many years. There is also a little white seed in the metal, just what would have been expected from an old coal or wood fired furnace. One of the old catalogues, believed to be of Molineaux Webb, shows a range of finger bowls. The copy I have seen is very faded but this appears to match the "Etonian." Diameter 14 cm, density 2.93 g/cc, uranium 0.56% wt. I will say *probably* Molineaux *about* 1870. Value $70 -$90.

Photo 87. Made in a two-piece mold, this candlestick is a sister of one shown in *BBVG* 77, left hand side, *BBVG*, except that the underside of the base has a starburst style molding, (probably because a different plunger was used) and is greenish yellow not amber. I suspect that it is also slightly younger. Height 14 cm, density 3.06 g/cc, uranium 0.25% wt. Date *about* 1860. Value $30 - $50.

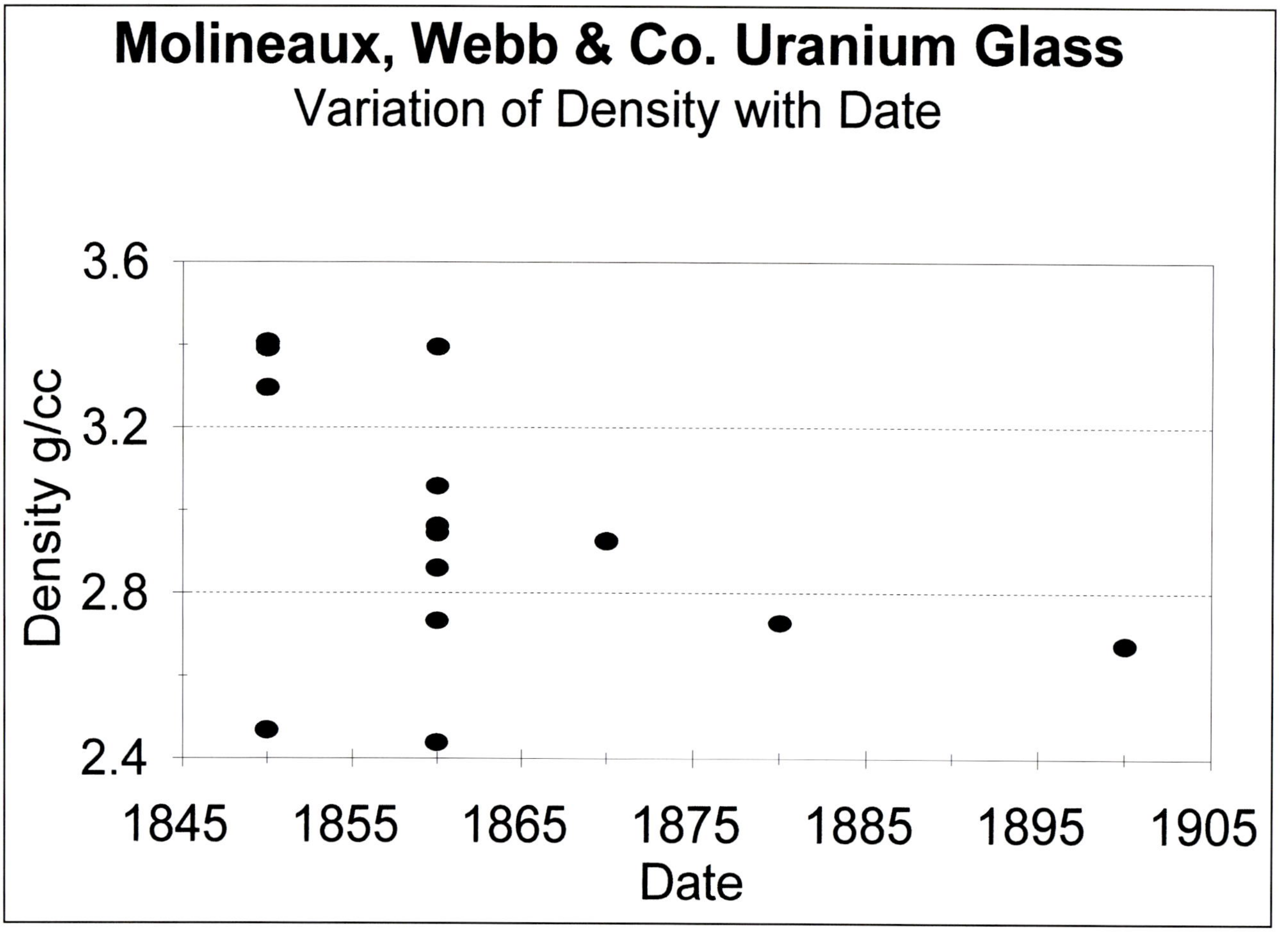

Molineaux, Webb & Co. Uranium Glass
Variation of Density with Date

Density g/cc
3.6
3.2
2.8
2.4
1845 1855 1865 1875 1885 1895 1905
Date

Figure 24

Chapter 18

Percival, Vickers & Co.

This Manchester Glasshouse, whose roots go back to 1844, was probably one of the most prolific producers of pressed and blown glass in the late 1800s. There is much scope for research about this company. However as my interest is in its use of uranium, I have nothing further to add to what I have already written in *BBVG* about its history. I have added a number of items to my collection, which may well have come from their furnaces and have illustrated and discussed them below. I have also reviewed the properties of their uranium-colored metal.

Photo 88. Another example of how difficult attributing a wine can be. There is strong evidence supporting Percival, Vicker's claim to this glass. The shape matches item 36 in their 1881 catalogue. The shape of the bowl, the two knops and the unusual flat tops on the six slices on the bowl all say so. On the other hand, Item 4528 in Webb's pattern book is the same shape and style but there the top of the slices are rounded. The density seems a little on the high side for the Lancashire firm, it would indicate 25% lead content which is more commonly found on the Continent. Also the height and diameter of the bowl (but not the foot) are more precisely metric rather than imperial. I will give it a *probably* Percival, Vickers. Blown foot and ground-out pontil, I date it *about* 1870. Height 13cm, density 3.07 g/cc, uranium 0.52% wt. Value $50 - $70.

Photo 89. The bowl of this wine has two rows of 13 oval dimples and as such appears identical to illustration 143 in the 1846 Percival, Vickers catalogue. The stem however is quite different. As this type of decoration is not unique to this firm, that alone is not enough to make even a tentative attribution. However, both the density and uranium content are consistent with other items attributed to that firm, which leads me to say *probably* Percival, Vickers. The base has the pontil dimple and has been blown. Because of the simplicity of this stem I would date this item later than the catalogue date and say *about* 1870. Height 12 cm, density 2.77 g/cc, uranium 0.3% wt. Value $30 - $40.

Photo 90. Another wine to ponder over. The stem and double knop, the uppermost of which is cut with multi-facets, as well as the six flats on the base of the bowl closely resembles item 212 in the Percival, Vickers 1846 catalogue. However, the bowl is a different shape. Both density and uranium would be consistent with other items attributed to this firm, however I am troubled by the height that is exactly 13 cm, the diameter of the bowl that is exactly 6 cm, and the base that is exactly 6.5 cm. I have included it in this section because of its similarities to the catalogue but I suspect it may be Continental. Density 2.79 g/cc, uranium 0.28%. Value $30 - $50.

Photo 91, The pattern of base and top is very close to a "take to bed" candlestick I gave a *"could be"* to in *BBVG*. However the density is too low for this firm. The design is very close to an Edward Moore pattern but the density is a little too high for that glasshouse. Perhaps it was a Percival, Vickers mold that someone else acquired, I can only speculate. Height 19.5 cm, density 2.55 g/cc, uranium 0.3% wt. Value $30 - $50.

Photo 92. A 1881 catalogue from the Glasshouse shows a "take to bed" candlestick which has an elongated circle pattern on its candle cup. This also has that unusual feature. It also has thin elongated circles on the stem. This taken together with the density, which is what I would expect from Percival, Vickers, I think I can safely give this a "*could be*." Date *about* 1885. Height 17.5 cm, density 2.86 g/cc, uranium 0.4% wt. Value $30 - $50.

Photo 93. I have shown another salt like this in *BBVG* (p 199) without an attribution. I referred to a pair and pointed out they were of slightly different size. This is one of another pair, each of which are of a slightly different size but whose sizes match those mentioned in *BBVG*. Since drafting that book, I have found these illustrated in a 1881 Percival, Vickers catalogue and now have no hesitation in attributing them to that firm. The densities are a little higher than I would normally expect from that glasshouse so I think these could be earlier than the 1881 catalogue suggests. Width 8.7 cm, height 4 cm. Density 3.13 g/cc, uranium 0.27% wt. Date about 1880. Value $30 - $40.

Photo 94. Photo 80 of *BBVG* shows three piano insulators of this pattern but with different underside impressions. I am including this one, as it is the twin of the one shown on the left hand side in that illustration, but in yellow instead of green. While, without doubt, Percival, Vickers did make an insulator of this design, it is possible they may also have been made by other glasshouses. Diameter 10 cm, density 2.65 g/cc, uranium 0.43% wt. *Could be* Percival, Vickers, *about* 1895. Value $30 - $40.

Photos 95a and 95b. This piano foot insulator is similar to the blue/green one shown in Photo 81 of *BBVG*. The difference is in the design of the base, which is more like that on the lefthand side of Photo 80 in *BBVG*. Its density is lower than I would have expected for Percival, Vickers, but then it matches some of the others. I now think that possibly the firm changed their metal in later years, using the cheaper low lead mix for more mundane items. Diameter 8.5 cm, density 2.5 g/cc, uranium 0.34% wt. *Probably* Percival, Vickers, *about* 1900. Value $20 - $30.

I have examined a sufficient number of items that I have high confidence came from this glasshouse to make a reasonable assessment of their uranium and density characteristics.

Fig. 25 shows the uranium concentrations in 12 examples of their yellow glass. The spread is fairly wide but the most common concentrations would appear to be in the 0.3%-0.5% wt range. The results are more definite for their green glass, Fig. 26. Here 23 items have been examined and it is seen that most have uranium concentrations in the 0.25%-0.3% wt range.

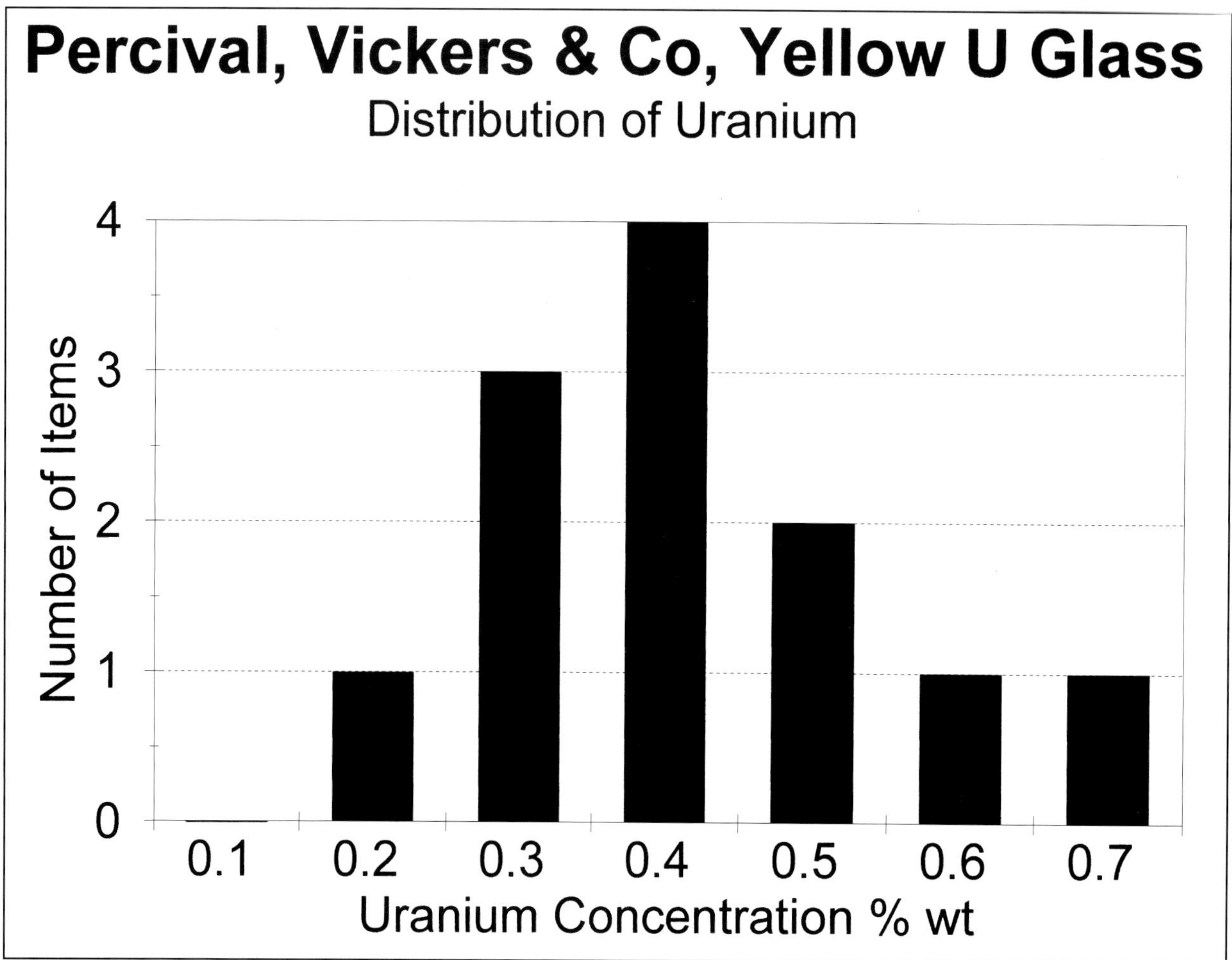

Figure 25

Fig 27 shows the density of uranium glass, both yellow and green, for some 40 items, plotted against their estimated date. Bearing in mind that the dating is not as precise as the uranium concentration estimate, it would seem that about 1880 there was a considerable reduction in the lead concentrations of their mixes. It is quite possible that those items with densities at 2.5 g/cc or below were not made by Percival, Vickers, but by another glasshouse using old Percival, Vickers moulds.

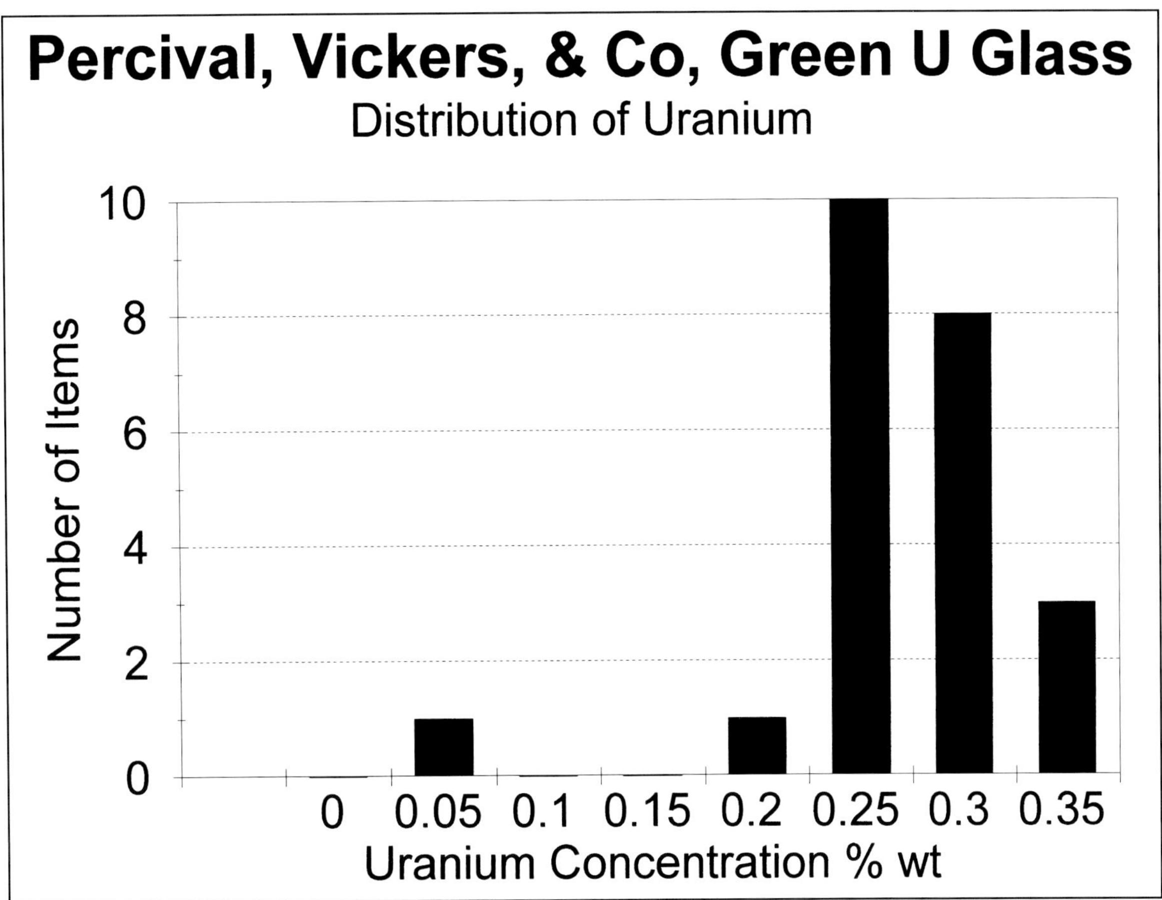

Figure 26

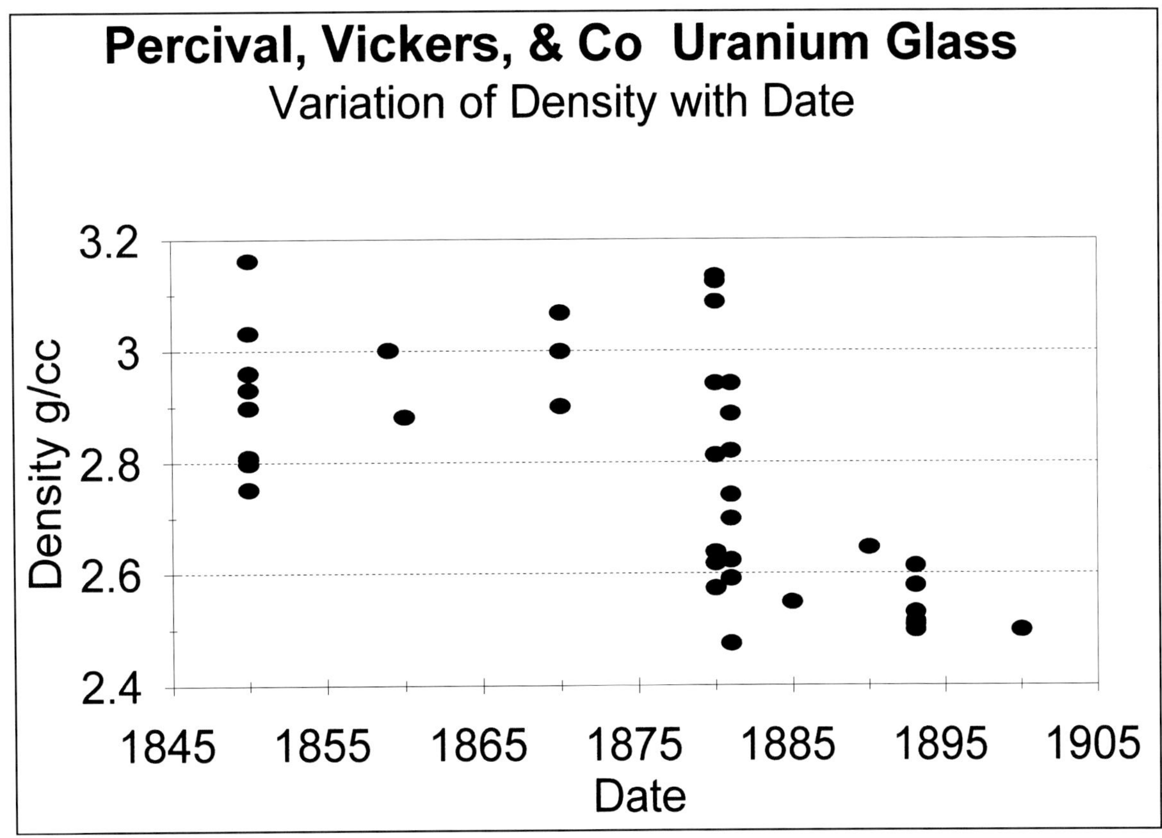

Figure 27

Chapter 19

London

Even given the several years since I drafted *BBVG*, I have to confess that I have only identified one other firm in this area that used uranium in their melts, although I have added a few pieces from Nazing and Whitefriars. I feel sure there must be others. My analysis of the Design Registrations for the years 1873 – 1875 which I referred to earlier, shows thirty-eight different companies or individuals with London area addresses had registered designs. With perhaps a couple of exceptions I do not recall any of them as being known glasshouses. Without doubt, some were designers and some, like G V de Luca, were marketing products made for them. But this surely can not account for such a large number, amongst these there must have been glasshouses that are now long forgotten.

Buckley[1] describes seven. The Falcon Glassworks took its name from the Falcon Stairs, near what is now the south end of Blackfriars Bridge. It moved to the Old Kent Road in 1877 and then in 1895 to Stourbridge. The other six were the Gravel Lane Glasshouse, The Old barge Stairs Glasshouse, St Mary Overies Glasshouse, The Tooley Street Glasshouse, The Stony Street Glassworks and The Bankside Glasshouses, none of which made it into the uranium era.

Chapter 20

Nazing Glass Works

Since *BBVG* was drafted, Geoff Timberlake[1] has published the results of his research, which provides a good deal more about the history and development of this Company. It also has many illustrations of their products, which is a great help to the collector making attributions. The range of products is much wider than I had thought based on one ashtray I have quoted shown in *BBVG*. It includes a range of cloudy and bubble glass, some of which could easily be confused with Grey-Stan or other glasshouses of that time. However, it is worth noting that Nazing made for local dealer H Elwell of Harlow, who insisted that only his name and not that of the manufacturer went on the piece.

Photo 97. Although this ashtray does not contain uranium, I include it because it represents a benchmark in dating. On the underside it carries the "Nazing Regicor Made in England" mark. On the top it has "xxxth International Rally 1969". Nazing produced advertising ashtrays for "Reginald Corfield" and as such items were often marked "REGICOR" this must be one example. Diameter 15.2 cm, density 2.47 g/cc. Value $10 - $20.

Photo 98. This has to be an ashtray, even though it has no cigarette recesses. Apart from the obvious word "Pony" and the motif of a saddled horse painted on the outside, underneath are the molded legends, "Nazing Made in England" and "RegiCo(?)." (I think the last letter should be an "r", but it looks more like a "y".) Unlike the ashtray in Photo 97, this one is made with uranium in the mix. Length 14 cm, density 2.53 g/cc, uranium 0.28% wt. Date about 1960. Value $20 - $30.

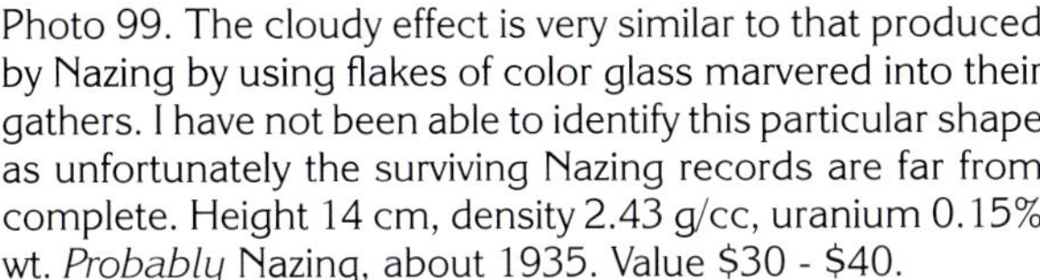

Photo 99. The cloudy effect is very similar to that produced by Nazing by using flakes of color glass marvered into their gathers. I have not been able to identify this particular shape as unfortunately the surviving Nazing records are far from complete. Height 14 cm, density 2.43 g/cc, uranium 0.15% wt. *Probably* Nazing, about 1935. Value $30 - $40.

Chapter 21

International Bottle Company Ltd.

Although this Company must have played a major role in the supply of glass bottles in the earlier part twentieth century, it does not appear to have caught the eye of the glass collector and little has been written about it.

John Maier founded the Company some hundred years ago. It imported glass perfume bottles and ornamental glassware from Germany and France. Unfortunately the Company's offices, located in the City of London, were bombed during WW2 and most of their history lost. To what extent they were manufacturing during this early period is not known, but in terms of design registrations they were prolific. According to my count, between their first registration of 24th July 1908, and the outbreak of WW2 they registered some 400 designs. In this context they were most active between the mid-1920s and 1939. Only two designs were registered in 1908, by 1920 the number had risen to 53. Another four were added in the next three years. In 1924 fourteen were registered, sixteen in 1925, twenty five in 1926, and 288 between 1927 and May 1939.

Although known as a bottle company, the Photo 266 in *BBVG* shows they were making table ware as well (Photo 266 is of an egg cup in the shape of a hen.) From this and the item shown here, it is clear that they also used uranium in some of their products.

During WW2 Maier continued to run the Company from temporary offices at Roehampton, South London, despite many of his key staff being called up for active service. In 1946 the Company moved to Park Lane in the West End of London to be near the principal perfume houses. Maier died in 1951, but the Company carried on and continued to grow. From the mid 1950s until the 1980s they had semi-automatic production at their Waterstone factory near Rotherham. In 1956 they developed a relationship with the Belgian Verlica Momignies, which as Nouvelles Verreries de Momignies remained a significant supplier through the ensuing years.

With many of their customers moving out of Central London, the Company closed its office in Park Lane in 1982 and moved to its present location in Hertford.

Despite all the design registrations, I have only come across two of their items made from uranium glass. One has already been mentioned, the other is shown in Photo 100.

Photo 100. I suspect this old bottle was recovered from a tip by an enthusiast, then cast aside as being of little value. It bears the Design Registration mark 723257, which was lodged by the International Bottle Company on 13th August, 1926. Height 16.5 cm, density 2.5 g/cc, uranium 0.12% wt. Value, in this condition, nominal.

Chapter 22

James Powell, Whitefriars

Much has already been written about this firm which can trace its origins back to the early 1700s. As I described in *BBVG*, it was a leader in the use of uranium to color glass. Apart from the examples below, which I have added to my researches, I have nothing else of significance to add.

Without doubt, to collectors, Whitefriars is the major London glasshouse and it is currently enjoying a period of popularity. The items, now colloquially known as the "Drunken Bricklayer" and the "Banjo" vases, appear to be attracting quite high prices. As I have not found any evidence of uranium being used in their melts I have been immune from the urge to collect them.

Photos 102 and 102a. An 1852 Pattern Sheet from Whitefriars, held in the Museum of London, shows a glass identical to this not only in style of cutting but also with a grapevine pattern. The only small difference I can detect is in the arrangement of the grapes in the bunch. Logic says this is an "*almost certainly*" if not unqualified Whitefriars wine glass. The problem I have is with the density. I have no other evidence that Whitefriars used anything other than leaded metal. The glass has a blown foot, a polished pontil, and a moderate amount of wear. I don't think it is a 1930s repro. So did Whitefriars make it in 1852, or did someone else copy the design? Another of the unanswerable questions. Height 12.1 cm, density 2.46 g/cc, uranium 0.25% wt. Value $30 - $40.

Photo 103. This is not an eighteenth century piece as might be supposed. The quality of the metal in the clear bowl is probably too good for that period but more to the point, the green has uranium. I think it is an example of Whitefriars "Glass with History" but it could have come from Stevens and Williams or another glasshouse. However after studying the available information, it more closely resembles an illustration in Whitefriars records. Height 15 cm, density, after allowing for the hollow stem, 3.03 g/cc, uranium 0.14% wt. Date *about* 1920. Value $50 - $70.

Photo 104. Although I have not seen this shape or size of glass in a Whitefriars catalogue, the faint diamond pattern is illustrated in a vase set in their 1931 catalogue. The top of the glass has been finished with a silver metal band. Although worn, the word "sterling" is readable. It is a quality piece. I will say *probably* Whitefriars, *about* 1930. Height 5.75 cm, density 2.66 g/cc, uranium 0.31% wt. Value $20-$30.

Photo 106. After twenty years of collecting uranium glass I thought I could tell a piece without the aid of my Geiger counter. This piece proved me wrong. Despite its delicate color it is devoid of uranium. But is it Whitefriars? The evidence says yes. The design and shape is, as far as can be seen, identical to a piece shown by Jackson[3], plate 23. It has a perfect pontil dimple indicating a quality glasshouse, and its density shows indicates it has about 30% lead. The illustration in Jackson indicates a date 1877 to 1910. I don't know how this color was formed but at that date I would have expected it to have been uranium based. So I will put forward the following theory. The moderate amount of wear suggests it is not of recent years, but somewhere about 1930-40. We know (*BBVG*) that Whitefriars made repro. so perhaps this is another example. Diameter 13.3 cm, density 3.28 g/cc, uranium nil. Value $50 - $70.

Photo 105. Although this is not uranium glass, I include it because the wave pattern is so similar to that of Webb. Like a Webb's piece, it has a perfectly circular pontil dimple. It could easily be mistaken for a product of that factory. In the 1930s Webb produced their Sunshine Amber using uranium. Sometime later and probably well after the end of WW2, Webb seems to have dropped this color in favor of a duller amber, which did not contain uranium. This piece lies somewhere between the two, probably closer to the Sunshine metal. If you don't have a Geiger counter handy look down the edge of the glass, if uranium is present it will be seen as a green sheen. Shown in a 1940 catalogue as No 8473 and also by Jackson[2]. Height 20 cm, density 3.199, uranium nil. Value $80 - $120.

Chapter 23
English Midlands

A major centre of glass manufacture in Britain was the English Midlands. Regrettably I have to use the term in the past tense because many of the famous names that sent their products all round the world are no longer in existence. Even between drafting *BBVG* and this book, changes have taken place and the industry has shrunk. Royal Brierly (Stevens & Williams) have sold off their original site and moved to a much smaller one. Stuart Crystal has gone into receivership.

The centre of this activity probably started in what was then a small village, known as Oldswinford. As Ravenscroft's leaded metal became the vogue, a number of glasshouses were built in the area around Stourbridge. When the industry expanded, it extended to Birmingham with such firms as Osler and Walsh Walsh. While most collectors refer to these products as "Stourbridge Glass", I prefer the more accurate term of "English Midlands" perhaps because I was born in Birmingham.

One of the outstanding characters during the nineteenth century development was John Northwood. Without doubt it was through the efforts and enterprise of men like him that the area gained a world wide reputation for glass of the highest quality. He was born in Wordsley in 1836 and started work at W H B & J Richardson, learning the art of painting and gilding. When the partnership split and production ceased, he tried his hand in the building industry but was later re-employed by Ben Richardson. In 1860, in partnership, he started a decorating glass business and achieved some outstanding successes with the Elgin Vase, Portland Vase and Milton Vase. He developed acid etching to a fine art. Early in the 1880s, he joined Stevens & Williams as their Art Director and Works Manager. He spent the rest of his working life with that firm, developing techniques and studying the properties of glass and so consolidated the name of Stevens and Williams as one of the greats of that area. The full story of this remarkable man is told by his son John Northwood.[1]

In *BBVG* I also included "Edinburgh Crystal" with Thomas Webb in the English Midlands section. I now apologize to every Scotsman for this error. It is true that Edinburgh Crystal was part of the same group as Thomas Webb for some of their existence, but they were independent both before and after that period. This time they will have a chapter to themselves!

The present day collector will only associate a handful of glasshouses with this area. However *Pottery Gazette*, July 1891, p 643 discusses the number of Flint Glassmakers in the late 1830s and for areas I would now call the English Midlands, they name 20 different firms. My analysis of the Design Registrations from 1873 to 1875 show 28 different individuals/glasshouses registered from this area. I only recognize 6 names, i.e. Hodgetts Richardson & Son, Philip Pargeter, Joseph Webb, Woodall & Sons, Boulton & Mills and Thomas Webb & Sons. In *BBVG* I only show examples of 5, this time I will show examples from 6. Clearly there must have been many more, but their identification has been lost with the passage of time. Their identifiable items are few and far between, other items probably being wrongly attributed or simple described with the generic term "Stourbridge."

The great characteristic about glass from the English Midlands is that is nearly always heavily leaded. In Fig. 28 I have plotted the densities of glass against their estimated date of manufacture. I have only included items whose glasshouse I have been able to identify with a high degree of confidence. The distribution is for 154 items. It will be seen they divide roughly into three groupings:

1 - Those with densities greater than 2.9 g/cc and extending nearly to 3.6 g/cc. An equivalent lead content of about 25% - 40%.

2 - Those with densities in the 2.7 g/cc – 2.8 g/cc bracket. These are mainly Webb's Burmese and the occasional Walsh Pompeian.

3 - Those with the lower densities in the 2.4 g/cc to 2.6 g/cc. These are mainly Stevens and Williams/Royal Brierley products.

It is also important to bear in mind that with such a large number of pieces, even with confidence levels at 98%, there are likely to be a few, perhaps 2–4, which will be rogues.

English Midlands Uranium Glass
Variation of Density with Date
Date
1960
1940
1920
1900
1880
1860
1840
2.4
2.6
2.8
3
3.2
3.4
3.6
Density g/cc
Figure 28

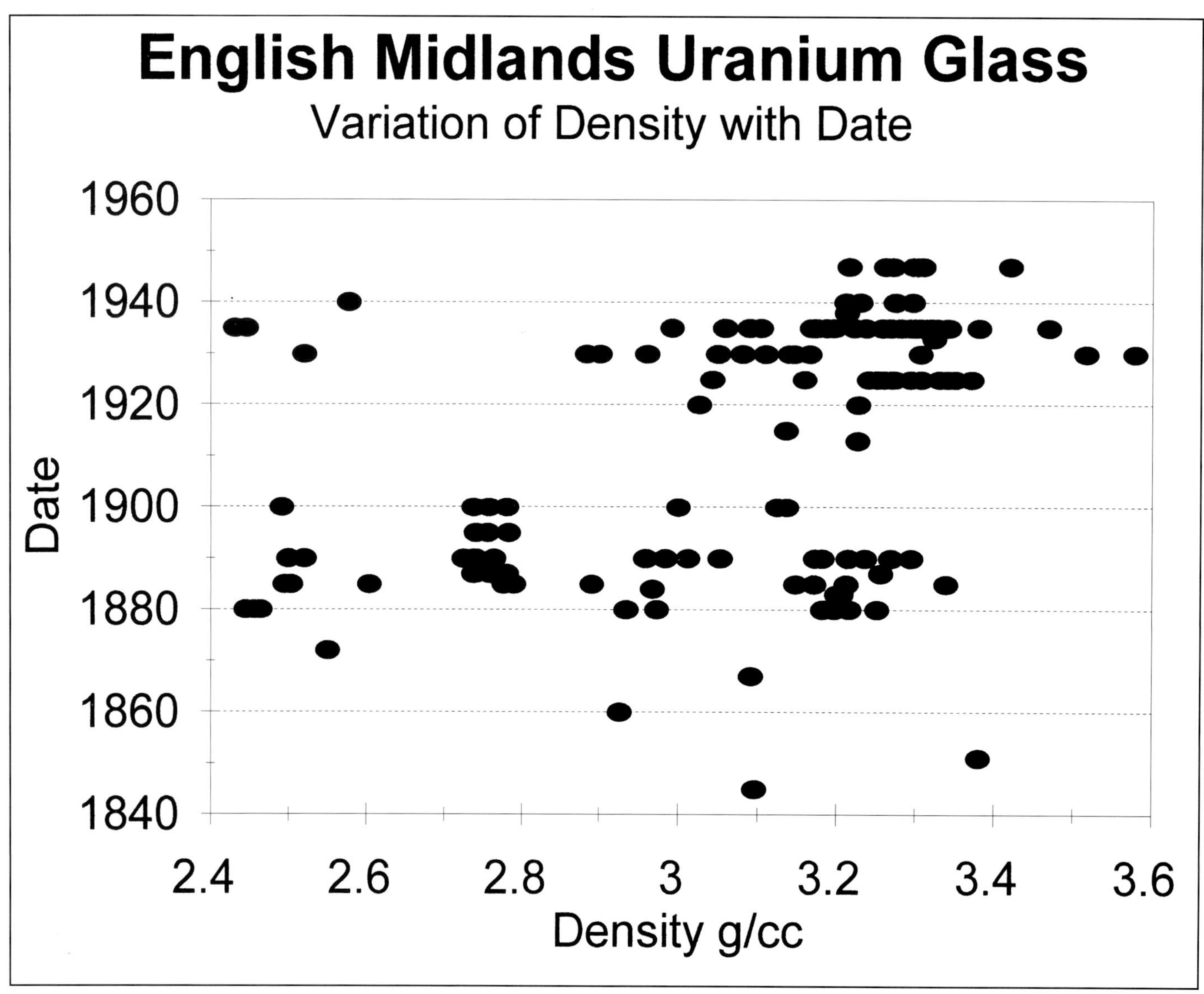

Chapter 24

Etna Flint Glass Works, Birmingham

Virtually nothing is known about this glasshouse. It may only have existed as such for a few years. It would appear from the registration mark on the item below, Photo 107, that the firm was operated by George Joseph Green. Who was he and where was his "Etna" glassworks in 1851? I do not know. It would seem that it was in business in the early 1850s.

The 1851 Census shows a George Joseph Green, Glass Manufacturer, aged 59, living at 8 Yew Tree Road, Edgbaston. (I will designate him GJG1.) However, there was probably another George Joseph Green (GJG2) around at the same time, this one was born 30 June 1815, at Dudley St Thomas, son of George James Green (GJG3) who probably linked with Bacchus & Green. GJG1 would have been born about 1792, which makes him old enough to be GJG2's father, that is, the same person as GJG3. But which one registered the design in Photo 107?

There is an entry in a Birmingham Trade Directory of 1855 giving a George Joseph Green, glass manufacturer at 42 & 45 Broad Street - could this be the Etna Glass Works? Apart from the plate below, there are two other Design Registrations that may or may not be relevant, namely by Joseph Green, 2nd Oct. 1848 and by George J Green, of Broad Street, Birmingham on 24th July 1850.

Pottery Gazette, June 1894, describing exhibits at "The Glass and Pottery Exhibits at the Imperial Institute" refers to exhibits by "Messers James Green & Nephew" but whether this firm has any connection with the Etna Street family is not established.

The mould for this plate must have represented a considerable investment for G. J. G. and on that basis it is likely his was not a "fly by night" operation, but possibly another of those glasshouses lost to the modern day collector for want of information.

To complicate matters further, Werner[1] reports that the Wyllie family, a firm of glass cutters in London, were buying glass from Green, George Joseph of Stoner Glass works Birmingham from 1841 to 1854 and from Green & Son, Joseph of Stoner Glassworks Birmingham, in 1843. Was there any connection between the Etna Glass Works and the Stoner Glass Works?

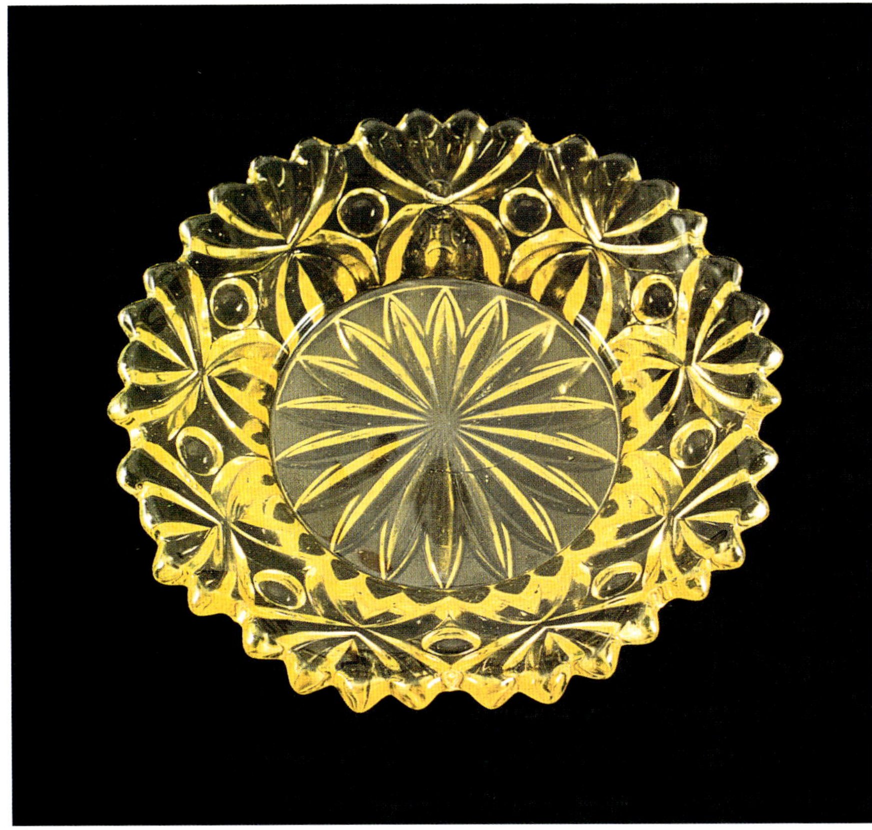

Photo 107. This humble plate is one the most interesting in my collection. It bears a nice crisp Design Registration lozenge mark indicating a registration by the little known George Joseph Green of Etna Flint Glass Works, on 21 July 1851. Diameter 17 cm, density 3.38 g/cc, uranium 0.31% wt. Value depends on the demand for this rare but mundane piece of glass. That aside, I would say $80 - $120.

Chapter 25

Richardsons of Wordsley

The history of this firm, founded in 1829 has been written up by Hajdamach[1] and is also discussed by Manley[2] It is ironic that its life started with Webb and ended with Webb. Thomas Webb was a founder of the firm together with William Hayden and two Richardson Brothers. A decade or so later Thomas Webb left. Just under a hundred years later, in 1930, Thomas Webb & Sons took over Richardson's. According to Eveson,[3] who told me he well remembered the time, Webb's made use of the old plant and moulds and for some years, continued with the name using their own metal. Glass production ceased with the takeover.

I have not added to my knowledge of the history of this glasshouse since I drafted *BBVG*, but am able to show and discuss a few more relevant specimens.

With only a limited number of high confidence attributions, I have not graphed any density information. However the average density of 8 such items is 3.045 g/cc, with a range of 2.93 g/cc to 3.22 g/cc. Those items in the upper part of this range hail from the later dates. The suggestion is that the earlier pieces, i.e. late 1800s, have slightly lower densities.

Photo 108. This small bowl, possibly used for sugar, comes from an 8 rib mold. The trail work is uneven and by hand. The crimp work has an unusual herringbone pattern on its underside. Closely resembles Richardson's Pattern Book entries 20029 and 20743. Weak response to uv light on the opalescence, strong on the crimpwork. 12.5 cm diameter. density 2.93 g/cc, uranium 0.06% wt. (CF Photos 105 and 106 *BBVG*). *Probably* Richardson's, *about* 1880. Value $100 - $140.

Photo 109. The pattern looks very similar to Richardson's No 19148 but this item would have to be a truncated version. The pattern book describes it as ruby and opaline. There are 3 drop waves and 6 vertical pillars. Diameter 11 cm, density 3.12 g/cc, uranium (not in the ruby), 0.12% wt. Date *about* 1880, *almost certainly* Richardson. Value $100 - $140.

Photo 110. Obviously the sister of Photo 104 *BBVG*. The same pattern but in different and less attractive colors. There is one difference, this vase has a perfect pontil dimple while that in Photo 104 has the broken pontil mark. Did Webb, I wonder, make this piece after they had taken over Richardson's in 1930? Was it a reproduction piece? There have to be doubts, but the considerable amount of wear on the base suggests it is older than the 1930s, so I'll stay with an *almost certainly* Richardson attribution. Date *about* 1890. Height 9.5 cm, density 3.17 g/cc, uranium 0.16% wt. Value $80 - $120.

Photo 111. Small vase with 8 vertical ribs. The top is finished British style but there is no pontil or gadget mark. The density suggests English Midlands or Whitefriars. The Richardson's Pattern Book shows very similar items in several places, i.e. Nos. 18621 and 21081. Because the design is very simple I cannot be sure that they were the only firm to make this type of vase and I will therefore give it a "*probably*." Height 10.5 cm, density 3.25 g/cc, uranium 0.13% wt. date *about* 1900, value $30 – $50.

Photo 112. This dish is identical to the one shown in Photo 106 in *BBVG* except for the milky effect, which is in a different place. The size, density and uranium contents are effectively the same. They must be from the same glasshouse. As I attributed that one to *probably* Richardson, I must do the same for this. I have concern over the lack of wear but this is at least partly offset by traces of ingrained dirt where the crimp work joins the body of the bowl. Despite the logic, somewhere I have a gut feeling that this may be one of my 5% errors. Diameter 13.7 cm, density 2.96 g/cc, uranium 0.12% wt. Date *about* 1890, value $80- $120.

Photos 113 and 114. This poor little salt has clearly been abused at some time in its life. However I like it so I will pretend it is perfect. The shape closely follows that shown in *BBVG* Photo 105. (The stand has been borrowed for this display.) The raspberry prunt appears identical. The uranium is only in the prunt and the crimpwork. Diameter 6.5 cm, density 3.0 g/cc, uranium approximately 0.2% wt. *Probably* Richardson *about* 1900. Value, if perfect, $50 - $70.

Photo 115. At first sight I thought this Grecian style vase was French but closer examination raised doubts, which were reinforced with reference to Manly's "Decorative Victorian Glass." The vase shows all the signs of age. Had it been French of that vintage I would have expected the whole piece to have been blown in a mold and the top cut and ground. While I cannot be sure, it looks as if the foot, which is open and hollow, has been added separately, the ring at the base covering the joint. The base has been cut and ground, the top has been heat finished. The artwork is by transfer and the red appears to have been glazed probably by painting on then baking. The density, which because of its size was difficult to measure and could be a slight under estimate, shows a significant lead content.

Manley (pages 56-57, item 35) shows a vase that has some similar characteristics, particularly the unusual red glazing. Manley (p 57) explains that vases of this type were sold as French, but sometime in the 1950s, a lot of similar, albeit broken, vases were found in a field belonging to Richardson's. "*And since then the peculiar brick colour and archer design have been found on other vases made by the firm...*" The density could be accounted for if the basic mix had a full lead content that was diluted by the addition of an opacifier. Thus, relying heavily on Manley, I would give it a "*could be* Richardson's *about* 1890." Height 36 cm, density 2.86 g/cc, uranium 0.15% wt. I cannot put a value upon it, much depends upon whether it is a Richardson, I have not seen similar sold on the open market. I know what I paid and I am not saying!

Photo 116. I am not attributing this vase to Richardson but have included it here to keep Photo 115 company. Again the question arises, "Is it Continental?" I think a lot of authorities would say "yes" but I have serious doubts. Perhaps it is not Richardson's, it does not have that brick red color to which Manley refers, but it does have a couple of telltale signs suggesting it is British. The base has not been formed in same blow mold as the body, but has been applied separately. On the underside of the base there is a "7" If it had been Continental, especially French, I would have expected the "7" to be crossed, this one is not. It has a Greek key pattern in gold, which has resisted the years of wear. The gold on the base shows considerable wear, which I believe indicates its age. The motif, whose features I do not recognise, appears to be made of a ceramic while it is mounted on a piece of black glass. Height 29.3 cm, density 2.49 g/cc, uranium 0.28% wt. Date *period* 1900. As for value, see Photo 115.

Photo 117. A great example of uranium Vaseline glass. It looks as if it ought to have come from the North East of England and my best guess, based on density would have been Greener. However a jug of similar shape, with an apparently identical stem and base, and a similar but not identical pattern on the body, is shown in Richardson's pattern book, close to the tumbler which I mentioned in *BBVG* and which referred to Davidson. Methinks now that perhaps Richardson's were making for Davidson. Date *about* 1880. Height 12.6 cm, density 2.57 g/cc, uranium 0.43% wt. Value $30 - $40.

Photo 118. This large green bowl carries the Richardson trademark. The union flag is surrounded by the words "Richardson British" as shown in Photo 109 in *BBVG*. I am not sure of the period for which this trademark was used but it was probably about 1930, the time that Webb took over Richardson. After the takeover, Webb continued to make Richardson products and use their name, although I understand that production stopped at the Richardson factory. So, did Webb or Richardson make this? The only clue may be in the color. It is slightly darker than the then current Webb's Eau de Nil and has less uranium than expected from that formula, my guess therefore is that this was made by Richardson before the take- over. Diameter 25 cm, density not measured, uranium 0.19% wt. Date *about* 1930. Value $80 - $120.

Chapter 26

Stevens & Williams - Royal Brierley

Stevens & Williams is one of the famous glasshouses of Stourbridge and in collectors eyes probably ranks alongside Thomas Webb. They changed their name to Royal Brierley about 1930. At the time I drafted *BBVG*, the firm were operating from their original site in North Street, Brierley Hill, but alas, since then they have seen troubled times. The Company went into administrative receivership in the Millennium year. The old site has been sold off and Royal Brierley now operates in association with the Dartington Group from Tipton Road, Dudley, in the West Midlands. Fortunately the old Description (pattern) books are in the public domain care of Dudley Metropolitan Borough Council. The new site offers the public the opportunity of factory tours, as well as visits to their own museum.

A little while ago I had a call from Malcolm Drown. He is in the lighting business and told me how his late father, Edward Fredrick Drown, was a customer of Stevens & Williams back in the 1930s. He originally bought lighting glass from their factory in Tipton and supplied hospitals and schools before they went over to fluorescent lighting. He got to know the Williams-Thomas family and bought Brierley Crystal to sell in his shops. Malcolm tells me he has a large engraved bowl that Royal Brierley presented to his father to mark some 50 years of business, at that time he was their oldest customer.

Although a thoroughbred Stourbridge firm there is evidence that they did not always work with leaded glass. Fig. 29 is a plot of density against date for 55 items of which I have high confidence in my attribution. While the bulk clearly lie between 3 g/cc and 3.4 g/cc, there is a grouping in the 2.45 g/cc to 2.55 g/cc bracket. With the early items this may be due to the opacifier, in the later items it would be due to using a non-lead melt.

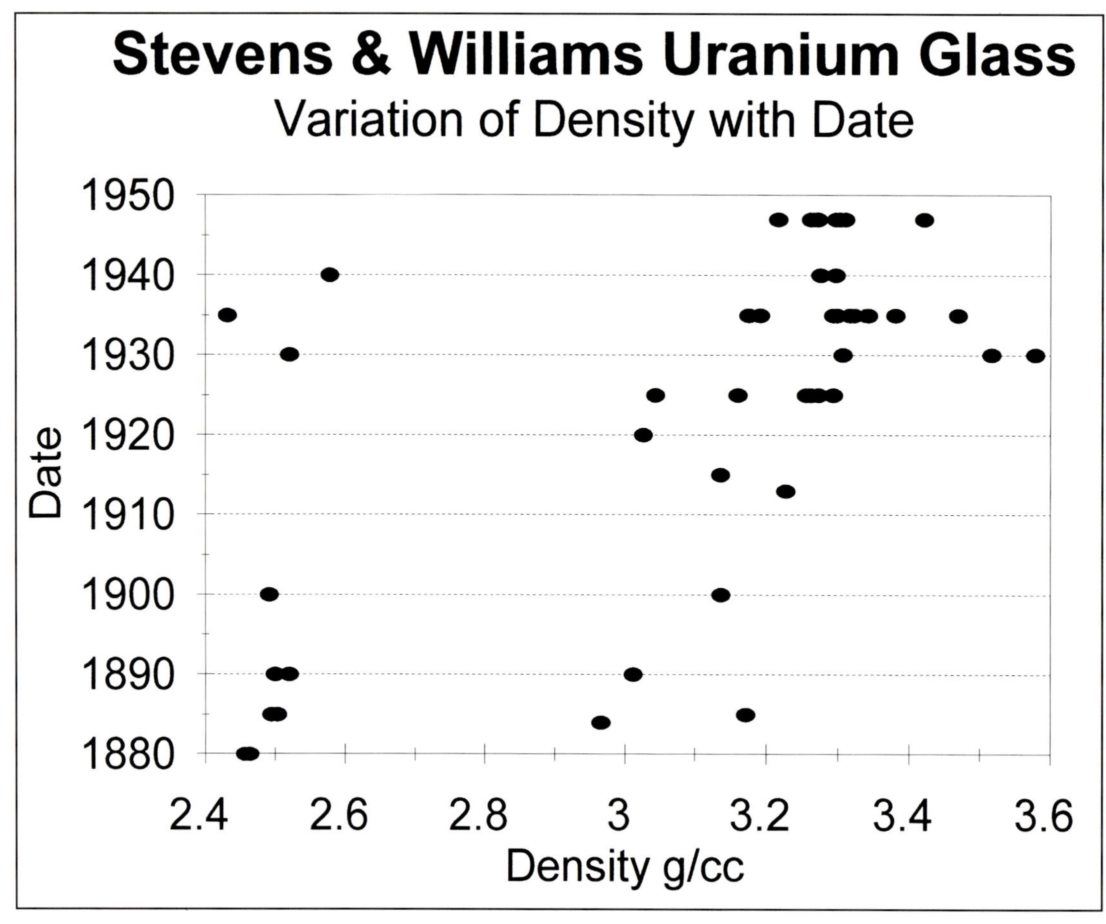

Figure 29

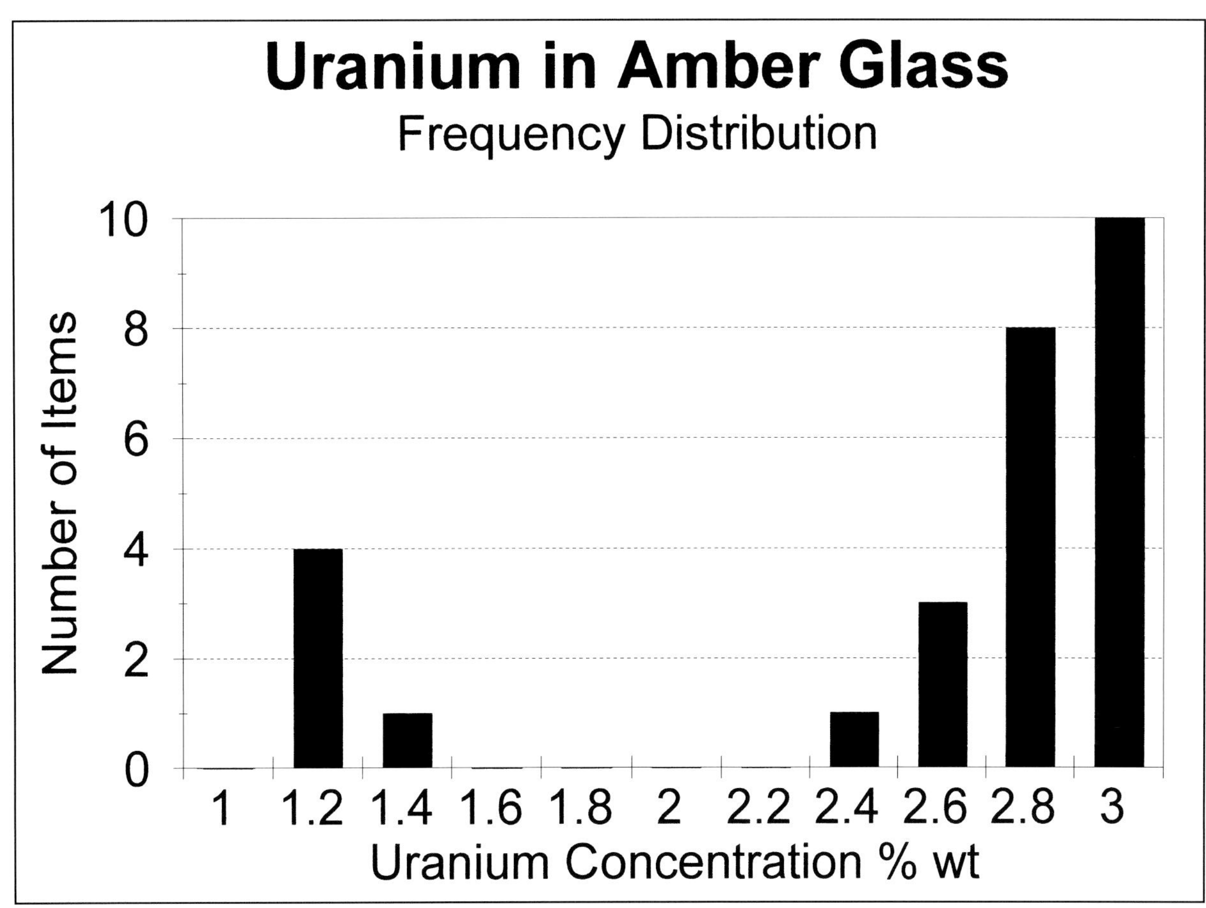

Figure 30

Their products exploited a range of colors but two predominate in my collection. They are the ambers and the primrose on white. Fig 30 shows the uranium concentration in the amber glass. Out of 27 items, the bulk lies between 2.6% wt and 3% wt. However there is a smaller group in the 1.2% wt – 1.4% level. This latter group is more akin to Webb's "Sunshine Amber" although it does not capture the warm glow of that metal. The higher levels of uranium are unusual and in my attributed items I have only found this level in Stevens & Williams.

With regard to their primrose on white items I have only examined seven. The average density is 3.27 g/cc with a range of 3.04 g/cc to 3.29 g/cc. The uranium, which is only in the primrose, has an average concentration of 0.84% wt with a range of 0.6% wt to 0.9% wt.

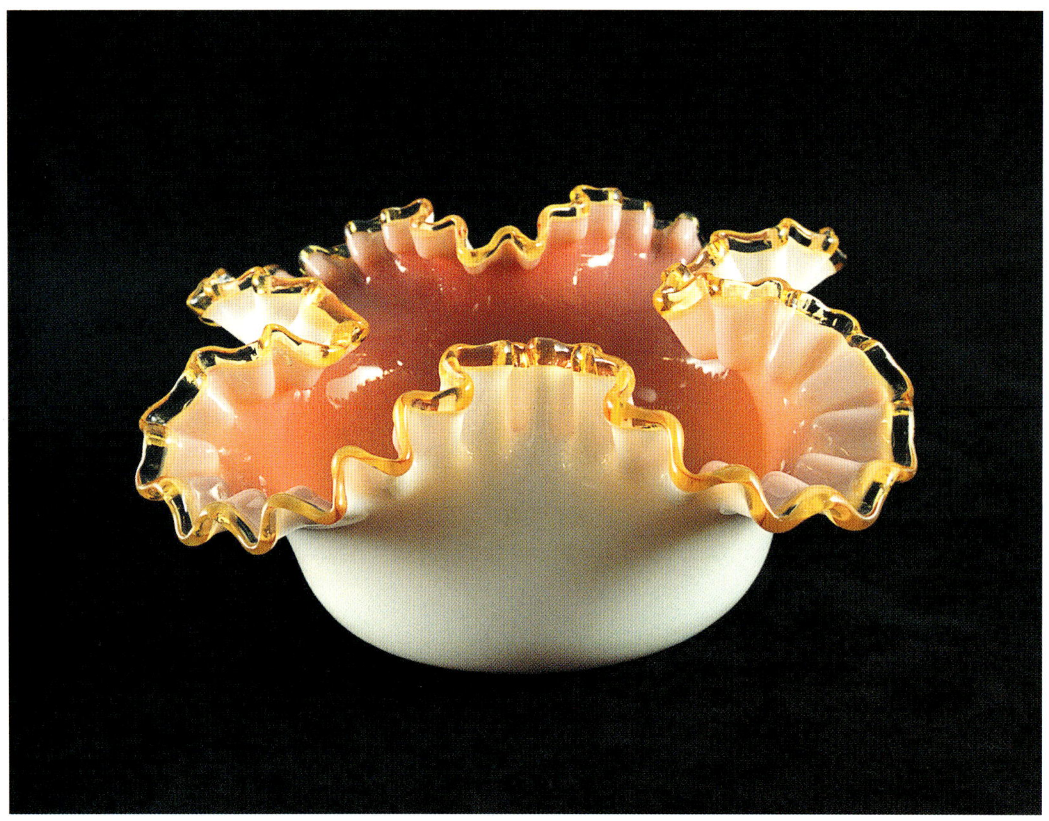

Photo 119. The striking thing about this item is its shape. I think it would have been difficult to think up a more impractical one! I have seen items illustrated in the Stevens and Williams description books which closely resemble this shape, i.e. Nos. 7883 and 9316. It would seem that in the 1880s they made a variety of items with odd shapes and crimped tops with trail work. The color of both the pink inside and the amber trail on the rim are, as near as the eye can tell, identical to Photo 116 in *BBVG*. Much the same can be said for the uranium and densities. On the base there is a perfect dimple where the pontil would have been attached. Height 8.5 cm, density 2.5 g/cc, uranium 0.2% wt. *Almost certainly* Stevens and Williams, *about* 1885. Value $160-$200.

Photo 120. This is one of those pieces I sometimes wish I had never found, as it raises more questions than it answers. At first I thought it was identical to Photo 122 *BBVG* but with the colors reversed. Closer examination shows it is not. The crimps are shorter than those in Photo 122; they are also slightly irregular. The metal is thicker and less translucent. The pontil dimple is oval not circular and the pink, a shade darker. Furthermore the Geiger only responds to the white (ivory) and not the pink. It is tempting to say this is not from the same glass-house as Photo 122, but when the metal is compared with Photo 116 *BBVG* there is a close resemblance. Diameter 13.8 cm, density 2.49 g/cc, uranium, (inside only),0.28% wt. *Could be* Stevens and Williams *about* 1885. Value $40 - 30.

Photo 121. The reason for including this jug vase in this chapter is based on some of its characteristics being close to other items. As glasshouses tended to crib patterns from others, there has to be caution. The pontil mark has been reduced to a smooth and circular dimple, usually the sign of a skilled operator. The shape of the leaves closely resembles those on items in Photos 117 and 119 *BBVG*. The trail work is much the same color. Finally the densities and uranium levels match. I have not been able to find a match for the flower either on the other items or in the Stevens and Williams pattern books. Maybe I should look harder. The dating is supported by the ingrained dirt in the leaves and the wear on the base. Height 14.5 cm, density 2.49 g/cc, uranium 0.12% wt. *Could be* Stevens and Williams, *about* 1895. Value $60 - $80.

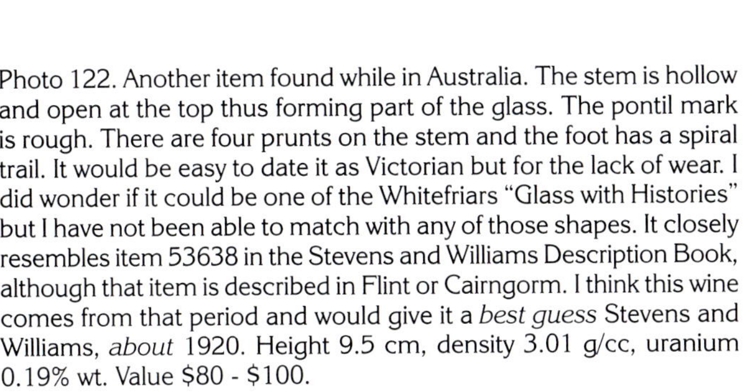

Photo 122. Another item found while in Australia. The stem is hollow and open at the top thus forming part of the glass. The pontil mark is rough. There are four prunts on the stem and the foot has a spiral trail. It would be easy to date it as Victorian but for the lack of wear. I did wonder if it could be one of the Whitefriars "Glass with Histories" but I have not been able to match with any of those shapes. It closely resembles item 53638 in the Stevens and Williams Description Book, although that item is described in Flint or Cairngorm. I think this wine comes from that period and would give it a *best guess* Stevens and Williams, *about* 1920. Height 9.5 cm, density 3.01 g/cc, uranium 0.19% wt. Value $80 - $100.

Photo 123. This liqueur is the same shape and size as the small glass shown in Photo 37, *BBVG* but it has 8 flats cut in its stem. The shape, although occasionally used by other glasshouses, appears in a number of places in the Stevens and Williams Description books for the 1930s, (i.e. number 64825). Like the pieces shown in *BBVG*, I date this *about* 1940. Height 5 cm, density 3.28 g/cc, uranium 2.48% wt. Value $20 - $30.

Photo 124. A superbly hand made glass which could easily be mistaken for the Georgian piece it is intended to replicate. As with other examples, the give away is the molded foot and the presence of uranium. An interesting and unusual feature is the double ring knop at the top of the stem. An item apparently identical to this is shown in the Hill Ouston catalogue of 1934. They were glass merchants not manufacturers and I cannot find this design in any of the reference documents I have searched. The density says it is probably from the English Midlands. The uranium is amongst the highest I have found in this color of glass. This and its density compares closely with Photo 130 in *BBVG*. Considering this glass with the one in Photo 125 below, which is the same shape, and which matches Stevens and Williams dark amber metal makes for an *almost certainly* Stevens and Williams. Height 11 cm, density 3.28 g/cc, uranium 1.86% wt. Date *about* 1935, value $40 - $60.

Photo 125. The shape of this goblet is identical to wine Photo 124 and all I have said about that piece applies here. The color and characteristics match closely those of other examples of Stevens and Williams dark amber. Height 16.8 cm, density 3.3 g/cc, uranium 2.8% wt. *Almost certainly* Stevens and Williams, *about* 1934. Value $30 - $50

Photo 126. It is with some trepidation that I put this candlestick under Royal Brierley. The basis is simply its dark amber color, density and uranium content. Although they made candlesticks with some similarities, I have not found this pattern in their books, but then I have only inspected a sample. Diameter of base 12.4 cm, height 5.3 cm, density 3.42 g/cc, uranium 2.6% wt. *Could be* Royal Brierley, "Dark Amber" *about* 1925 Value $30 - $40.

Photo 127. The coarse diamond pattern appears identical to other items in the Stevens and Williams Description book, as No 64341. It is not a complex pattern and could well have been used by other glasshouses. However the book says the items were made in "Auburn" and measurements of density and uranium content on other Stevens and Williams items come close those for this decanter. Height 22 cm, density 3.47 g/cc, uranium 1.2% wt. *Almost certainly* Stevens and Williams *about* 1935. Value $50 - $70.

Photo 128. This jug and bowl are, as near as makes no difference, identical to those shown in Photo 133 of *BBVG*, the only difference is that these items are held in a silver plated cradle clearly made especially for them. The plate bears the mark "EPNS" and "BH Ld." Unfortunately I have not been able to identify this firm. These pieces are illustrated in the Stevens and Williams *Description Book* as items 53105. Written in ink at the side of the sketch is "BH Ltd" which confirms these are Stevens and Williams and not look-a-likes made by Walsh, etc. Height 7 cm, density 3.26 g/cc, uranium 0.93% wt. Date *about* 1925. Value $50 - $80.

Photo 129. I have shown some similar shaped pieces in *BBVG* they, with one exception, are all cased in pink. I have not found an exact match for this piece, but there are very similar ones shown in the Stevens and Williams Description books with white cased on primrose. It would seem that from the mid 1880s until the 1930s, Stevens and Williams were making small bowls and dishes with this long crinkled edge. The pontil dimple on this piece is not a perfect circle. Response to uv light is a little odd. When shined on the surface it gives very little fluorescence and could easily be missed. However when the light is shone through this opalescent material it glows with the expected uranium response. The wear is in my slight to moderate range. Oddly, there is no uranium in the green edging. Diameter 13.5 cm, density 3.16 g/cc, uranium (as measured on both sides) 0.15% wt. *Probably* Stevens and Williams, *about* 1925. Value $40 - $60.

Photo 130. When I first saw this vase I thought it would be Whitefriars, for they have a reputation for producing bubble glass. So do other firms. This item has a perfect dimple and is almost certainly comes from a quality British glasshouse, but which one? I have not been able to associate this shape with Whitefriars. Nazing, in the 1950s, produced a range of bubble glass in their "Waterlilly Suite" and this could possibly have come from there. However it more closely matches illustrations in the Steven and Williams Description book from the 1935 period, i.e. item No 66477. Judging from the wear on the item I would favour dating it from the '30s rather than the 50s and I would therefore give it a cautious *probably* Stevens and Williams from that period. The density indicates that it is not a leaded glass, but then I have seen other items I attribute to this firm, that are in non-leaded glass, see *BBVG* p 110. Height 11.7 cm. The density measurement gives 2.43g/cc, which is probably lower than the actual value due to the presence of the air bubbles. Height 11.7 cm, uranium 0.23% wt. Value $24 - $36.

Chapter 27

Stuart Crystal

I briefly reviewed the history of this stalwart of Stourbridge in *BBVG*. Sadly, since I drafted the book, Stuarts have gone out of business. Their demise came in 2001. Glass is no longer made on this historic site, which is now being redeveloped. Happily the Red House Glass Cone, which was part of Stuart's and had been used as a museum, still remains and is leased to the Dudley Metropolitan Borough Council. It is open to the public as a museum. It dates back to the end of the Eighteenth Century and was used to manufacture glass until the mid 1930s. It is one of only four left in the UK.

Photo 131. The crimp work on the top of this bowl is an unusual shape. A similar style of finish is shown in Stuart's pattern book, item No 12584. It was made in a 24-rib mold and has 11 crimps on the lip of the bowl. The uranium level is also consistent with a formula in an old batch book believed to be Stuart's. Height 8.5 cm, density 3.07 g/cc, uranium 0.43% wt. *Probably* Stuart *about* 1900. Value $60 - $80.

Photo 132. Another example of how tricky making an attribution can be. The pattern on this wine has all the appearances of being identical to that shown in a Leerdam catalogue of 1910, although the shape of the wine is slightly different. However the same pattern is to be found in a Stuart's pattern book of the 1870s (item No 642) and in this case the complete wine appears identical to the illustration. So who did make it? If the glass were made in the 1870s we would expect a ground off pontil and a blown foot. This has neither. It does have a moderate amount of wear. I would date the foot from the 1930s. An ex-Stuart employee has told me that the Company did not generally use uranium at that time, but is this an exception? I think this is Stuart and I suspect it was made by them in the 1930s as a repro. They would simply have pulled the design out of their old pattern book and made it according to the practice of their time. Here density is the crucial factor. The Leerdam glass I have examined has all had a much lower density. This item has quite a lot of lead in it and is more consistent with Stourbridge. Height 11.5 cm. Density 2.96 g/cc, uranium 0.3% wt. Value $20 - $30.

Chapter 28

Walsh Glass (John Walsh Walsh)

As explained in *BBVG* this Birmingham glasshouse was founded by Samuel Shakespeare at the beginning of the nineteenth century and was not acquired by John Walsh Walsh until 1850. Little or nothing is known of these early days.

Like most collectors, Eric Reynolds, since publishing his book,[1] has continued his research. This includes access to some hither too unknown batch formulae from Walsh during the nineteenth century. These he is currently working on and I look forward to the ultimate publication of his findings, which I understand will include uranium.

Eric has also furthered his research into Walsh's connection with silver smiths and silver platters. Consequently, the item on the right hand side of Photo 149 *BBVG*, which I now reproduce below as Photo 133, Eric has confirmed is Walsh and that the silver smith was W J Myatt & Co of Birmingham.

Since I drafted *BBVG* I have seen items advertised on E-Bay as being "Walsh's Autumnal Glass", the characteristic being an acanthus leaf in autumnal colors. In *BBVG* I had shown a few items that might have come into this category and I reproduce one example in Photo 134; this I attributed to Stevens and Williams. I have not changed my mind. Reynolds[2] has pointed out that Walsh were advertising "Autumnal Ware" in Pottery Gazette during 1886 but also conceded that other firms may have produced this style of decoration. Indeed Kiesow & Co, of Basinhall St. London, had a full-page color advert in Pottery Gazette for August 1885 in which one piece has ripe cherries and two pieces have a brown acanthus leaf. Photo 116 *BBVG* shows a vase with an autumnal acanthus leaf and in which I have high confidence came from Stevens & Williams. Photo 135 shows a close up of the edge of that leaf. With regard to Walsh I have only been able to reference the item shown in *BBVG* Photo 154, which unfortunately has a lower confidence level. Here there is a clear acanthus leaf and Photo 136 is a close up of the edge of that leaf. Comparing Photos 135 and 136 it can be seen that the Stevens & Williams has plainer crimp work than the one on the assumed Walsh item. It also has to be pointed out that the Stevens & Williams Description Books show examples of items with this sort of decoration. My conclusion? Be ware of anyone claiming a piece is Walsh because it has Autumnal type decoration.

Photo 133. Three examples of Wash "Crushed Strawberry" taken from *BBVG*. See above for discussion.

Photo 134. An illustration from *BBVG* of a piece of Stevens and Williams which could be mistaken for Walsh Autumnal Ware. See above for discussion.

Photo 135. Close-up of the edge of an acanthus leaf on a piece of Stevens and Williams glass.

Photo 136. Close-up of the edge of an acanthus leaf on a bowl thought to be Walsh.

Fig 31 is a graph of density against date for some 49 examples of high confidence level Walsh glass. These include the cased pink on ivory, yellow primrose on white, Pompeian, and other colors. It is seen that, with two exceptions from the 1930s, all have densities greater than 3 g/cc. In fact most are greater than 3.1 g/cc. The lower density items from the 1930s are Pompeian, the lower density no doubt due to the trapped air.

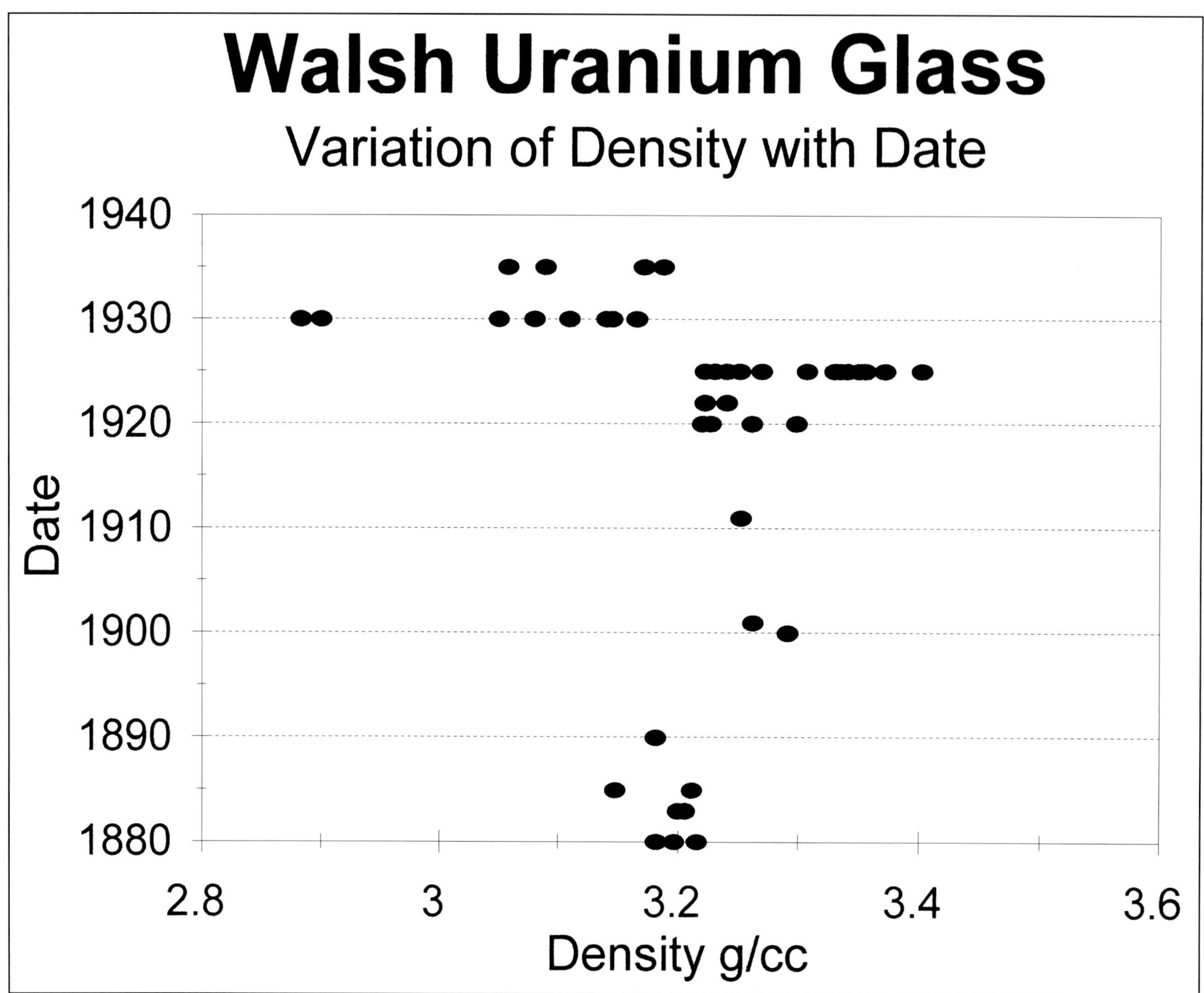

Figure 31

I have not analyzed the uranium content with relation to color as so many of my examples are cased where the thickness is too thin to be "infinite depth". However, excluding the Pompeian because of its trapped air, the results on a few amber glasses indicate a uranium content of about 1.24% wt. Which is close to some examples from Stevens & Williams and also Webb's Sunshine Amber.

Photo 137 and Photo 138. This item is a perfect match to the illustration in the advertisement in *Pottery Gazette*, Nov. 1883, for Walsh "Crushed Strawberry" ware. Maximum height 11 cm and maximum width 20 cm. Density 3.15 g/cc, uranium 0.5% wt. It has a raspberry prunt over the pontil mark. Walsh *about* 1885. (Similarity of this item to those in Photo 150 page 112 of *BBVG*, remove the very slight doubt that I had that those pieces might not have been Walsh.)
The two fish on the edge of the bowl are unusual, but it would be wrong to assume that Walsh were the only glasshouse to use this design. The Thomas Webb's pattern books show similar fish like decoration, i.e. Nos. 13346, 13347, 13518. Unfortunately age is telling with this item and it has a stress crack. This is not surprising considering its construction. Value without damage $160 -$240..

Photo 139. A good example of Walsh "Crushed Strawberry" - the shape is illustrated in *Pottery Gazette* Nov. 1883 but in "Electric Blue." Like other examples, it is made from layers of metal with pink on the outside and amber inside. It may well be that the uranium is only on the inside, the geometry makes it difficult to determine. Height 11.5 cm, density 3.21g/cc, uranium Geiger reading 5 cps. Date about 1890, value $40 - $60.

Photo 140. I have not found any direct evidence that this is from Walsh but the circumstantial evidence, if not convincing is strongly suggestive. The density says it is likely to have come from the English Midlands. The raspberry prunts are similar to some seen on Walsh glass (but other glasshouses used prunts like these). The blue, which does not contain uranium, matches as near as the eye can tell, the blue seen on a marked piece of Sateen Glass (see Photo 141) and the shape of the bowl of the vase is the same as that shown in the *Pottery Gazette* advert of Nov. 1883. Height 18 cm, density 3.15 g/cc, uranium (on the inside) 0.43% wt. Somewhere between *could be* and *probably* Walsh, *about* 1885. Value $100 - $160.

Photo 141. This piece does not contain uranium. It has a satin finish. It carries the Design Registration Number 86318. This is not a glass registration but for the silver plate holder, not shown, into which it fits. Renolds[3] identifies this as being a piece of Walsh Sateen glass. Height 4.1 cm, density 3.09 g/cc, Value $40-$60 Date *about* 1886.

Photo 142. At first sight this appears identical to the wine shown in *BBVG* Photo 171. The pattern is the same but on this item the metal of the bowl has only been flashed as a thin layer on the inside, giving a paler lemon appearance. The Geiger reading is only 10 cps, which would equate to 0.6% wt, but I suspect it is in fact the same uranium glass as used for *BBVG* Photo 171, the difference in the Geiger reading being due to the thinness of the uranium layer. Height 14 cm, density 3.22 g/cc, date *about* 1930. Value $24 - $30.

Photo 143 and 144. I suspect that this green Pompeian bowl, which has the Walsh England trademark (see Photo 144 below), started life with a lid. It has a perfect pontil dimple. Diameter 11.5 cm, density 3.09 g/cc, uranium 0.34% wt. Date *about* 1930, value, (without lid), $10 - $20.

Photo 146. Another of the "Primrose" pieces, but did Walsh make it? An article in *Pottery Gazette*, April 1922, shows a stand with the Walsh Primrose Glass. Just discernible are some epergnes of similar, but not the same, shape. They also have metal work that closely resembles this piece. Height overall, 23 cm. The density could not be measured. The uranium levels appear to vary, possibly because the primrose layers are not exactly the same thickness. I recorded them as 7 cps, 10 cps and 12 cps. The higher reading would equate a uranium concentration if at "infinite depth" of 0.7% wt *Probably* Walsh, *about* 1925. Value $100 - $145.

Photo 147. I have not been able to relate this shape to Walsh, but the silver plated top suggests it may well be connected with that firm. Unfortunately the only mark is EPNS, which is not very helpful. Diameter of base 5.6 cm, density 3.54 g/cc (this is probably a high measurement because of the contribution from the metal top) uranium 0.9% wt. *Best guess* Walsh, date *about* 1925. Value $30 - $40.

Chapter 29

Thomas Webb & Sons

The name Thomas Webb is synonymous with Stourbridge. Although the firm existed for a little over 120 years, well it depends just exactly when you choose to claim it started and when it finally closed, it made an impact, which will long survive its demise. Ask any collector to name the most famous of the Stourbridge firms, and the name Webb is likely to be at the forefront of their reply. I have outlined briefly the story of Thomas Webb & Co in *BBVG*, and the story has also been written about by other authors so I will not repeat it here, but instead pick up some of my research where I left off.

Thanks to Eveson,[1] we have knowledge of the composition of many of Webb's mixes. I show my interpretation of these, in terms of density and uranium content, in Tables 2, 3 & 4 in *BBVG*. However, as they are helpful in understanding and attributing, I have reproduced a condensed version below in Table 1. This only shows mixes that contain uranium.

Color / Description	Est. Density g/cc	Est. Uranium % wt.	Period	Comment
Cyrysoprase	2.55	0.85	19th c	
Lemon	2.55	1.1	19th c	
Lemon	3.15	0.14	19th c	
Ivory	3.15	0.35	19th c	
Yellow Ivory	3.15	1	19th c	
Tricolor	3.45	0.26	19th c	Contains gold
Carmine	3.43	0.41	19th c	Contains gold
Oriental	3.41	0.72	19th c	Contains gold
Aquamarine	3.18	0.07	19th c	Lead Crystal based mix
Emerald Green	3.18	0.28	19th c	Lead Crystal based mix
Rich Topaz	3.18	2.2	19th c	Lead Crystal based mix
Burmese	2.7	0.67	19th c	Contains gold
Burmese Mt Washington USA	2.88	0.91	19th c	Contains gold
Burmese opalescent green	2.72	0.49	19th c	No gold in mix
Lemon	3.18	0.13	19th c	
Russet	3.4	0.48	19th c	
Dark casing green	3.1	0.26	19th c	Lead Crystal based mix
Rich golden amber	3.1	2.3	19th c	Lead Crystal based mix
Chrysoprase green	3.12	2.3	19th c	Lead Crystal based mix
Lemonescent	3.18	0.23	19th c	Lead Crystal based mix
Amber sunshine	3.12	1.13	20th c	Lead Crystal based mix
Bristol green	3.15	1.15	20th c	Lead Crystal based mix
Eau de nil	3.18	0.23	20th c	Lead Crystal based mix

Table 1. Estimated density and uranium concentration of some known Webb's mixes. The Mount Washington Burmese is shown in italics.

One of the interesting aspects of writing a second book is that it provides an opportunity to re-examine work already covered. The piece of Queen's Burmese, shown in Photo 159, gave me cause to take a closer look at my other pieces. Amongst those with artwork, a number appear also to have been made from two different gathers, one with gold and one without. The Burmese technique requires that part of the item which is to turn to a shade of pink, to be reheated at a glory hole. It is the presence of gold in the mix that causes the change of color with the second heating. Clearly it is just not possible to reheat the inside so precisely as to leave a defined change of color on the rim. I can only conclude that in this piece the inside contained gold the outside did not. In such cases the pinkie glow, which appears when viewed from the outside, is due to the translucent nature of the metal. Geiger counter readings are the same for both the inside and outside of this vase, thus suggesting the two melts are different only in that one has been doped with gold.

While on the subject of Queen's Burmese, in *BBVG* Photo 185 I show an example of a Clarke's Fairy light in Webb's Burmese. This is correct but it has since come to my attention that the Clark's moulds were being used in the late 1950 – 1960 and "repro" Clarke's Fairy Lights were coming onto the market. These had tapered and ground top openings and were in amber, light green, pale blue, crystal and ruby. It is unlikely that any were then made in Queen's Burmese, however it seems that some look-a-likes may have been made in an Italian version of Burmese.[2] These should not give the astute collector any problem, but in view of item Photo 167 I cannot guarantee that the uranium and density alone will resolve any dilemma.

With the exception of Burmese and a few special metals, it would seem that Webb worked only with high leaded glass. Fig. 32 shows the density distribution of 35 pieces of Webb's uranium glass, excluding Queen's Burmese, in which I have high confidence, i.e. 98%. The bulk of their glass has a density in the 3.2 g/cc to 3.4 g/cc, that is 32% to 38% lead. This is independent of the color of the glass.

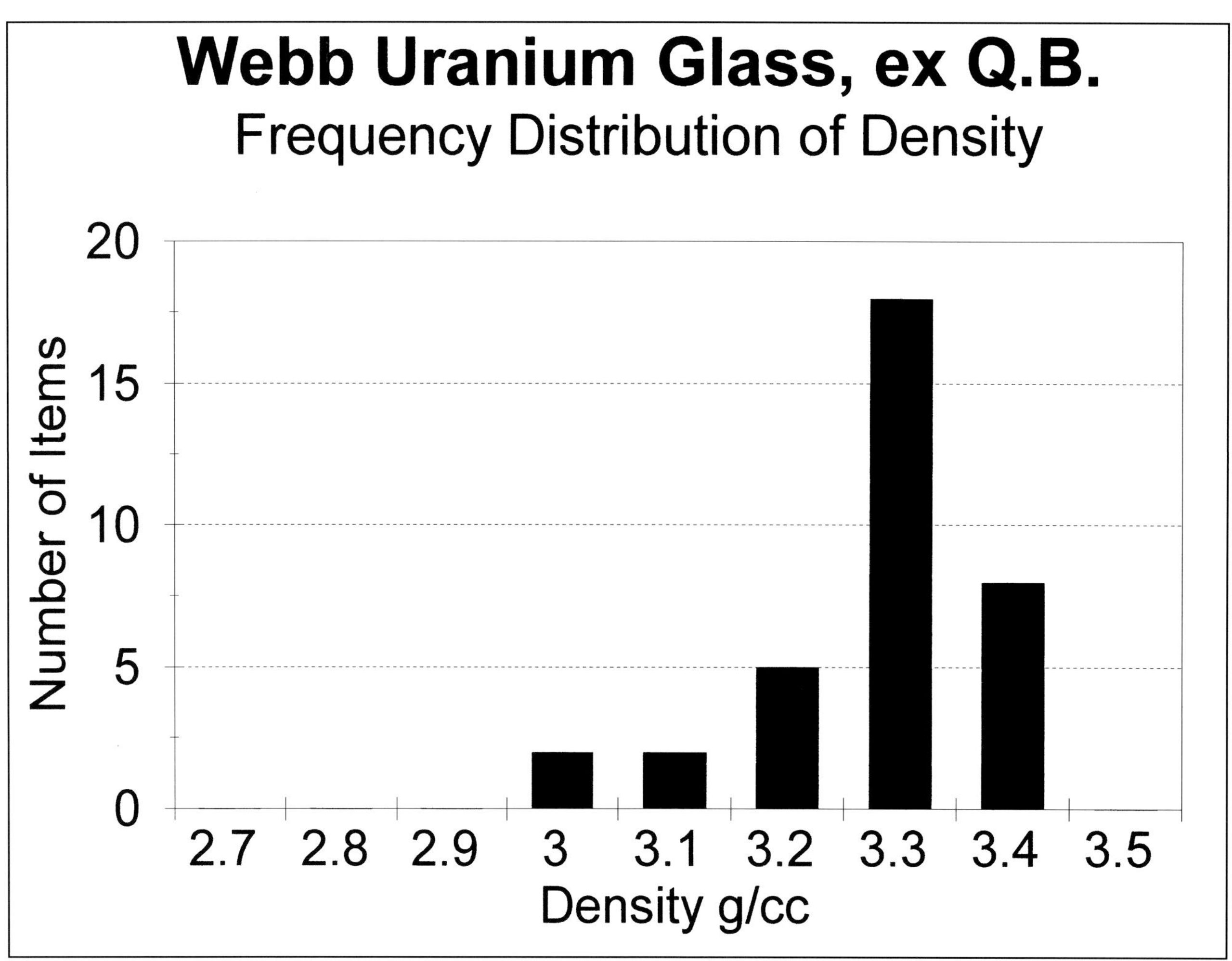

Figure 32

Fig 33 shows the density distribution of 21 pieces of Queen's Burmese. Not all are signed but I am satisfied that they were made by Webb. The density of these are considerably lower than for the other Webb metal and with one exception are in the 2.7 g/cc to 2.8 g/cc range. Any Burmese that does not fall within this bracket should be treated with great suspicion if it claims to be Webb.

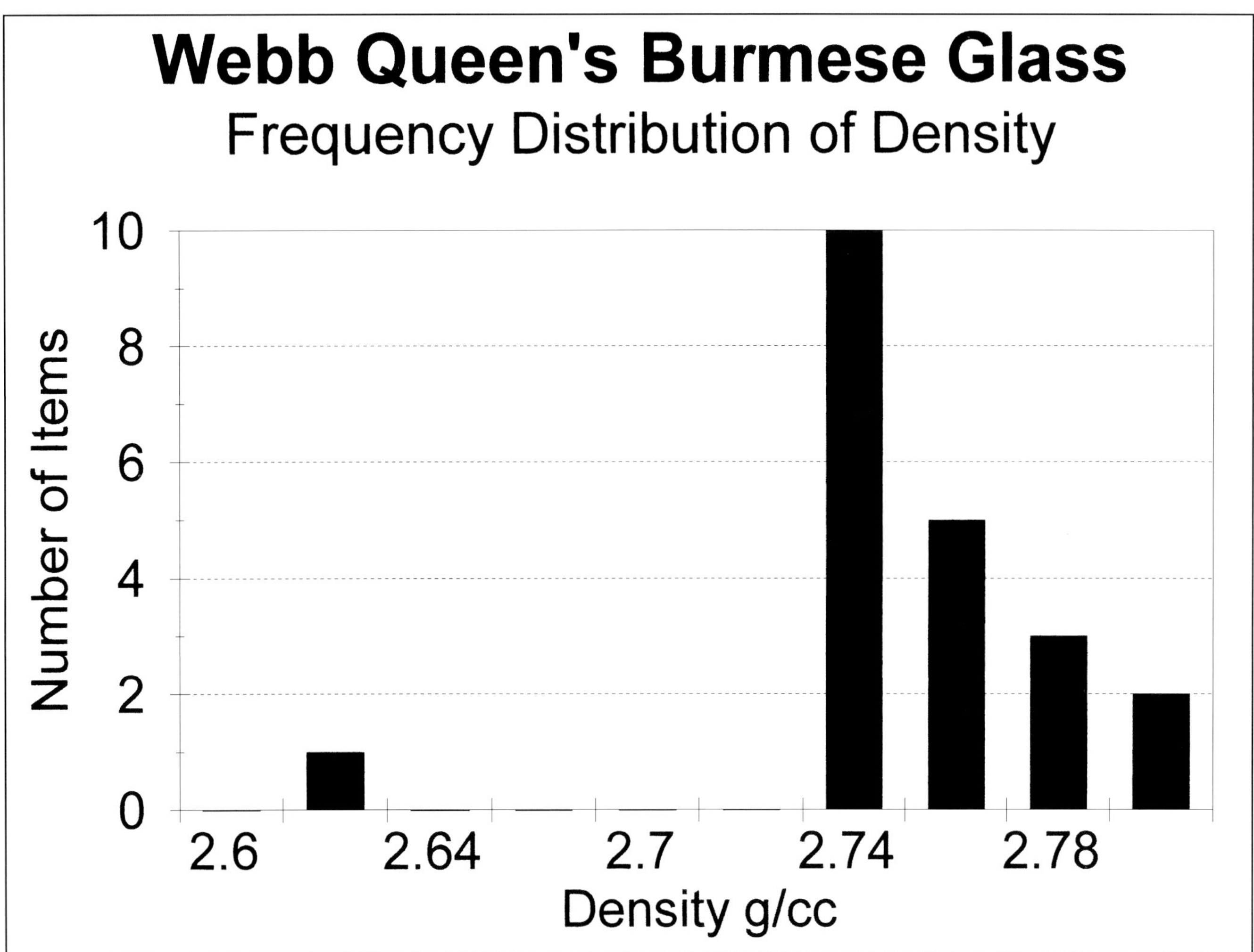

Figure 33

With regard to uranium concentrations I have only been able to make a meaningful interpretation of two colors, namely the Amber and Queen's Burmese.

Fig 34 shows the uranium concentration distribution in 20 pieces of Amber. The bulk fall within the range 1.1% wt to 1.3% wt. This compares well with the estimated value from the published formula of 1.13% wt. Joining the tops of the bars on this distribution would produce a curve expected in a random distribution.

Fig 35 shows the uranium concentration distribution in 24 pieces of Queen's Burmese. The most common value is in the range 0.4% wt to 0.5% wt. This compares with the estimated value from the published formula of 0.67% wt. The most likely explanation of this is that, according to Eveson,[3] Webb reduced the uranium concentration by as much as half in the later years of production.

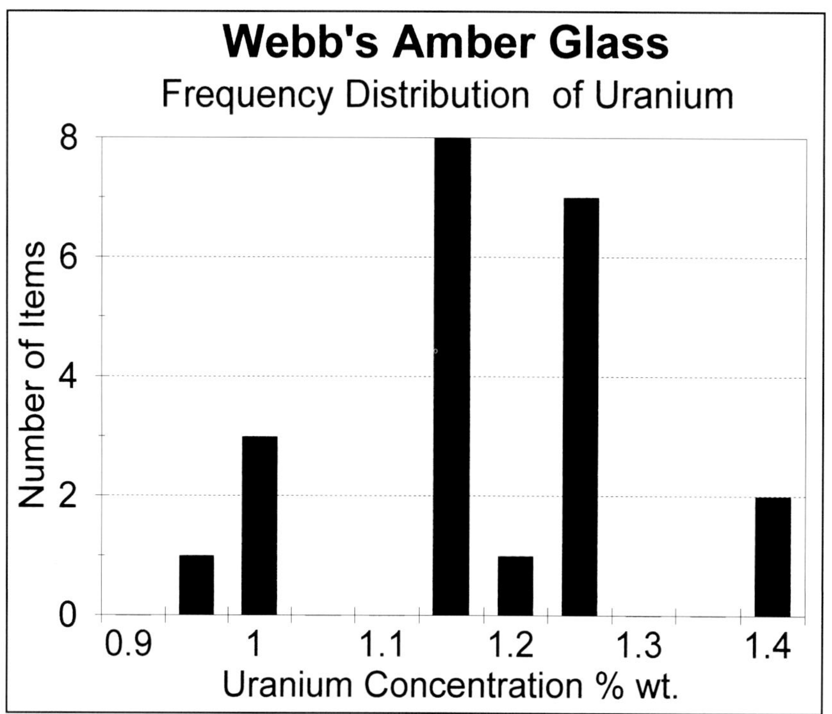

Figure 34

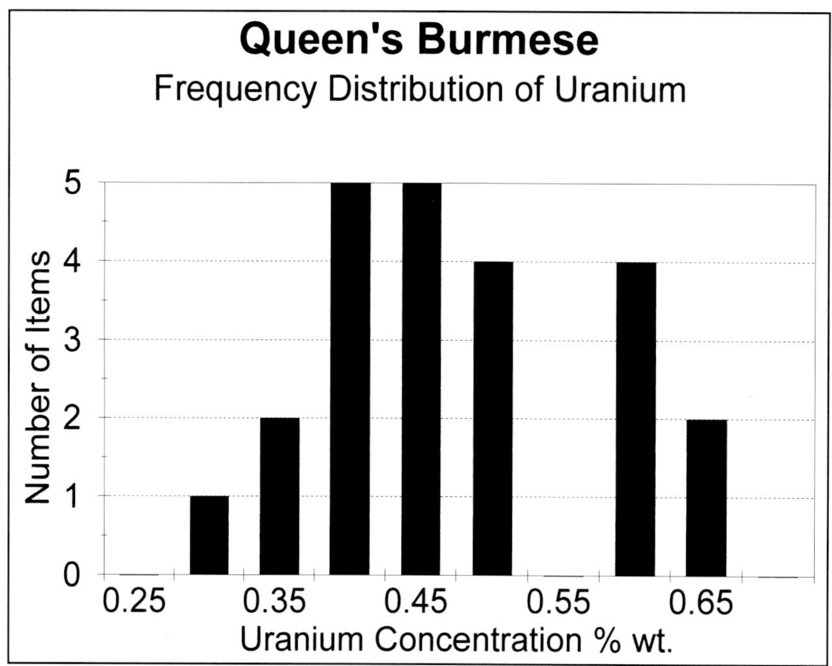

Figure 35

Photo 148. This is a good example of how difficult attributions can be. In all appearances it is the same as the wine in *BBVG*, Photo 304, and while its uranium is a little higher, the densities match. I have to conclude that they probably came from the same glasshouse in the same era. The foot of this wine is blown. I have revisited my notes on Webb's pattern books and find close, but not exact, matches to several wines in the Nos. 2300 - 2500 range. The uranium and densities match exactly those of the wine in *BBVG* Photo 172. Now I think both this one and its twin in *BBVG* Photo 304, *probably* came from Webb *about* 1850. Height 14 cm, density 3.22 g/cc, uranium 0.33% wt. value $80 - $120.

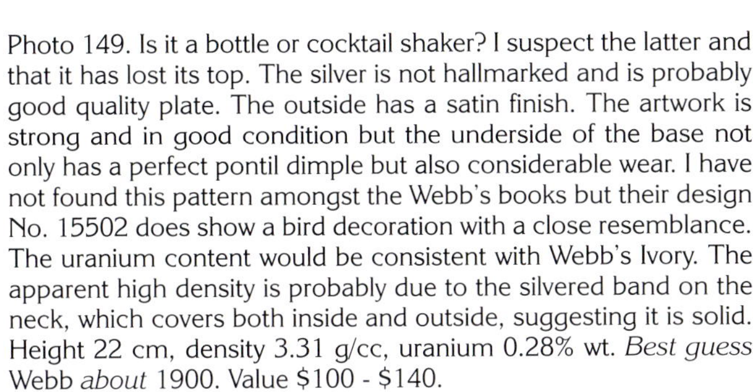

Photo 149. Is it a bottle or cocktail shaker? I suspect the latter and that it has lost its top. The silver is not hallmarked and is probably good quality plate. The outside has a satin finish. The artwork is strong and in good condition but the underside of the base not only has a perfect pontil dimple but also considerable wear. I have not found this pattern amongst the Webb's books but their design No. 15502 does show a bird decoration with a close resemblance. The uranium content would be consistent with Webb's Ivory. The apparent high density is probably due to the silvered band on the neck, which covers both inside and outside, suggesting it is solid. Height 22 cm, density 3.31 g/cc, uranium 0.28% wt. *Best guess* Webb *about* 1900. Value $100 - $140.

Photo 150. Although I have not seen anything like this in the Webb's pattern books I have studied, I feel fairly sure this specimen vase came from that factory. The shape of the crimped "petals" is typical of Webb's Design Registration 80167 already mentioned in *BBVG*. The uranium is only in the green. Height 17 cm, density 3.05 g/cc, uranium 0.05% wt. *Almost certainly* Webb, *about* 1890. Value $120 - $200.

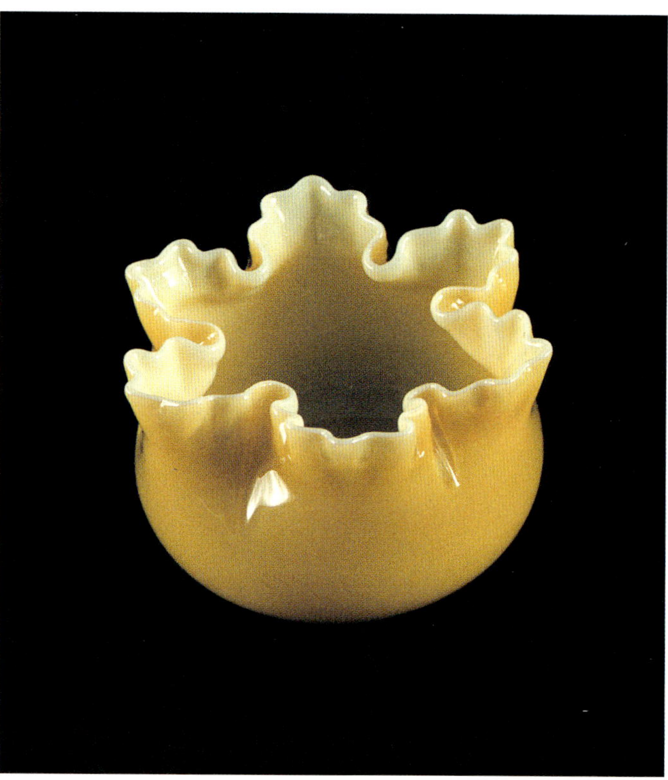

Photo 151. There is quite a lot about this piece that says it came from Webb's works and nothing to say that it did not. It has a perfect pontil dimple, items of very similar design are seen in their Pattern Books. No 14659 appears identical, but unfortunately the drawing is not too explicit. Finally, both the density and uranium would be as expected for Webb's "Yellow Ivory" (See Table 1 above.) On that basis I would rate it somewhere between a *probably* and *almost certainly* and date it *about* 1885. Height 5 cm, density 3.38 g/cc, uranium 1.2% wt. Value $80 - $120.

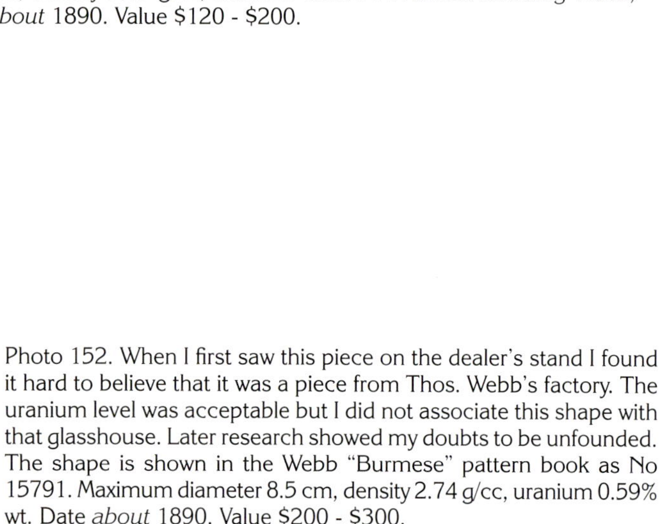

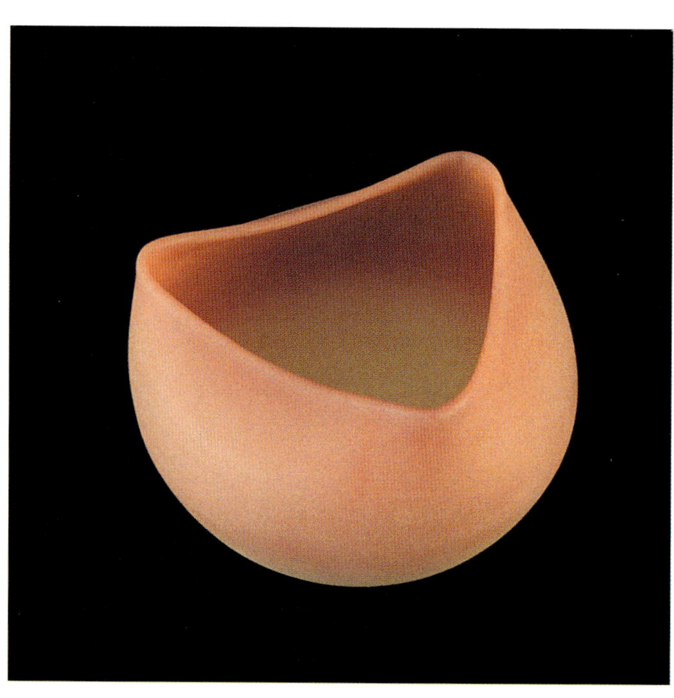

Photo 152. When I first saw this piece on the dealer's stand I found it hard to believe that it was a piece from Thos. Webb's factory. The uranium level was acceptable but I did not associate this shape with that glasshouse. Later research showed my doubts to be unfounded. The shape is shown in the Webb "Burmese" pattern book as No 15791. Maximum diameter 8.5 cm, density 2.74 g/cc, uranium 0.59% wt. Date *about* 1890. Value $200 - $300.

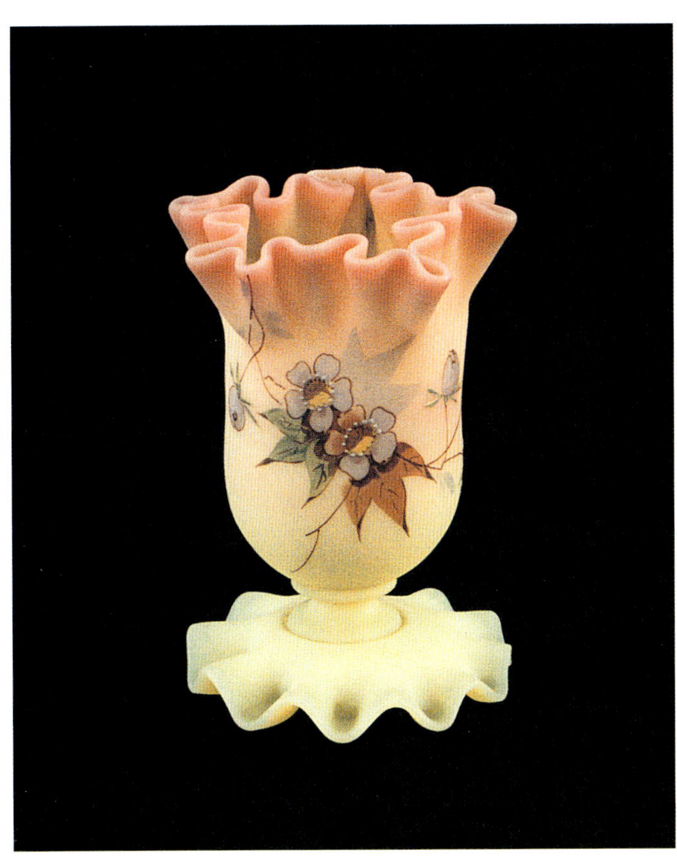

Photo 153. No doubt about this beautiful piece of Burmese coming from the Thomas Webb factory. A similar piece used to be on display in their factory museum. The shape is the same as shown in *BBVG* Photo 175. Height 9.75 cm, density 2.74 g/cc, uranium 0.62% wt. Date *about* 1890, value $300 - $400.

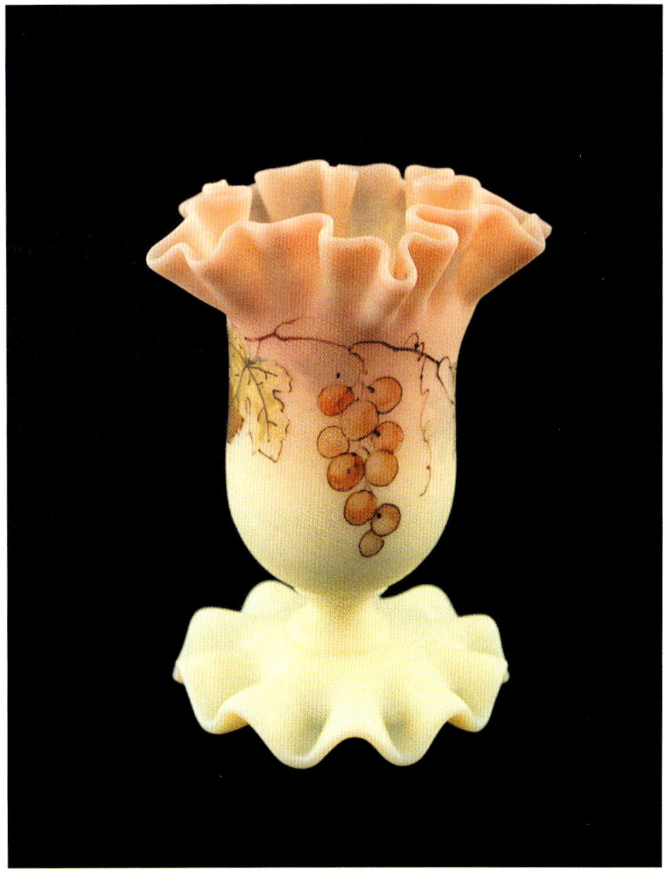

Photo 154. Almost identical to the piece in Photo 153, except for the painted pattern. The uranium is lower but within the range that we have come to expect in this product. Height 10.5 cm, density 2.76 g/cc, uranium 0.43% wt. Date, *probably about* 1900, a little later than the previous item as Webb reduced the uranium content for their later mixes. Value $200 - $300.

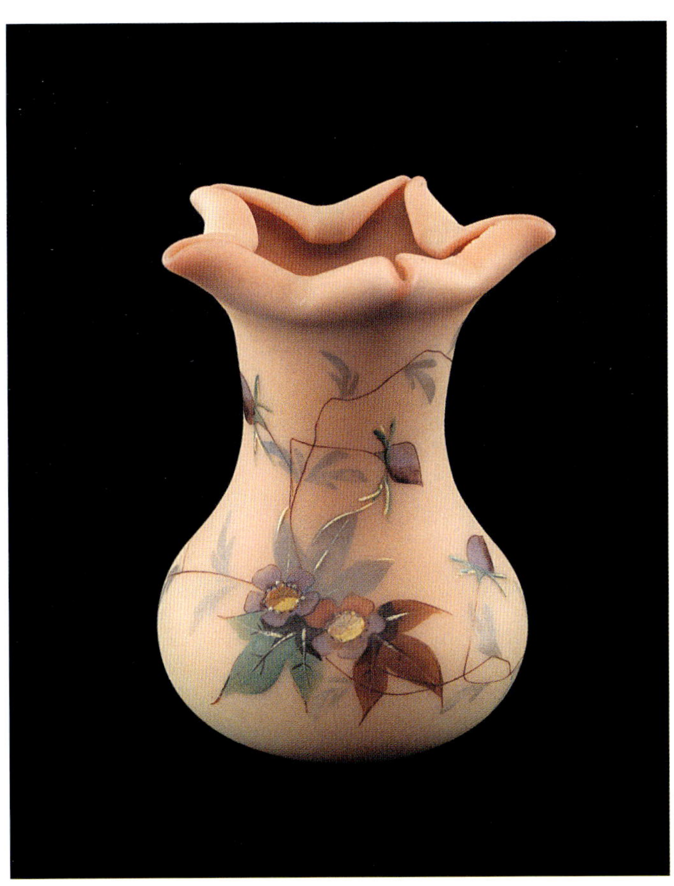

Photo 155. There is no doubt this piece is the genuine Queens Burmese. It has the Webb mark on the pontil dimple. Curiously there is also Rd 676, this is an incomplete registration number. Height 10 cm, diameter 7.25 cm, density 2.74 g/cc, uranium 0.5% wt. Date *about* 1890, value $245 - $350.

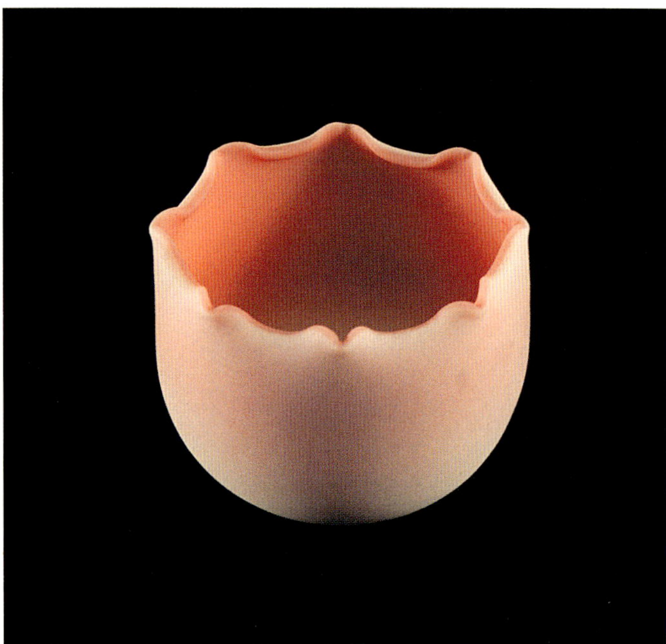

Photo 156. Although unsigned, I have no doubt this is a piece of Webb's Queen's Burmese. I have seen an identical shaped piece in an auctioneer's catalogue that was decorated and signed. Diameter 7.4 cm, density 2.74 g/cc, uranium 0.3% wt. Date *about* 1890, value $120 - $200.

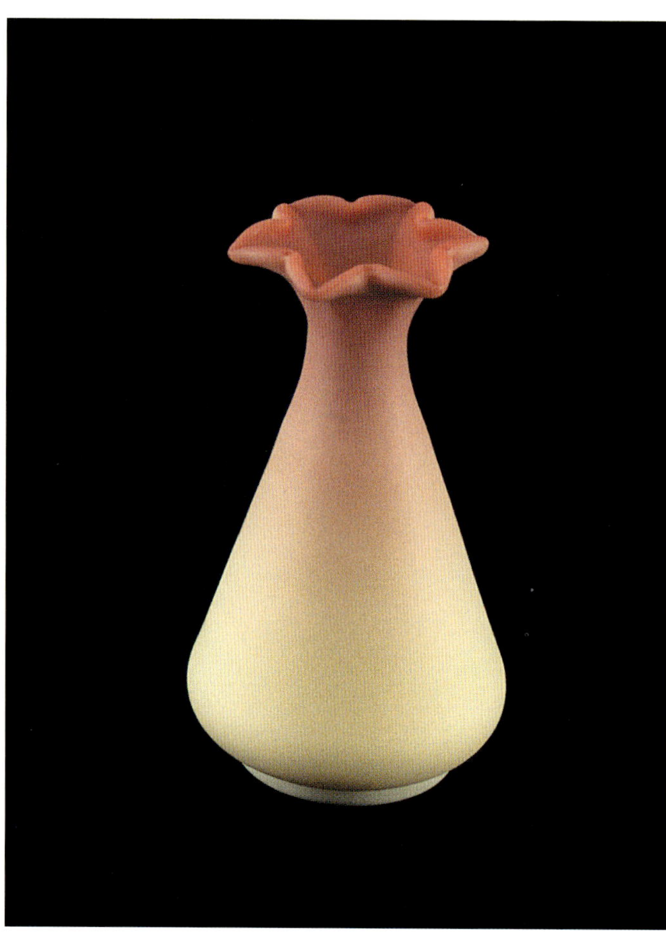

Photo 157. The top of this spill vase is finished with the Webb registered design. The shape is also shown is Webb's pattern book, No 18516 (1890). It has a perfect pontil dimple. Height 11.4 cm, density 2.77 g/cc, uranium 0.37% wt. Not marked but Webb Queen's Burmese, *about* 1895. Value $180 - $240.

Photos 158 a, b, c. I will take these three items together; they are nearly identical. Their style and size is as for the items shown in *BBVG* Photos 190 and 191. They are *almost certainly* Webb's Burmese. The shape is simple and may have been used by other glasshouses in their own version of Burmese, but the way the pontil dimple has been formed, density and uranium content all shout Webb. What this Photograph illustrates quite well is how no two pieces of Burmese are the same color. As already mentioned in *BBVG*, this is because the red color is formed when the item is reheated at a glory hole. Statistics, reading left to right; diameter 6.7 cm, 6.7 cm, 6.7 cm. Density 2.76 g/cc, 2.74 g/cc, 2.74 g/cc. Uranium 0.56% wt, 0.56% wt, 0.62% wt. Date *about* 1895, value (each) $100 - $160.

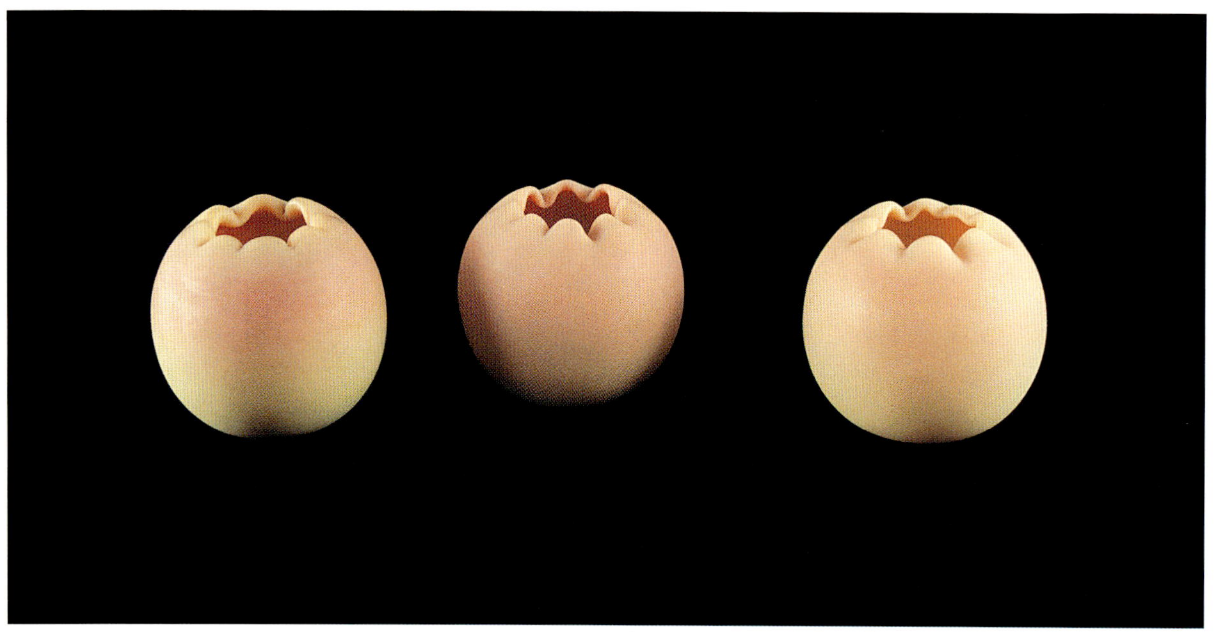

Photo 159. Although not marked, this has to be a piece of Queen's Burmese. The density and uranium content are consistent with Webb's later production and although not marked it has the Webb's design-registered petal top and a perfect pontil dimple. Only the inside is rose pink and close inspection appears to show that the metal is layered. See Photo 160. The outer layer showing no sign of the pink must be devoid of gold. The artwork is also interesting, both the small blue forget-me-not and the white flower are thick and raised. Height 8.3 cm, density 2.76 g/cc, uranium 0.37% wt. Date *about* 1900. Value $200 - $240..

Photo 160. Close-up of the top of Photo 159, showing a sharp delineation between the inside and outside color, indicating separate layers of metal.

Photo 161. This is a most peculiar piece of Burmese, it is made in two layers both of which appear to be a Burmese mix. Unlike the other Webb pieces it has a smooth but not glossy finish. The pontil dimple is not quite perfect in symmetry. Height 8.75 cm, density 2.74 g/cc, uranium (outside) 0.37% wt, (inside) 0.5% wt. I think the balance of probability favors Webb, but I have a doubt so I will settle for *could be, about* 1900. Value $120 - $200.

Photo 162. Another case where all the evidence says Webb's Queen's Burmese. The smooth satin finish, the delicate texture of the glass, the perfect pontil dimple and the Webb patented petal top finish and its density. However there is a curiosity, which is well illustrated in Photo 163. The red does not gradually merge into the lemon on the rim of the petals but is in sharp contrast. This suggests that the rim of the petals is formed from a different metal to the remainder of the body, the former being the standard Queen's Burmese, the latter being the same but without the added gold. Perhaps this was intended as a cost cutting exercise for although only a little gold is used, it is largely wasted in the body of the vessel, which is not reheated. Height 7 cm, density 2.76 g/cc, uranium 0.31% wt. Date *about* 1900, value $120 - $160.

Photo 163. Top view of Photo 162 showing the limited Burmese effect on the rim.

Photo 164. When I saw this pin holder I did not think it could be Webb. It has a glossy finish and again lacks the gradual merging of the red into the lemon as would be expected from the reheat process. However I have now seen a signed Queen's Burmese advertised on eBay, which had a glossy finish. I have also found this shape illustrated in Webb's pattern Book as No 18531. It also has a perfect pontil dimple and is of the density expected for Webb's Queen's Burmese. There is a curiosity. The red is sharply defined on the top of the mushroom. However it does not fully penetrate to the underside, see Photo 165. I get the impression this piece is also made from two different gathers, while both would be the basic Queen's Burmese mix, only one would contain gold. As for the glossy surface, it should be remembered that the more usual satin finish is obtained by additional acid treatment. Height 7.5 cm, density 2.76 g/cc, uranium 0.31%. Date *about* 1900, value $160 - $200.

Photo 165. The under side of item Photo 164 showing how the red has not penetrated and must be layered.

Photo 166. Although not marked this is, without qualification, a piece of Webb Queen's Burmese. It has the perfect pontil dimple associated with their Burmese. The shape is also shown in the Webb pattern book for Burmese as pattern number 15740. Height 8.5 cm, density 2.61 g/cc, uranium 0.37% wt. Date *about* 1890. Value $120 - $160.

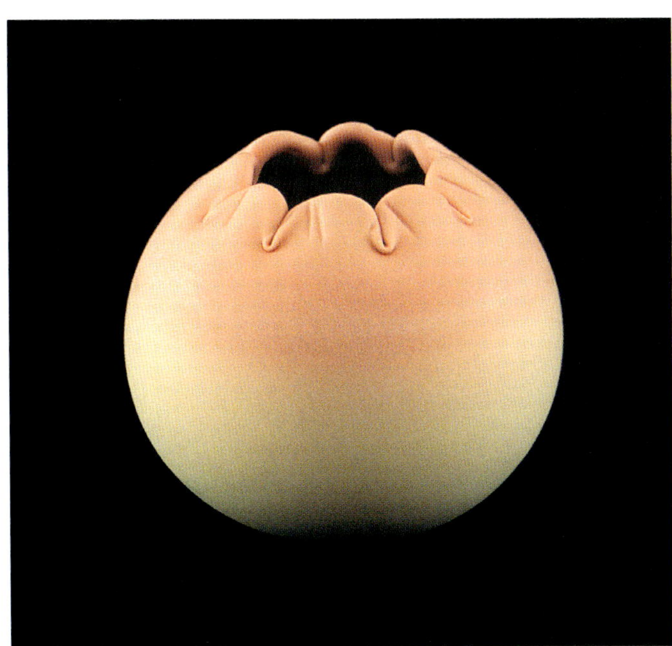

Photo 167. The only reason I have included this in the Thos. Webb chapter is because the dealer who sold it on eBay claimed it to be a piece of Webb's Burmese. I have no doubt that it is not. Oddly the density and uranium content are consistent with the Webb Queen's Burmese formula but several other factors say it is an imitation. The red color extends over all the inside while that on the outside only goes down half way. It is difficult to see how this could come about by the traditional reheating at a glory hole. It is far too thick, Webb's Q.B. is always thin and delicate. The crimp work is to crude. The pontil has not been fully ground off, although there is a dimple. The shades of red and lemon are not quite Webb. I don't know who made it but I feel confident it was intended to deceive the unwary. As to when it was born, I am also mystified. The absence of wear makes me think it is not all that old, so best guess is *about* 1950. Height 7 cm, diameter 8.5 cm. Density 2.78 g/cc, uranium 0.37% wt. Value $40 - $60 as a curiosity.

Photo 169. This sherry bears the typical Thomas Webb trademark for the period 1936-49. In view of the demand for uranium during WW2, it is more likely that this particular item was made in the earlier part of that period. It is another example of the Webb Eau de Nil color. My calculated density and uranium values for this mix, see Table 1, are 3.18 g/cc and 0.23% respectively. These are close to the measured values quoted below and give an idea of the consistency between estimated and measured values. Height 7.75 cm, density 3.23 g/cc, uranium 0.23% wt. Value $16 - $24.

Photo 168. This is not what I would have thought of as being Webb's "Ball Glass," but that is how the dealer described it. To me the "balls" are too small for that description. However it does carry the Webb trademark for 1935-49. Height 13.2 cm, density 3.21 g/cc, uranium 0.17% wt. Webb "eau de nil" *about* 1940. Value $40 - $60.

Photo 170. These three glasses come from the Webb's intaglio "Water Lily" range. They are in Sunshine Amber. All are trademarked with the 1935-44 mark, but as they contain uranium, it is most likely that they were made before 1940. Height 15 cm, 12.7 cm and 11 cm. For the largest, density 3.2g/cc, uranium 1% wt. Value $50 - $90 each.

Photo 171. Close-up of the Water Lilly pattern shown on items appearing in Photo 170.

Photo 172. Both the decanter and 6 spirit glasses carry the Webb 1935-44 trademark and is an example of their "Wave Pattern". Heights, decanter 20 cm, spirits 9.2 cm. Density 3.28 g/cc, uranium 1.1% wt. Value for the set of decanter and six spirit glasses $180 - $240..

Photo 173. Although made in thick glass this is another example of Webb's wave pattern in "Sunshine Amber". Unusually it is not marked however, it has a slight blemish on the side of the bowl and the perfectly circular pontil dimple is slightly off-centre. It could well be a factory reject. Height 11.2 cm, density 3.33 g/cc, uranium 1.21% wt. Date *about* 1935, value $40 - $60.

Photo 174. This goblet, unlike the preceding one, is marked "Webb Made in England." It is in Sunshine Amber, *about* 1935. Height 11.4 cm, density 3.33 g/cc, uranium 1.24% wt. Value $50 - $70.

Photo 176. Although the density and uranium are a little low, I am fairly confident this is a piece of Webb's Sunshine Amber. The pattern matches that on item in Photo 197 *BBVG*. There are a few slight blemishes on the rim of the mushroom and I suspect it was a "factory second" and as such would not carry the Webb trademark. Diameter 17.5 cm, density 2.99 g/cc, uranium 0.93% wt. *Probably* Webb, *about* 1935. Value $50 - $70.

Photo 177. A large, unusual, and superb example of Webb's "Sunshine Amber" in the Horizontal Wave Pattern. The bowl carries the already described Webb trademark, it is too large for me to weigh or measure density. Diameter 15.5 cm, height 27 cm. Uranium 1.12% wt. Date *about* 1935. Value $120 - $180.

Chapter 30
The Remaining Items

The foregoing Midlands glasshouses are a few for whom I have found samples of their products. There are also interesting examples of glass, which I feel sure came from this area, that I can not reasonably attribute. I have already shown a number in *BBVG*. The Photographs that follow will show some more.

Photo 178. A simple finger bowl in "Bristol Green." How old is it and who made it? This is another unresolved "whodunit." The uranium tells us it is later than 1830, the perfect pontil dimple says it is from a quality glasshouse. The excessive wear and the blemishes in the metal make it unlikely to be a 1930s reproduction. The design is too simple to make it worth looking through pattern books. The density indicates it has a lot of lead in the mix. I'm going to say *probably* English Midlands, *period* 1860. Height 9 cm, density 3.1 g/cc, uranium 0.37% wt. Value $60 - $80.

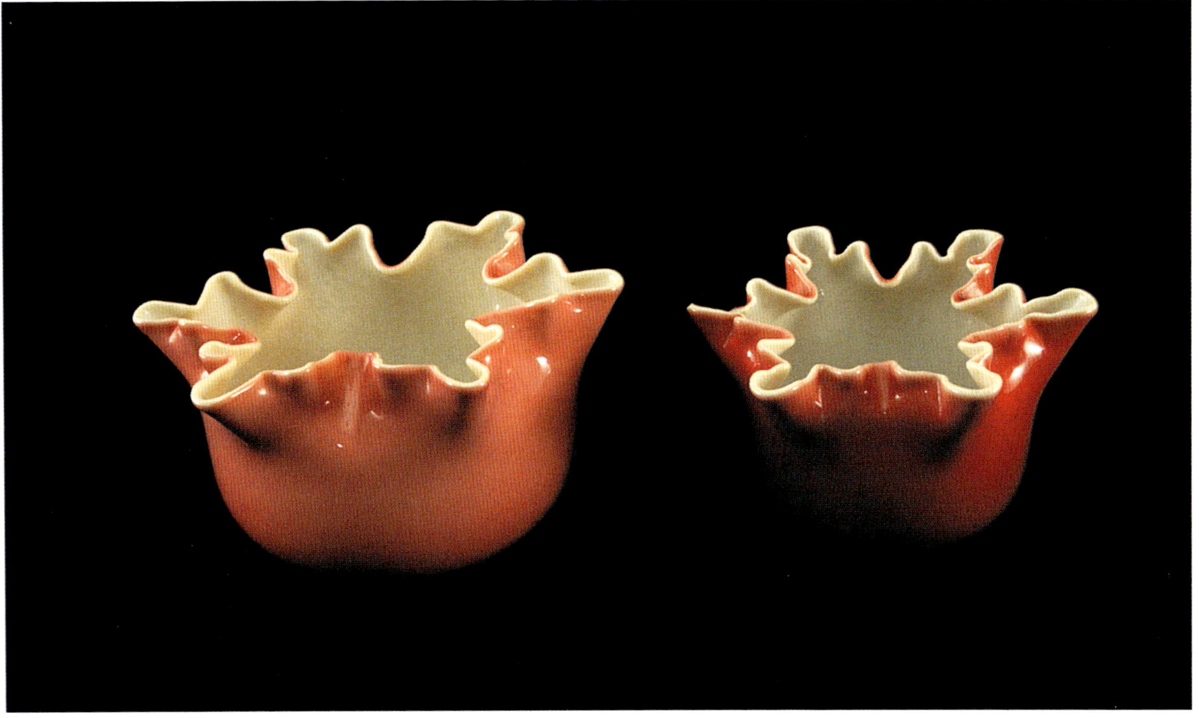

Photos 179 a and b. I have shown these two pieces together. The shape of the top and other measurements indicate they came from the same factory. A number of glasshouses, especially in the English Midlands, went in for this fancy style of finish about the turn of the nineteenth century but this particular pattern is so unusual that it must be as good as a signature. Unfortunately I have not been able to establish who made them. Webb, Stevens and Williams, Richardson and Stuart pattern books all show this type of work, but I have not found a match. I have Photographed them side by side to show the slight difference in colors. The largerleft hand side item is paler than its sibling, but I suspect this is because the outer casing is thinner. The uranium appears to be in the inner ivory. Both items show considerable wear on their base and have good quality pontil dimples. Unfortunately the one on the right hand side has a chip off its rim. Diameter (lhs) 13.7 cm, (rhs) 11.4 cm. Density (lhs)3.18 g/cc, (rhs) 3.19 g/cc. Uranium measured on the inside, (lhs)0.29% wt, (rhs) 0.25% wt. Value each, in good condition $60 - $100.

Photo 180. The shape closely resembles of the three pieces in Photo 181. The uranium is only in the applied trail work round the neck. This is rather crude and not becoming of a quality glasshouse. The density is a little lower than the others are but this may be due to the different metal from which it has been made. Height 9 cm, density 2.99 g/cc, uranium not measured. Date *about* 1890, value $30 - $40.

Photo 182. Three gathers of glass have been used to make this spill vase. The outer is clear uranium primrose, next is a brilliant white and finally on the inside, pink. It is the opaque white, which shows through the primrose making that look opaque. On the underside is a broken pontil mark. Victorian? I don't think so, it is more akin to the Walsh and Stevens and Williams products of the early 1920s, but the lower uranium concentration says it probably did not come from either of those glasshouses. Height 10.5 cm, density 3.18 g/cc, uranium 0.4% wt. Value $40 - $60.

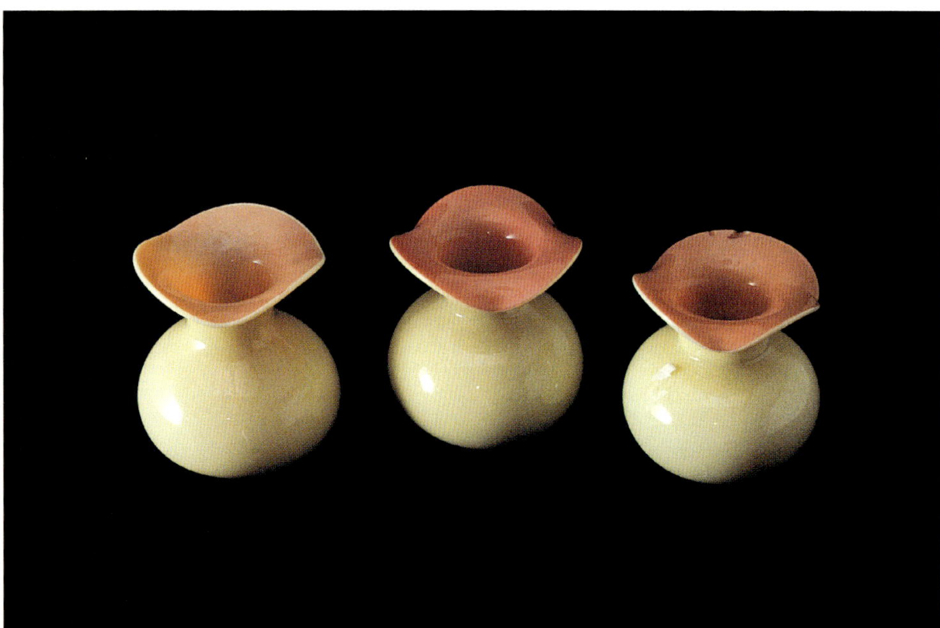

Photos 181 a, b, c. These three little items look like triplets, but I doubt their sibling relationship. Are they another example of almost identical items being made by different glasshouses? If they are, then it shows little consideration for collectors! The middle piece is illustrated as Photo 220 in *BBVG*. I have not changed my mind with respect to its origin. The two outside pieces have the same densities but slightly lower uranium levels, by itself this difference is not significant. However the lefthand side item has a rough, un-ground pontil while the right hand side has a crudely ground pontil dimple. Furthermore the pinks are not the same shade, that of the centre piece being darker than the other two. My *best guess* is still that the centre is Webb but the other two are English Midlands of another glasshouse. Reading left to right; height 8.25 cm, 8 cm, 7.75 cm; density 3.3 g/cc, 3.3 g/cc 3.26 g/cc; uranium 0.81% wt, 1.1% wt, 0.92% wt. Dates are likely to all be much the same *about* 1890. Value $30 - $50 each.

Photo 183. This is a most unusual piece. A deep pink gather has been cased with two or more layers. Incorporated are air and silver flakes. There is a perfect dimple where the pontil has been ground out. It is not marked. The uranium is in the pale lemon outer casing. Almost certainly from the English Midlands. It could have come from a variety of firms but the pontil dimple suggests it was one of quality. Walsh, Webb, Stevens and Williams come to mind. My *best guess*, based only on the shade of the pink is Stevens and Williams. The density is lower than might be expected because of the trapped air. Date *about* 1890. Diameter 8.6 cm, density 3.08 g/cc, uranium 0.25% wt. Value $80 - $120.

Photo 184. The interesting aspect of this little vase is its color. It is not unique but an unusual bluish green for uranium glass. It has been produced in a 12 rib dip mold, the pontil has been ground out leaving a near perfect dimple. The base shows considerable wear, which helps me make up my mind on dating. Height 9 cm, density 3.19 g/cc, uranium 0.17% wt. A similar color is seen in Photo 110, the density, and uranium of that item are very close to that of this piece. I cannot pin it down to any particular firm with confidence, so I will say *Almost certainly* English Midlands, *could be* Richardson, period 1890. Value $40 - $60.

Photo 185. When I decided to include the item in Photo 228, *BBVG*, I thought I would never see another piece like it, which is why I thought it must be a friggers piece. Now this one has turned up. It is not the same color, but for all intents and purposes the same shape and size! The rough edge at the top strongly suggests it was never finished off, unless some mount was intended to be cemented on top. Height 6.5 cm, density 3.13 g/cc, uranium 0.19% wt. *Probably* English Midlands and this example has, perhaps, a little more than rummage sale value than the piece in *BBVG*.

Photo 186. Is this a jam pot or a vase? I don't know, but does it matter? This simple but attractive piece probably started life in an eight-pillar dip mold. It would have been expanded in a smooth wall spherical mold before the base was added. The shape of the base and the fact that it is not a perfect circle, its radius varying by 1 mm, suggests it was not shaped in a mold. It has a ground out pontil, which is not quite a perfect circle. Although it cannot be seen in the Photograph, the top of the bowl has a "bud" where the cut would have been made. All these characteristics are typical of a piece of British glass. It could well have come from Stevens and Williams but I have not found any clues, except its density, to confirm its birthplace. Height 10 cm, density 3.24 g/cc, uranium 0.15% wt. Date *period* 1920, value $20 - $30.

Photo 187. The interesting aspect of this little dish is that, despite appearances, the uranium is only on the inside, in the form of a thin layer. The grape vine patten is very similar to that used by Stephens and Williams and my gut feeling is that this item came from that firm. Logic says that other Midland glasshouses used similar patterns so that is where I must place it. Dimensions 9 cm square, density 3.09 g/cc, uranium 2.2 cps. Date *probably about* 1925. Value $10 - $20.

Photo 188. A toilet water bottle with all the attributes I expect from the English Midlands. The lower ribs would have been formed in a dip mold, but the upper part and the stopper have been hand cut and polished. The pontil dimple is perfect in shape. There are some similarities to Webb pattern 2668 and to some Richardson patterns. These are not close enough for an attribution. Height 17.5 cm, density 3.16 g/cc, uranium 0.31% wt. *Almost certainly* English Midlands, date *about* 1880. Value $100 - $160.

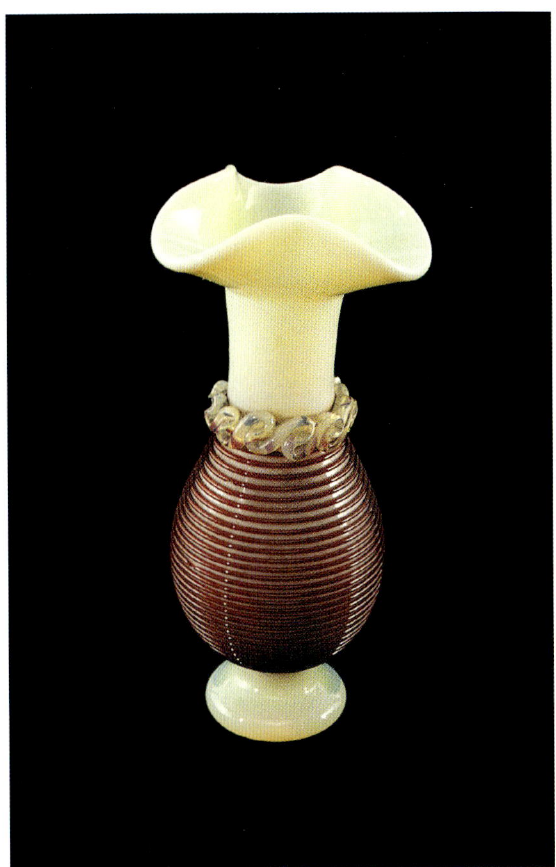

Photo 189. I have very little doubt that this piece came from Stourbridge but who made it? The uranium level is not close enough for me to associate it with Webb's Ivory, it is however near enough the same as that in item Photo 112 (*BBVG*). The applied trail work round the necks of the two items is also the same, so could this have come from Stuart? Their pattern books do show threading and also pieces whose shape vaguely resembles this piece. However Richardson's and Webb's books also show similar trail work. My *best guess* is Stuart *about* 1880. Height 11 cm, density 3.2 g/cc, uranium 0.24% wt. Value $60 - $100.

Photos 190 and 191. I bought the biscuit barrel shown in Photo 190 in Sydney, Australia. The lid carries the mark HARDY. This almost certainly indicates that it was retailed by Hardy Bros., now a major jewellers. Mr John Hardy arrived in Australia from Nottingham, England. In 1853 he started trading from his rooms in Jamison Street, Sydney but two years later opened a showroom in Hunter Street which became the home of the business for 80 years. Later other showrooms were opened. It would seem that most of the high quality goods came from the UK and it is highly probable that this piece was no exception. I would go as far as saying it *almost certainly* came from the English Midlands, with a *best guess* it was from Thos. Webb. The barrel is a basic Ivory metal with a brown criss-cross overlay. The base, Photo 191, is formed with an added disc of topaz. The uranium content is consistent with the Webb's formula for "ivory", while the topaz disc is close to the topaz on the vase shown in Photo. 174 of *BBVG*. The density is only indicative because of the metal band and handle. Height 13 cm., density 3.4 g/cc., uranium on Ivory 0.45% wt, on Topaz 0.56% wt. Date *about* 1880. Value $200 - $300.

Photo 192. In this version of the Victorian table centre piece, the spiky logs form a tripod. Height 11.5 cm, density 3.24 g/cc, uranium 0.12% wt. Both density and uranium match the items in Photos 225 and 226 *BBVG* Date *about* 1890. Value $80 - $100.

Photo 193. Another first sight deception. From appearance this table piece looks very much as if it has come from the English Midlands, however the density raises doubts. I have included it in this chapter because of the similarities to other pieces I have seen but, while I don't think it came from abroad, there is a chance it originated somewhere else, perhaps Lancashire. Date *about* 1890. Height 16 cm, density 2.8 g/cc, uranium 0.9% wt. Value $50 - $70.

Photo 194. Made to look like a Victorian table piece, the green uranium glass has been cased with clear overlay. The cut top suggests it is Continental. I am reluctant to date it but would say *probably period* 1930. Height 20 cm, density 2.45 g/cc, uranium approximately 0.25% wt. Value $10.

Photo 195. This centrepiece is unusual in as much as it is a white opaque glass cased over with uranium glass. This would suggest to me either Walsh, or Stevens and Williams, who we know used a brilliant white in their primrose lines in the 1920s. Height 10 cm, density 3.22 g/cc, uranium 2.5 cps. Date *about* 1900, value $50 – $70.

Photo 196. The only uranium in this jam dish is in the crimp work. The metal stand is EPNS. The ruby dish has a perfect ground pontil and was made from a 16 rib mold. The crimp work pattern is not unlike that on Photo 108 and could be Richardson's but I can find no other indication. Webb's 1880 pattern No 13212 shows a 16 rib mold and an item of this shape but there is no evidence for their using a double layer of crimp work like this. Diameter 12.25 cm, density 3.17 g/cc, uranium approximately 0.24% wt on crimp work only. Value $160 - $200.

Photo 197. The density and style of this Jack in the Pulpit says this *probably* came from the English Midlands. There is no pontil mark and the foot has been molded. The considerably amount of wear on the base shows something of its age. I doubt if it would have come from one of the quality glasshouses and have not found it illustrated during my researches. Height 17 cm, density 3.16 g/cc, uranium, only in the ivory, 0.19% wt. date *about* 1915. Value $40 - $60

Chapter 31

Edinburgh Crystal

Scottish glass should deserve an introductory chapter in its own right. However I have found very few examples of uranium colored glass that I can attribute to that country. Those that I have found have come from Edinburgh Crystal. Ungraciously, in *BBVG* I included Edinburgh Crystal with Thomas Webb & Sons because at one time they were part of the "Webb's Crystal Glass Company." However "Webb" now exists in name only and, ironically at the time of writing, that name is owned by Edinburgh Crystal. The development of the glass industry in that part of Scotland, and the part played in it by Edinburgh Crystal, has been told by H W Woodward,[1] in his book *The Story of Edinburgh Crystal*, which takes us as far as the early 1980s.

The origins of crystal glass in this part of Scotland can be traced to the 1600s. By 1867, The Edinburgh and Leith Glass Company was a going concern at their Norton Park factory in Leith. The Company became associated with Thomas Webb & Sons in the depression years. It became the "Edinburgh Crystal Glass Company" in 1955. In 1964 Crown House Limited acquired Thomas Webb and the Edinburgh Crystal operation. This brought a temporary respite to what was otherwise a declining industry as Crown House were able to finance modernization.

Edinburgh Crystal moved from Norton to a larger site at Penicuik just south of Edinburgh. Another change of ownership occurred in 1988. Edinburgh Crystal, along with Thomas Webb, was acquired by Coloroll as part of Crown House Tableware. They established a Crystal Division with its Head Office at the Thomas Webb site. Edinburgh Crystal, in Penicuik, was part of that Division in the role of a satellite manufacturing facility. A couple of years later Coloroll went into receivership and, in 1991, the crystal operation in Edinburgh was the subject of a management lead buyout, backed by funding from Caledonia Investments who are now the major shareholder.

The new company "The Edinburgh Crystal Glass Company", established its head office at Penicuik, meanwhile the Webb factory was closed. Edinburgh Crystal bought the Thomas Webb brand name and in April 2004 acquired Caithness Glass, the renowned paperweight and art glass company. However by the summer of that year the Edinburgh Crystal closed down their furnaces at Penicuik to concentrate of cutting rather than making their pieces. Now, as I write the final draft of this book, in the summer of 2006, the news is that this old established firm, part of Scottish heritage, has gone into administration.

Although I have only had opportunity to examine a few samples of this glass it seems that, for items made in the 1930 era, while the dark ambers have a density of about 3.1 g/cc, the greens and yellows have a density of about 2.8 g/cc.

Photo 198. Toothpick holder (or small vase) in a classical uranium yellow carries the Edinburgh Crystal trademark (see Photo 199). It has been blown into a mold and has 12 flats on the inside. The top has been cut and polished. Height 7.5 cm, density 2.83 g/cc, uranium 0.22% wt. Date *about* 1930, value $40 - $60.

Photo 199. The mark of Edinburgh and Leith Crystal, as shown on the item in Photo 198 and elsewhere.

Photo 200. A rare example of a blown bucket vase from Edinburgh and Leith Crystal. It may have been formed in a dip mold to obtain the pattern, then expanded by the blow pipe. On the underside of the base is a perfect ground dimple where the pontil would have been attached. It bears the "Edinburgh E and L Crystal" signature, a product of the 1920/30s. It is possible that the quality of the pontil dimple shows Webb influence, but the metal does not. While the uranium content could be that of "Eau de Nil," the density is much lower. Height 20.5 cm, diameter at top 15 cm, density 2.82 g/cc, uranium 0.29% wt. Value $60 - $100.

Photo 201. This mini-tumbler has 20 shallow internal flats. It would have been formed in a dip mold then blown into the final mold to reverse the flats and make its final shape. I have not positively identified it in the Edinburgh Crystal pattern books, but I have seen similar shapes, with fewer flats, shown as part of a cocktail set. It seems likely that the original dip mold may have come from Richardson. The uranium and density is so close to the item in Photo 198 that, even though this item is not marked, I will say *probably* Edinburgh Crystal. Height 7 cm, density 2.87 g/cc, uranium 0.22% wt. Date *about* 1935. Value $20-$30.

Photo 202. Edinburgh Crystal are well known for their "Thistle Design" of wines and sherries. However, although I have found similar shapes in their pattern books and carrying their signature, I have not found an exact match to this glass. Unfortunately I have not been able to trace any of the Company's old batch books and have no evidence that they used metal with such a high uranium content. A shape similar to this is shown in Webb's pattern book (no 39341), which dates to 1928. However at that time Webb was very close to joining with Edinburgh Crystal, so it is quite possible they were working closely together. However all the information I have indicates Webb used a mix with much less uranium. A further complication is that an identical shape, with a different cut design in the cup of the wine, is shown in a Richardson's pattern book, the date of which is uncertain but probably dates from the time that Webb took over Richardson, which loosely links all three firms. On the other hand, the uranium content would be consistent with Stevens and Williams dark amber. For these reasons, although I have put this piece in the Edinburgh Crystal chapter, I am not going to attribute it to this or any other firm. Height 13.8 cm, density 3.34 g/cc, uranium 2.98% wt. Date *about* 1930, value $40 - $60.

Chapter 32

American and Continental Glass

When I researched the use of uranium, I thought examples would be few and far between. I had also read in several books about glass that the use of uranium was discontinued after WW2. I soon discovered that both these concepts were false. As a consequence, I had to restrict the area of my researches to mainly English Glass. However, I have allowed my attention to wander to the products of some other countries to confirm the world-wide use of this element. As in *BBVG*, in the following chapters, I will show more examples of uranium glass from sources other than the UK. I have not collectively analyzed them in terms of density and uranium concentration because they are too few and varied for such treatment. I have quoted vales for individual items so the reader can form their own opinion of the characteristics of the products of these glasshouses.

Notwithstanding there are some general qualities which appear to come to the fore. There appears to be much less use of leaded metal on the Continent and all the Bohemian items I have found have low densities. Much the same applies to French glass. Generally the Continental glassworkers had a fundamental different approach to that of the UK glassblowers. When it came to taking the near finished vase etc off the blowpipe, instead of transferring it to a punty and finishing the top at a glory hole, they would cut it off and grind the rim flat. Thus, as I frequently point out in the captions, the rim of the vase and sometimes the drinking glass will be flat with a sharply defined edge. The English equivalent will be rounded where it has been reheated. The Continental glassblowers made more use of moulds to form the foot of their items. That is to say the whole vase, etc, would be blown in one mould, which also formed a hollow base as part of the body of the item. The English version would be to add on a solid base after the body had been formed. These techniques should not be regarded as "finger prints" but rather as being indicative.

With regard to Burmese, I have not found any genuine Mt Washington examples but quite a few by Fenton. The Fenton are easy to distinguish from the Webb's as they are marked "Fenton". However I have seen an example where the Fenton mark has been erased. The density of Fenton Burmese is much lower than that of Webb's Burmese. The quality of the item is also different with Fenton Burmese being thicker and less translucent.

Chapter 33

American Glass, Examples

Photo 203. A very good example of Fenton Burmese, in their Rose Pattern. It is marked on the underside with the Fenton trademark and "Hand painted by Dona R." Height 10.5 cm, density 2.53 g/cc, uranium 0.62% wt. *About 1980*, value $60 - $80.

Photo 204. I am only including this vase under the heading "American" because the e-Bay dealer who sold it described it as "Antique Mt Washington Victorian Glass Vase." I think this was a genuine misunderstanding of this type of glass, rather than an attempt to deceive. The formula for Mt Washington glass is described in Chapter 29 Table 1. The metal of this item is nothing like it. In the first place, the radioactivity is only on the inside, the demarcation between the pink and lemon is well defined and not as graded as would be expected from reheating at a glory hole. It has a darker ring on the edge round the top, which is quite uncharacteristic of true Burmese. Finally, it shows no sign of the wear that would be expected on an item of that age. Height 9.5 cm, density 2.53 g/cc, radioactivity 6 cps. I would date it *about* 1990 and, except to a collector of fakes, give it only a nominal value.

Photo 205. This shoe is marked with a Fenton stick-on label as well as being signed by the person who did the hand painting. "Blue Rose on Custard Satin" 1981. Length 13 cm, density 2.54 g/cc, uranium 0.1% wt. Value $20 - $40.

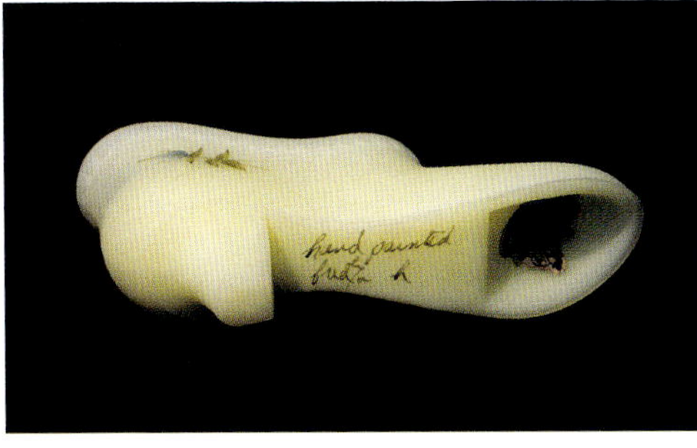

Photo 206. The Fenton label and the decorator's signature clearly visible on item Photo 205.

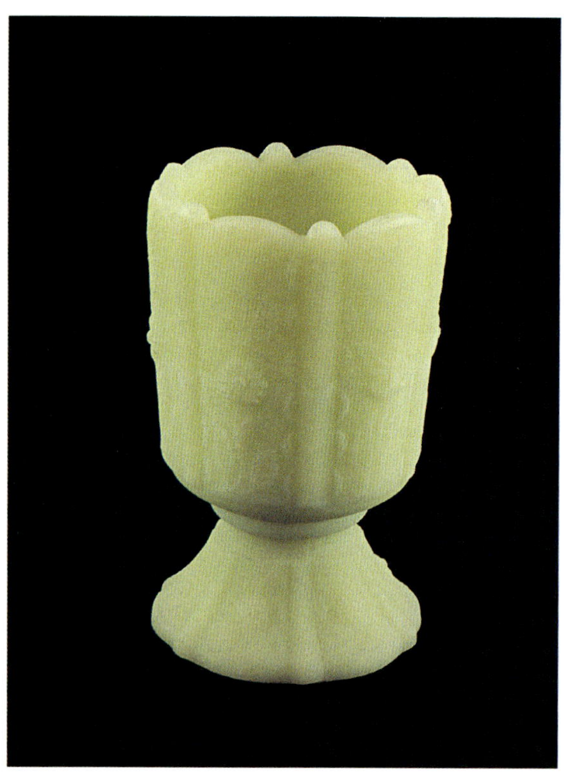

Photo 207. A salt, in lime green, with the Fenton trademark. Height 9.2 cm, density 2.55 g/cc, uranium 0.4% wt. Date *about* 1975. Value $20 - $30.

Photo 208. A boot, in lime green, from the Fenton factory. Marked on the underside with the usual Fenton trademark. Height 11 cm, density 2.55 g/cc, uranium 0.3% wt. The lime green color was not produced until 1973, this piece *about* 1975. Value $20 - $40.

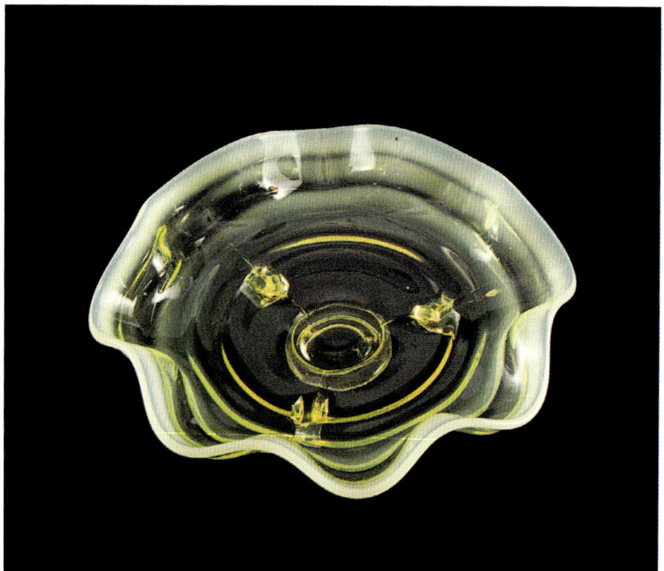

Photo 209. The plate has four horizontal rings and eight flutes on the rim. This item shows moderate wear and has one seed. Peterson[1] illustrates an identical dish as Fenton circa 1929. Diameter 18.5 cm, density 2.45 g/cc, uranium 0.28% wt. Value $40 - $60.

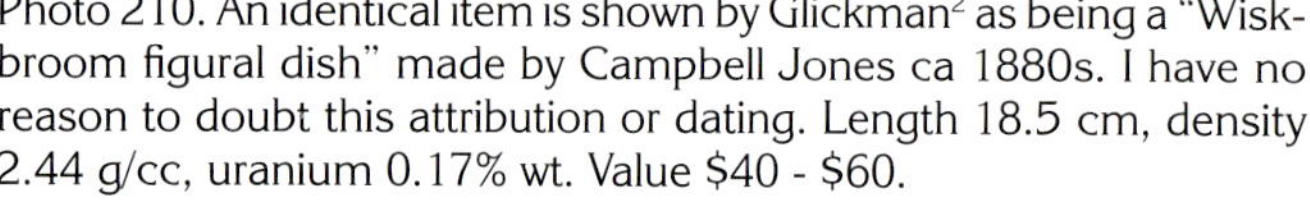

Photo 210. An identical item is shown by Glickman[2] as being a "Wisk-broom figural dish" made by Campbell Jones ca 1880s. I have no reason to doubt this attribution or dating. Length 18.5 cm, density 2.44 g/cc, uranium 0.17% wt. Value $40 - $60.

Photo 211. Presumably this Top Hat was designed to be a tooth pick holder. The daisy button pattern appears identical to Photo 209 but the uranium content is significantly different, probably indicating that it did not come from the same glasshouse. Glickman[2] also shows a Top Hat but there are small but significant differences. I am going to say *probably* American, *period* 1910. Height 7 cm, density 2.44 g/cc, uranium 0.23% wt. Value $30 - $40.

Photo 212. One of the more mundane pieces of uranium glass. This mixing bowl bears the mark "McK" and McKee used this mark 1935-40. Height 9 cm, density 2.5 g/cc, uranium 0.26% wt. Value $20 - $30.

Photo 214. A graphite rubbing of the mark on the horse shown in Photo 213.

Photo 213. Not exactly the sort of animal the cowpokes or Indians would ride but I think it can only have come from the USA. Glickman[3] attributes an identical piece to "New Martinsville - Viking" and dates it ca 1960. I have no reason to question either this attribution or dating. New Martinsville Glass Manufacturing Company was founded in 1901, it dropped the "manufacturing" from its title in 1938 and became the Viking Glass Company in 1944. Curiously this item has a "M" inside a circle molded into its base (see Photo 214, which is a graphite rubbing.) Pullin[4], shows three examples of an "M" inside a circle but they do not match this. Glickman quotes it as being "Mosser mold mark." Height 14.5 cm, density 2.44 g/cc, uranium 0.31% wt. Value, whatever you are willing to pay for it!

Chapter 34

Continental Glass, Examples

Belgium Glass

Photo 215. This wine has two rows of twelve slices, a hollow stem with two knops, and a hexagonal base. It matches the pattern of Val St Lambert, "Prince de Galles" design. Height 12 cm, density (approximate because of the hollow stem) 2.88 g/cc, uranium on the green bowl, 0.56% wt. Value $40 - $60.

Photo 216. I bought this wine at an English antique fair from a Belgium dealer. It has a distinctive engraved pattern on the bowl but I have not been able to identify its origin. I think the top of the bowl has been cut (Continental style) and then fired to round it off, but I could be wrong. Height 11 cm, density 3.18 g/cc, uranium 0.22% wt. My *best guess* for the origin and date is Belgium *about* 1910, value $20- $30.

Photo 217. This has the words "VERRERIES DE SCAILMONT MANGE" molded into the inside. The glasshouse was located in the Hainaut area of Belgium. It was operational from 1901 to 1972. They made a quantity of pressed glass, I am not aware of what happened to their molds. This item is free from any signs of wear which makes me think it was made in recent years, either just before the factory closed or by someone else who has acquired the mold. Width 12.6 cm, density 2.463 g/cc, uranium 0.081% wt. Value $20 - $30.

Czechoslovakian Glass

It may seem ironic that I have said so little about glass from this country which some consider to be the originator of uranium glass. I can only plead that the subject is so wide, that the use of uranium has been so extensive, that I have specialised in British glass and neglected detailed study of other producers. Notwithstanding, I would now mention the Ornela Company. According to information given on their Web Site it is situated at Densa v Jizerskych Horach, near the boarder with Poland. The origin of glass production in this area goes back to the sixteenth century, with the major growth occurring in the nineteenth century in an area around the present day town of Desna. The Ornela Company is the successor of the glasshouses that established their businesses during that period.

The site where the Ornela Company complex exists today, at Doini Polubny, is where Ignatz Friedrich built a glass factory in 1847 and not long after sold it to the legendary Josef Riedel (Snr.) The site developed to supply glass to other companies in the area. These included Heinrich Hoffmann, Curt Schlevogt, Gebruder Feix and Rudolf Rabik. Curt Schlevogt founded his company and began producing luxury pressed glass in the 1930s.

Amongst the products from the Ornela Company is the Desna Classic range. These are based upon old designs and in some cases use old moulds. Some of these items are produced in uranium glass.

Photo 219. Cover of the packaging for the turtle in Photo 218.

Photo 218. This piece comes from the Ornela Co. Ltd at Densa V Jizerskych Horach and is an example from Desna Classic range, The Turtle is from the original design by Curt Schlevogt. They make a range of items, reproducing designs from original molds. The company of Curt Schlevogt was founded in 1928 and began producing luxury pressed glass in the 1930s. Length 20.5 cm, density 2.45 g/cc, uranium 0.24% wt. Date current.

Dutch Glass

Leerdam, near Rotterdam, has long been the site for glass manufacture. Those who can read Dutch will find a mine of information about this site in "Leerdam Glass 1878 -1930" by A Van der Kley-Blekxtoon, ISBN 90-352-1355-6, 1990. Its more recent history may be traced back to 1878 when an existing bottle factory expanded to make table glass. Both blown and pressed items were produced and marketed not only in the Netherlands but also in Britain and as far away as South America. The firm is still in existence but now (since 1938) is part of the Dutch "United Glassworks" which also acquired Maastricht Glass in 1959.

Photo 220. A water set from N V Kristalunie Maastricht, illustrated in their 1932-3 catalogue. The jug would have cost 1.75 Fl, and the glasses 0.25 Fl. Height of jug 17 cm, glass 9 cm. Density 2.52 g/cc, uranium 0.25% wt. Value for jug with set of six glasses $40 - $60.

Photo 221. Water jug and tumbler *probably* from Holland. In 1992 the Leerdam Museum had a similar tumbler on display credited to C. Lebeau 1924/5. Jug height 13.5 cm, tumbler height 8.4 cm. density 2.45 g/cc, uranium 0.27% wt. Value for a set of jug and six tumblers $40 - $60.

Photo 222. Made in three pieces, the bowl has a ground top, and the foot shows no sign of a pontil or gadget mark. It would have been made in classical Continental style of holding the item on the blow tube until all work is complete, then cracking it off and grinding flat the resulting edge. The 14 elongated flats have been hand ground. When I first saw it, I dated it about 1910 and later found it illustrated in a Leerdam Catalogue of 1902 as William Tell. Height 10 cm, density 2.43 g/cc, uranium 0.3% wt. Value $10 - $20.

Photo 223. Made in two pieces, the stem having been drawn from the bowl. There is no pontil mark on the foot but evidence of a gadget. The foot is molded. It could be English but the etched pattern on the bowl, especially the upper multi-wave band, has resembles to some shown in the Leerdam 1902 catalogue so I will say *best guess* Dutch. Date *about* 1910. Height 10.5 cm, density 2.47 g/cc, uranium 0.15% wt. Value $20 - $30.

French Glass

One of the most prominent of French Glass producers is "Baccarat". The glasshouse was founded in 1765 by the Bishop of Metz in an attempt to bring work to the little village. All kinds of domestic glass was made including windows. In 1815 Aime-Gabriel D'Artigues bought the glassworks and operated it in conjunction with his other glassworks at Voneche, which was by then part of Belgium, as Voneche-Baccarat and concentrated on producing items in lead crystal. He sold out in 1822 and the new owners established it as Compagnie des Cristalleries de Baccarat. It quickly established itself as a quality glasshouse and today is one of the leading glass producers in France. It is particularly renowned for its paperweights but, regrettably, I have not had opportunity to study any, with or without uranium. It is interesting to note that the two items shown below have densities indicating high lead content, although the green opaline bowl, *BBVG* Photo 262, has a much lower density.

Photo 224. When I first picked up this "stick" and ran my fingers under the base searching for a registration mark, I thought I might be able to confirm it as a piece from Ed Moore. Then I found the "Baccarat Depose" mark. Height 17 cm, density 3.17 g/cc, uranium 0.12% wt. Value $40 - $60.

Photo 225. Like the candlestick in Photo 224, this jar, which has probably lost its lid, bears the legend "Depose Baccarat". The uranium content and densities are so close as to proclaim them brothers. It has 16 swirling gadroons. I have little evidence to go on with regard to dating but on the basis of wear and style I would say *period* 1930. Diameter 7.3 cm, density 3.17 g/cc, uranium 0.14% wt. Value $20 - $30.

Photo 226. Another example of a Pernod Ashtray (CF Photo 261r *BBVG*) but this one is much larger. Although the densities match, the uranium in this piece is a little lower but probably within the margin of variation that could be expected. Width 18 cm, density 2.49 g/cc, uranium 0.37% wt. Value $20 - $30 Made by Verrerie Louard, *about* 1970.

German Glass

I know very little about German glass. August Walther & Sohne appears to be quite collectable and has been commanding relatively high prices for their Deco pieces on Internet sales. I am told that a number of Walther designs were registered in the UK under the Patent and Design Act of 1907. I also understand there is a lot of similarity between some products from this firm and those of well known English firms like Davidson, Sowerby and Jobling. Examples of Walther's items can be seen on the web site www.pressglas-korrespondenz.de So far, I have not come across any such examples.

Photo 228. According to information I obtained over the internet this is an example of Walther Fische range. It is a quality molding and small bubbles are skilfully molded coming from the weed shown on the side of the jar. Height 11.3 cm, density 2.44 g/cc, uranium 0.13% wt. Date *about* 1935. As for value, a similar item sold on eBay for $110.

Photo 227. This green powder jar has a delicate mermaid molded into the top of the lid. I am assured that it is illustrated in an August Walther catalogue of 1934-5. Height 10 cm, width 9.5 cm, density 2.45 g/cc, uranium 0.16% wt. (CF *BBVG* p189 Photo 376, items centre and right) As for value, I have seen one sold on eBay for $436.

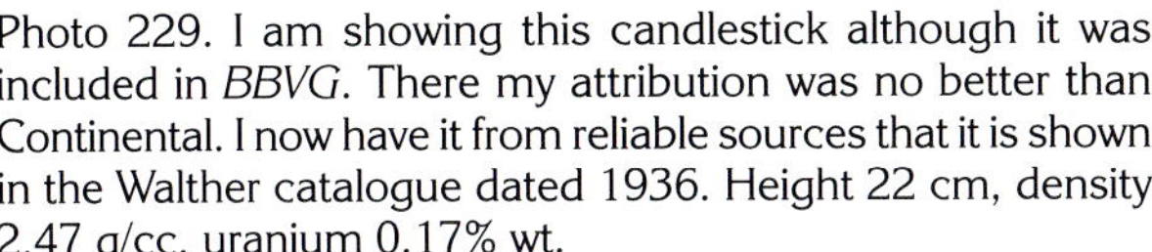

Photo 229. I am showing this candlestick although it was included in *BBVG*. There my attribution was no better than Continental. I now have it from reliable sources that it is shown in the Walther catalogue dated 1936. Height 22 cm, density 2.47 g/cc, uranium 0.17% wt.

Photo 230. An unusual type of vase in two parts. The base is just a deep plate. The centre piece has a watertight trumpet, the base of which has a small circular frog. Presumable the plate and trumpet held water but the flowers in the small frog must have to be very short! I am told it is illustrated in a 1937 catalogue, but I have not seen this so I will only give it a *could be* Ankerglas. Base 19.5 cm. Diameter, trumpet 15 cm high. Density 2.47 g/cc, uranium 0.04% wt. Value $30 - $40.

Photo 232. A larger version of Photo 231. On the basis of the fruit pattern I will attribute it to the same firm. Diameter 200.5 cm, density 2.44 g/cc, uranium 0.14% wt. Value $30 - $50.

Photo 231. Two small bowls from the depression period. The lefthand side has an outside starburst intaglio molded pattern on the base, the other a display of fruit. I have not been able to confirm these exact shapes in the information I have. Similar shapes for the bowls are not uncommon, but the clue to the origin of these comes from the design of the base. Bagley used both starburst and intaglio molded fruit display in this manner, but the fruit display shown in their catalogue does not quite match this one. However, an exact match for these bases appears in a 1932 Ankerglas Berdorf catalogue so I will attribute them to that firm. Diameter 10.2 cm, densities 2.51 g/cc and 2.49 g/cc, uranium 0.14% wt. Value $10- $20 each.

Venetian Glass

Photo 233. The adhesive label says "Murano Genuine Venetian Glass Italy." Unfortunately, it does not tell us when and by whom it was made. The item has been made from at least three layers. The uranium is sandwiched between two and hence it is not possible to estimate its concentration, but the Geiger counter and uv light shows it to be present. Although the green, which is the uranium layer, shows at the base it does run as a very thin layer right through the vase. This is clearly illustrated in Photo 234, which was taken looking into the top of the vase with uv light. Height 25 cm, density 2.5 g/cc, uranium 2.5 cps max. Date sometime after 1930. Value $40 - $60.

I recently had the opportunity to inspect another piece of Venetian glass, which the dealer confidently dated about 1970. It too was colored with uranium, although I was not able to estimate its concentration.

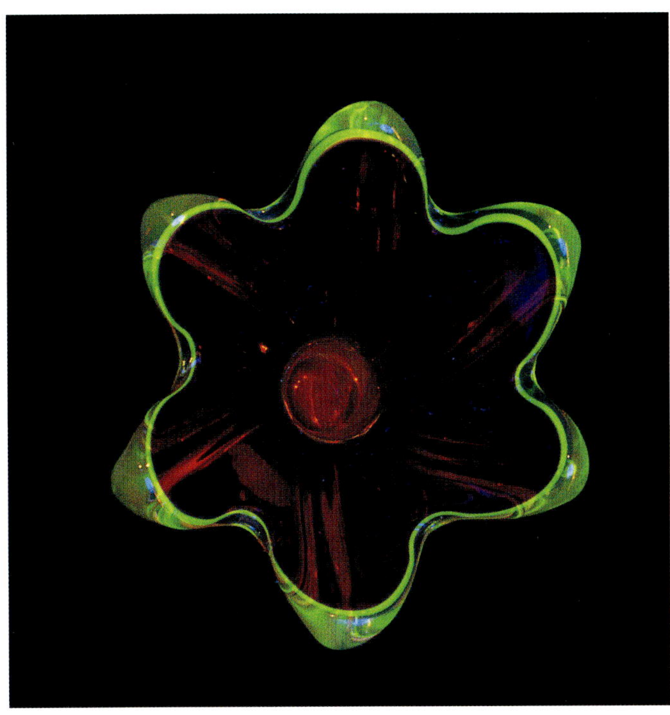

Photo 234. Item shown in Photo 233 taken from the top but in uv light. The uranium layer shows as a brilliant green.

Photo 235. Unlike Photo 233, this piece is not labeled, but its characteristics are so similar. It has three layers of metal, ruby, uranium green, and clear. Length 12 cm, density 2.5 g/cc, uranium 1 cps. Probably Murano about 1970. Value $20 - $40.

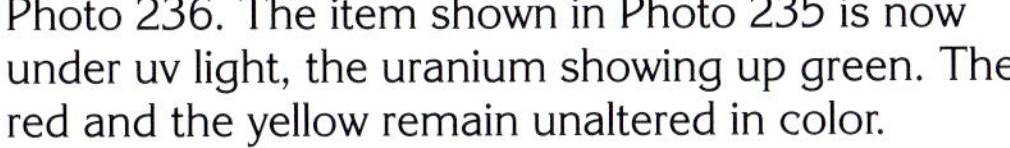

Photo 236. The item shown in Photo 235 is now under uv light, the uranium showing up green. The red and the yellow remain unaltered in color.

Section 3: Non-attributed Items

This is probably the saddest section of my book, for it represents all those interesting items that have successfully resisted my attempts to give them attributions. Chapter 35 shows items, which have marks for which I have not been able to discover their origin. The chapters that follow may be of benefit to those who collect according to the nature of the object rather than who made it. Never the less this Section is still with items that have uranium in their make up and illustrates just how wide spread the use of this element has been in the glass industry. Although I may not be able to make a confident attribution, or even a best guess I have been able to date most of these pieces.

There are several ways in which this miscellany of items might have logically be arranged. For the want of something better I have adopted the same layout as in *BBVG*. The first chapter of this section dealing with marked items then the remainder according to the nature of the item.

Chapter 35

Glass with Marks or Inscriptions.

Photo 237. This Art Deco style candlestick bears the Design Registration 796007. It was registered by Heppner Ltd on 28th August, 1934. Kelly's Trade Directory of 1944 quotes them as China and Glass Merchants, Audrey House, Ely Place, London EC1. I doubt if they made this piece, more likely it was contracted out. Unfortunately I cannot ask them, the firm went into receivership in May 2000. The uranium is low but the item fluoresces strongly under uv light. Height 17.5 cm, density 2.45 g/cc, uranium 0.03% wt. Value $20 - $30.

Photo 238. One of three salts all of which have identical marks on the base. I am not sure whether I found them in France of Belgium. The marks the figure 44 facing the reverse way but without the vertical stroke joining the diagonal. (see Photo 239). I am not at all sure whether this is a trademark or simply a maker's number. The metal is of low quality and the molding rough. In terms of color and quality it resembles the products of Jules Lang, see *BBVG* Photo 265. We know Lang was closely involved with Continental glass. They could be connected to that firm, but such a link is too tenuous for an attribution. Height 6.5 cm, average density 2.42 g/cc, uranium 0.4% wt. Date *period* 1900. Value $20 - $30.

Photo 239. A close-up of the marks on the base of the salt shown in Photo 238.

Photo 240. This humble bottle bears the words molded into the glass, "F.WOLFF and SOHN" on one side and "KARLSRUHE" on the other. It is likely that at one time it contained perfume but who molded it is not known. It would seem that some of the quality bottles used by this firm may have been produced by Baccarat but there is no evidence to suggest they made this bottle. Height 15.5 cm, density 2.45 g/cc, uranium 0.05%. The nature of the bottle suggests a date of about 1900-10. Value nominal except to a collector of uranium glass looking for an unexpected use of the material.

Photo 241. Another example where we might reasonably ask the question "why use expensive uranium glass and then cover it up?" These vases have been made with an opaque off white overlaid with a clear brown. The uranium barely adds any color except under uv light. The shading of the body is entirely due to the thinning of the brown layer. I have not been able to identify the marks on the base, see Photo 242. Height 15 cm, density 2.47 and 2.48 g/cc, uranium on both insides approximately 0.22% wt. Date *period* 1900, value each $24 - $40

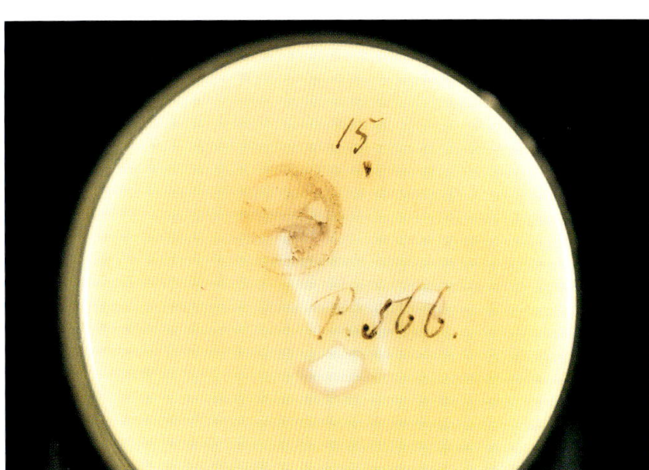

Photo 242. Marks on the base of the vase shown in Photo 241. Note the faint trefoil-like mark by the figure 15.

Photo 243. I would be tempted to attribute this delicate iridescent vase to the Continent but for the hallmark on the silver band. It was assayed in London in 1903. The outside is rough but the inside smooth and there is no pontil mark. Height 18 cm, density 2.5 g/cc, uranium 0.26% wt. Value $100 - $140.

Photo 244. The wear on this toilet water bottle gives witness to the hard life it has suffered. On the underside it bears the words "Registration Applied For" which implies its English origin. It has a Bakelite screw cap. Bakelite, the first plastic, was invented in the early part of the 20th century by Dr Bsekeland of Belgian origin. However its commercial exploitation is more associated with the 1920-50 period, after which it was superseded by other plastics. A factory at Tyseley Birmingham produced a lot of the British Bakelite from 1930 and it is possible that the cap of this bottle was made there. On the inside it bears 1012/17 HK, where the letters are joined by a common down stroke. Height 14.3 cm, uranium 0.12% wt. Value nominal.

Photo 245. The metal frame for this translucent jade green bowl is electroplated. It bears the inscription EPNS TW and Co. 15947. It could be Thomas White and Co. of Sheffield, or even T Wilkinson of Birmingham, or neither. The diameter of the bowl is 10 cm, density 2.523 g/cc, uranium 0.59%. It has a polished pontil dimple and a cut and ground top. The metal work is British, the glass may or may not be, but my hunch is that it is English. Date *about* 1920. Value $30 - $50.

Photo 246. When I bought this piece I thought I had a good chance to track down its origin. The silver band on the top was hall marked by the Birmingham Assay office in 1903. The silversmith's mark, which appears to be CM@Co, I cannot attribute. But with a Birmingham mark does this not mean the English Midlands? The density says probably not. The other curious thing is that it is cased, uranium on the inside and clear on the outside. The six pillars are of two different, alternating widths. Height 17.5 cm, density 2.44 g/cc, uranium on the inside, 3 cps. Date 1903. Value $40 $60.

Photo 247. The rather worn inscription reads *"I'll meet you 'at the Bristol.'"* Just why 'at the Bristol' is in inverted commas is not clear. It suggests it is a quotation or saying of the time, but either way its origin is to me unknown. When I found this piece I had expected it to have the Nazing mark on the underside, as advertising ashtrays were a speciality of theirs in the post WW2 period. However it is not so marked and remains un-attributed. Width 9.6 cm, density 2.44 g/cc, uranium 0.19% wt. Date 1930 -1960, value nominal.

Chapter 36

Radioactive Animals

Photo 248. Fido here appears to have lost his tail, but that is no reason not to love him! Can you guess where the uranium is? It is in the clear glass, which surprisingly does not produce a color. The quantity is much higher than some other pieces that show strong green or yellow. Only the Geiger counter and uv light indicate that this is another of those radioactive animals. Height 12 cm, density 2.51 g/cc, uranium 0.16% wt. *Period* 1960, value, without its tail, lets say $4.

Photo 249. I know little about dog breeds so I will not attempt to name this one. However it is radioactive. The uranium is only in the yellow. Height 8 cm, density 2.46, uranium approximately 0.6% wt. Date *about* 1955. Value $6-$10.

Photo 250. The shape of this little doggy makes it difficult to get a reliable uranium reading, I have quoted a figure just to give some idea of the probable uranium concentration. Height 8.2 cm, density 2.48 g/cc, uranium about 0.4% wt. Date *about* 1955, value $4- $10.

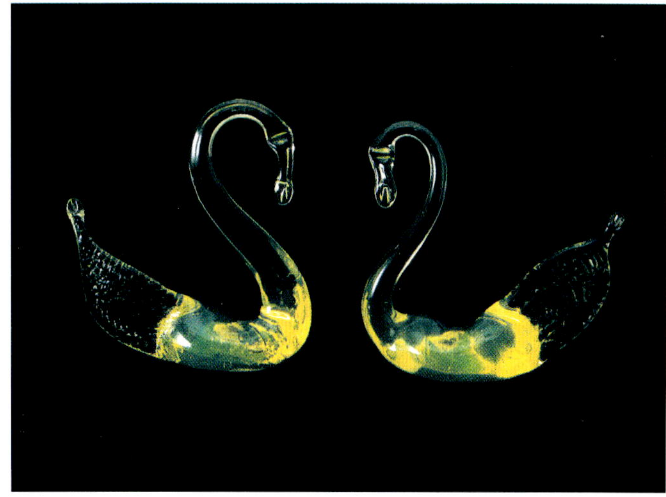

Photo 251. I cannot believe that these pair of swans were ever a production item from a commercial glasshouse. They are crudely made, one is significantly larger than the other, and except to a collector of uranium glass they are hardly things of beauty. Furthermore, more their density indicates a high lead content, so why use an expensive metal on such a poor item? The answer that comes to mind is that they are frigger's pieces. Maybe some young apprentice made them to take home to show Mum. I would have expected a better job from a skilled and experienced worker. Let's say *could be* English Midlands, *period* 1920. Height right hand side 12.5 cm, left hand side 11.25 cm; density right hand side 3.23g/cc, left hand side 3.22 g/cc; uranium (both) 0.17% wt. Value? Well, I paid $40 for the pair, so what do you think?

Photo 252. Not exactly a great work of art, but this swan qualifies to be in my collection by virtue of its radioactivity. The wear on it suggest the 1930s. I have no idea where it was born and the density, which is a little low for the English Midlands, does not help. Height 8.8 cm, density 2.95 g/cc, uranium 0.3% wt. Value $20 - $30.

Photo 253. I suppose we have to feel sorry for a little bird that has radioactive wings. However I don't think we can blame that on Chernobyl. It stands only 4 cm high in its bare feet and is too small to make sensible density measurements with the equipment I have to hand. I guess it was born in the 1960s and may be an immigrant. It clicks the Geiger counter at 2 cps, and its only value is likely to be to another bird seeking a partner with uranium in its wings.

Photo 254. I wonder if this was the inspiration for the song about the ugly duckling! It is composed of at least three gathers of glass; green, lemon and clear. As far as I can ascertain the uranium is only in the lemon, and as is covered by clear glass, it is not possible to estimate the uranium content. Best guess is Venetian Height 13.8 cm, density 2.39 g/cc, Geiger response 1 cps. Date *probably* post WW2 Value $10 - $20.

Chapter 37

Curiosities

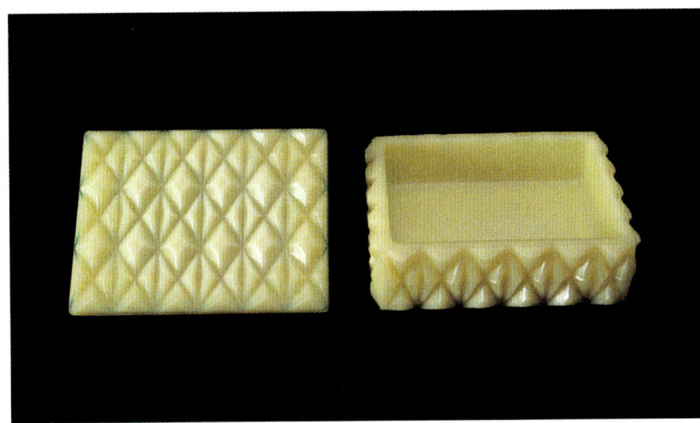

Photo 255. I am not sure for what purpose this opaline glass box was conceived. A trinket box? I think more likely it was for cigarettes at a time when it was fashionable to have them on the dining table for an after eating smoke. I also have difficulty in dating it. There is no sign of any wear and if it was not that the use of uranium is now very uncommon, I would have put it as being yesterday or last year. As it is, I think it is probably of similar vintage to the Nazing and Verrerie Louard ashtrays, say *period* 1970. The density of this metal is quite unusual but it tells me it was not made by either of the two aforementioned factories. Dimensions, 12 cm x 9.5 cm x 4.5 cm. Density of both lid and box 2.69 g/cc. Uranium of both 0.47% wt. Value, to a uranium glass collector, $20 - $40.

Photo 256. I suppose this glass ring could be used to support an egg, but I rather think it was intended for a napkin. The edges are cut and polished and the middle has traces of striation marks. My theory is that it was formed from a tube then cut into sections. Who made it? I wish I knew but it may well have been a factory specialising in industrial glassware. There is a slight taper of about 1 mm but I suspect this is by accident rather than design. Diameter 5 cm, density 2.64 g/cc, uranium 0.34% wt. Date *period* 1940, value nominal except to a collector of radioactive napkin rings.

Photo 257. Apart from being a glass rod with twist, what is this piece? The lady who sold it thought it was a bobbin, she might well be correct but who would want something as fragile as this for a bobbin and a radioactive one at that! It's small size (9.9 g) increases the error in the density determination, and the uranium concentration has a large "guestimate" content as it is small compared with the size of the Geiger tube. Length 11.5 cm, density 2.4 g/cc, uranium 4.5 cps (about 0.9% wt). Best guess at date *period* 1900. Value $20-$30, unless two collectors of radioactive glass bobbins both want it.

Photo 258. Apart from the novelty, why would anyone want to make marbles out of uranium glass? I bought them out of curiosity and believe they came from the USA or Canada. The low density suggests they may be a boro-silicate glass. In which case it may be they were never intended for the children's game but some process, which involved heating them. Diameter 0.4 cm, density 2.28 g/cc, uranium about 0.15 wt. Date current. Value nominal.

Photo 259. I count this as a "curiosity" because I don't believe it was seriously intended as an eye bath. With my usual caveat of "I may be wrong", I think this has been made, in modern times, to attract the collector. It is from a two piece mold and unsigned. It shows no sign of wear and the metal is without any blemish. Height 7 cm, density 2.51 g/cc, uranium 0.29% wt. Value, well it cost me $40 in Australian dollars, which is far too much but my curiosity got the better of my judgement.

Photo 260. Almost identical to the paperweight shown in Photo 296 *BBVG*, this one has a star cut into its base. The uranium is only flashed and cut away in the flats as is well illustrated under uv light. Density 3.03g/cc. Uranium 3cps.

Photo 261. This is the item in Photo 260 under uv light.

Photo 262. Was this a serious piece or just a novelty? Is it old or is it new? Does it really contain uranium? I don't know the answers to any of these questions. I find it difficult to believe that it was ever intended to be used to push needles through thick cloth, for despite the dimples on the end, I feel sure a needle would slip. It shows no wear but it does have signs of crizzling. As for uranium, it just makes the Geiger counter flicker and has a feint response to uv light. Height 3 cm, density 2.46 g/cc. Value whatever you are daft enough to pay for a glass thimble!

Photos 263 and 264 are the same item, the former being that of the jelly mold the right way up, the latter a view of it up side down. If you think there is nothing curious about this common jelly mold, take a closer look. All the pattern is on the outside. The object of a jelly mold is to produce a jelly with an interesting pattern, this would just give birth to a dull and uninteresting shape, so why bother with it instead of using a bowl? Why go to the expense of making an elaborate decorative mold for a mundane item that is going to spend its life in a kitchen cupboard? Consider the expensive uranium, and 40% lead, the question becomes more pertinent. It has been made in a one-piece mold, its tapered shape means it would simply have been tipped out after the plunger had done its job. The top has been ground flat. Adding all this together and taking account of the considerable wear, I am of the opinion this is a very early piece of press molding, probably from the English Midlands, as they tried out the "new" technology of its day. It was only later, after about 1865, that low lead glass was pressed. Length 15.5 cm, height 8 cm increasing to 8.5 cm. Density 3.49 g/cc, uranium 0.37% wt. Date *about* 1855, value $40 - $60.

Photo 265. I suppose we could call this a radioactive mine! It would appear to be a novelty menu or other cardholder. This is styled after the most common sea mine used in the First World War. The item shows considerable wear, has a small seed in the metal, and is starting to crizzle. On that basis I would date it *about* 1915. I can only speculate about its origin, it is not the type of menu holder normally seen and I wonder if it were made for some special Naval occasion, or Officers Mess or something of that sort. If it is British-made, then the top suspects, based on density measurement, would be Greener or Sowerby. Height 4.8 cm, density 2.58 g/cc, uranium 0.5% wt. Value $20 - $30.

Photo 267. At first I thought this to be an egg cup, but it is too delicate for that. It is too small for a sweet dish. Perhaps a salt or for holding a piquant sauce. At first sight it looks like it came from Stevens and Williams but density and uranium content say not. It looks as if the top has been cut and polished so let's plumb for Continental. Height 6.9 cm, density 2.65 g/cc, uranium 0.43% wt. Date *period* 1940. Value $10 - $30.

Photo 266. I suspect this barrel has lost its stand and stopper which is probably witness to an unhappy past. It would have held an alcoholic spirit. Judging by its volume and size of tap, it must have been for a liquid to be dispensed in small quantities. The surface has been subject to heavy grit blasting to give it a rough pitted appearance. Length 14 cm, density not measured because of the chrome plated brass fittings, uranium 0.08% wt. Date *about* 1930. Value, if complete, $40 - $60.

Photo 268. Is it a vase, a beaker, or a sundae? That is not the only thing curious about this item. It certainly looks Victorian. I have examined three such items and they are, as near as makes no matter, the same. The stems show twist, the effect expected from fire polishing. Height 16.5 cm, density 2.7 g/cc, uranium 2.8% wt. The problems with attributing and dating come to the fore on closer examination. The metal on all three is good and clear, not a seed to be seen. The base does have a sort of "poor quality metal" effect but I think this is more on the surface than in the metal itself. Non of the three show the sort of wear I would expect from a hundred years of use. A small, clean chip on the foot is not an indicator of age or wear. Finally there is no sign, on any of them, of ingrained dirt. I can accept that perhaps one had survived in Granny's cupboard in near pristine condition but surely not all three? My best guess is that these may well have been made from old molds but are post-WW2. Perhaps a reader will prove me wrong?

Photo 269. I am curious to know for what purpose these little pots were intended. At first I thought they were salts, but they are too small to allow reasonable access to the conventional salt spoon. Looking at them side by side is like one of those "spot the difference" games. The applied artwork looks the same but there are a few minor differences, the gold band on the lefthand side one is thinner, the base of the lefthand side piece is made from colorless glass while that on the right hand side is green. Notwithstanding, the uranium is only flashed on the inside of both pieces. The uranium count rates and the densities are also different. I can only conclude they were made by different glass-houses. I mention this in some detail as it is a good illustration of not jumping to a conclusion, just because two items appear the same. Left hand side h 3.5 cm, density 2.44 g/cc, uranium 4.5 cps. Right hand side height 3.3 cm, density 2.53 g/cc, uranium 15 cps. As for date and value, I haven't much of a clue!

Chapter 38
Coralene

Coralene is a special type of decoration, good examples of which are hard to find. It is formed from tiny glass beads, which may be colored or clear. In the latter case they are fixed over a colored background. In the better, and more expensive, examples these glass beads are heated at the furnace to fix them.

Photo 271. I have used side lighting to show up the tiny beads, which make up the decoration on the vase shown in Photo 270.

Photo 270. A very fine example of coralene decoration. The tiny glass beads have their own color, which catches the light. This is a quality item, which clearly comes from the Continent. The body would have been made in a blow mold, working all the time from the blow pipe. It has then been cracked off and the top cut and ground. Considerable skill must have been deployed to get the different colored coralene beads in the right place. The fact that they have survived so long strongly suggests that they were fired in position rather than just stuck. Although similar, this is not the same vase as shown in *BBVG* Photo 302. However the characteristics are so close they probably all came from the same glasshouse. Height 23 cm, density 2.48 g/cc, uranium 0.25% wt. Date *about* 1900. Value $120 - $160.

Chapter 39

Drinking Glasses

Photo 272. Product of a blow mold, has a cut and ground top, typical of a cheap continental product. The semi-opaque effect is from un-dissolved opacifier particles in the melt. Height 12 cm, density 2.4 g/cc, uranium 0.51% wt. *Almost certainly* Continental, *best guess* is Dutch, date *about* 1930. Value $10 - $20.

Photo 273. I am not sure whether this is a tumbler, vase or even a celery! I will treat it as the former. It has been made in a four piece mold and probably fire polished. It is not marked but has a moderate amount of wear. I can find nothing like it in my research material. However my hunch is that it came from the USA. Height 13 cm, density 2.56 g/cc, uranium 0.4% wt. Date *period* 1915. Value $30 - $40.

Photo 274. The goblet has been made in a four piece mold and probably acid polished. It has a rich uranium green color. I find it difficult to date, it shows only slight wear so I am going to put it about 1930. Height 12.7 cm, density 2.41 g/cc, uranium 0.28% wt. I would like to think it came from Tyneside but I cannot match density or uranium content with other known pieces from that area. Value $10 - $20.

Photo 275. The unusual pattern on this press molded tumbler defies my attempts to identify the maker. It is the style I would have expected to have come from the North of England. The wear and quality of the metal puts it in the third quarter of the nineteenth century, *period* 1870. The density and uranium, which matches very well with the lozenge marked basket in Photo 57 (*BBVG*), prompts me to *best guess* at Sowerby. Height 14.2 cm, density 2.55 g/cc, uranium 0.26% wt. Value $30 - $40.

Photo 276. This wine has been made in three sections, bowl, stem and foot. It has 16 shallow internal vertical ribs. The shape is a little unusual and resembles a design by A D Copier for Leerdam Glass in 1927. As far as I can tell from the illustration I have seen the match is not exact enough to suggest an attribution. This item shows a moderate amount of wear, which influences my opinion on the dating. Height 10.8 cm, density 2.76 g/cc, uranium 0.81% wt. Date *about* 1925. Value $14 - $24.

Photo 277. This attractive sherry has been made in three operations. The bowl with its vertical ribbing, the twisted stem and the molded foot. Height 12 cm, density 2.59 g/cc, uranium 0.16% wt. Deco period, value $10- $16.

Photo 278. This glass was bought in Belgium. It has a solid stem and the bowl has been cut and rounded in Continental style. Height 11 cm, density 2.45 g/cc, uranium 0.23% wt. Date *about* 1900. Value $20 - $30.

Photo 279. How I wish I could attribute this beauty. Delicately made from a 14 narrow rib mold, it has a blown foot and a ground out pontil mark. The top is rounded, not cut and polished. I would like to think it is British. Edinburgh Crystal pattern book R7 shows a similar wine with a slightly different shape to the lower part of the bowl with the caption "made from Richardson's 16 rib mold No 359" It is also dated 16/12/30. This again illustrates the link between the three companies of Richardson, Webb and Edinburgh Crystal. It also raises the question, did Richardson's have a 14 rib mold as well and, if so, did they make this piece before they were taken over by Webb? The low density suggests that this is not the case. Height 12.6 cm, density 2.47 g/cc, uranium 0.62% wt. Date *about* 1870, value $40 -$60.

Photo 280. The foot and stem appear to have been molded as there are remains of fins where the mold would have opened. I believe the bowl, which has 11 hand-ground and polished facets, was made separately. The top has been cut and fired over. Height 10.75 cm, density 2.51 g/cc, uranium 0.12% wt. Date *about* 1920. Value $10 - $20.

Photo 281. I bought two of these glasses in Belgium. They are identical except that one is slightly darker than the other and has a little more uranium. It would appear that although bought as a pair, they were not from the same mix. There are 6 flats on the hollow stem and 10 small scallops on the bowl. They have been hand cut and polished. The top of the bowl has also been cut and ground. Height 12.75 cm, density 2.46 g/cc and 2.52 g/cc, uranium 0.31% and 0.43% wt. Date *about* 1880. Value $30 - $40.

Photo 282. This glass has been made with a drawn stem and blown foot. It has a ground off pontil dimple. The amount of wear is consistent with an early birth date. It has been hand cut and polished. I have little doubt about the date of its origin. The pattern very closely resembles examples in the 1846 Percival, Vickers catalogue, but I cannot attribute it to that firm because of the density. Height 13.3 cm, density 2.43 g/cc, uranium 0.25% wt. Date *about* 1865, value $20 - $30.

Photo 283. Many glasshouses used variations of the "Greek Key" pattern but this is quite unusual and I bought it in the hope of being able attribute it on that basis. Unfortunately despite trawling through all my references I have been unsuccessful. It has been made in three pieces with an applied stem and blown foot. The pontil dimple is perfect. A delicate wine from *about* 1870. My gut feeling is it could well be Dutch but that is not an attribution. Height 12.7 cm, density 2.67 g/cc, uranium 0.28% wt. Value $20 - $30.

Photo 284. A closer view of the pattern on the bowl of the wine in Photo 283.

Photo 286. The flats on the bowl of this glass make it look very much as if it had come from Percival, Vickers or one of the Midland's glasshouses. The density suggests otherwise. The wine has been made from two gathers, the bowl and stem from one and then a blown foot applied. It is a quality piece with a good dimple where the pontil has been ground out. I was doubtful whether the foot had been blown until I checked it with callipers. The slight eccentricity confirms this assessment. Height 12.5 cm, density 2.46 g/cc, uranium 0.6% wt. Date about 1870, *best guess* is that it was made in England. Value $24 - $30.

Photo 285. Another green uranium glass added to the collection, how I wish I could resist them. This one has seven flats on the bowl, a ground out pontil and a blown foot. With a lead content of about 33% I would say English Midlands, but some of the continental factories also used such metal so I wonder. Hunch prevents me from attributing it to my Country. Height 12.5 cm, density 3.21 g/cc, uranium 0.18% wt. Date *period* 1870. Value $24 - $30.

Photo 287. I have examined four of these glasses. They are made in two pieces, the foot is molded and there is a ground off pontil. My first reaction was to date them about 1880 but second thoughts raise doubts. The lip of the cup shows no sign of a bud where it would have been cut. Furthermore, the four glasses examined are all near identical height, so were they cut on a turntable? Could they be 1930s repro? Height 12.5 cm, density 2.63 (average of two), uranium 0.3% wt. Value of each \$30 - \$40.

Photo 288. A delicate wine with a starburst cut pattern on the foot. It has been made in three pieces and has a molded foot. The top looks as if has been cut and finished on a turntable. There are only slight signs of wear. I will, with some hesitation, date it *about* 1935. Height 10.6 cm, density 3.0 g/cc, uranium 0.25% wt. Value \$20 - \$30.

Photo 289. The interesting point about these glasses is the hint of blue in the green. Under uv (near) they respond as expected for uranium glass, but to uv (far) they glow with a pale blue color. Height 9.5 cm, density 2.82 g/cc, u 0.14% wt. From the deco period, perhaps late 1930s or post WW2. Value \$6-\$12 each.

Photo 290. Readers of *BBVG* will find some similarities between this wine and one shown in Photo 129 in that book. The stems look much the same but it would be quite wrong to assume this came from their glasshouse. The base to stem joint is different and the top of the bowl has been cut and polished. More to the point the densities and uranium contents are different, those in *BBVG* were 3.07 g/cc and 0.16% wt. For this glass the height is 195 cm, density 2.44 g/cc, uranium 0.1% wt. It could be Continental. Date *about* 1935. Value \$10 - \$20.

Photo 291. A reproduction Georgian style with its broken-off pontil still leaving a ragged edge. It is likely that it came from the English Midlands, but I cannot say who made it. Its shape is seen in some of the Walsh patterns, but then this shape is hardly unique. Height 13.2 cm, density 3.17 g/cc, uranium 0.56% wt. Date *about* 1930. Value $30 - $40.

Photo 292. Uranium yellow wines are not easy to come by, this is a more recent example. The lip of the bowl has been cut and ground in Continental style. Height 13.5 cm, density 2.47 g/cc, uranium 0.62% wt. The foot says this does not have history so I am going to date it *about* 1950 but it could be later or just prior to WW2. Value $20 - $30.

Photo 293. The cut and ground lip says its Continental and the style that it is Deco. Height 13.25 cm, density 2.46 g/cc, uranium 0.22% wt. Value $20 - $30.

Photo 295. A simple but attractive conical wine from the deco period. It has 10 shallow flutes, which were probably induced during the forming of the bowl, rather than in a dip mold. The top has been cut, ground and possibly heat treated to round down the cutting. The foot is molded. I doubt if it was made in the UK and suspect it is Continental, with a hunch that it is Dutch. Height 8.2 cm, density 2.46 g/cc, uranium 0.19% wt. Date *about* 1935, value $10 - $20.

Photo 294. A quality glass made in three pieces. The top was probably cut then fired, rather than polished. The foot has been molded. On my scale, the wear is slight to moderate. The style is very close to that of a champagne by K P C de Bazel from Leerdam. Height 11.5 cm, density 2.65 g/cc, uranium 0.47% wt. Date *about* 1920. Value $16 - $24.

Photo 296. Arguably one of the most puzzling items in this collection. Take a close look at the handles on the cups. They are delicate and not joined to the body of the cup at the top. Too small to be tea cups, I would not risk holding them while filled with hot coffee. Anyhow, the density says they are not made from boro-silicate glass and would not like the thermal shock of a hot drink. A child's play set perhaps? I doubt it, far too delicate for that. A beautiful range of color, were they made for some exhibition I wonder? As might be expected, only the green and amber contain uranium. The odd one out however is the pink, which has a much lower density than the others. I have no idea why. Height 6 cm, densities; green 2.65 g/cc; amber 2.64 g/cc; blue 2.65 g/cc; mauve 2.7 g/cc; pink 2.48 g/cc. Uranium, green 0.09% wt, amber 0.47% wt. Date probably period 1930, Value $40 - $60.

Chapter 40

Sweet Dishes

Photo 297. An intriguing piece. The style looks as if it should have come from the English Midlands at the end of the 1800s, it compares with Photo 106 in *BBVG*. It has not. The foot is in a later style, the quality of the metal and its wear is without that age. My *best guess* is that it was made in the 1930-40 period from an old mold, possible bought up from another factory, which had gone bankrupt. Height 11 cm, density 2.83 g/cc, uranium 0.19% wt. Value $20 - $30.

Photo 298. The bowl, stem and foot are from different gathers of the same melt. Un-ground pontil mark is rough. Foot has been molded. There is considerable wear. Height 9.5 cm, density 2.55 g/cc, uranium 0.6%% wt. I would date this *about* 1880. Value $30 - $40.

Photo 299. This bowl is part of a set which includes a larger bowl and I think could well have been for trifles, fruit salad, etc. It contains only a trace of uranium and in artificial light appears almost clear. However, in natural light, the uranium gives it a greenish tinge. Close examination of the gold trim round the edge shows it to be worn, so is the base, but I suspect the bowl has not been subject to repeated use. Sowerby appears to have made a similar shaped and patterned bowl as part of their Service No 2266, shown in their 1907 catalogue. However I don't think this is quite the same pattern. Despite the lack of moderate wear I would date it *period* 1920. In the first half of the twentieth century it was common practice, especially amongst the working and middle classes, to keep things like clothes, crockery, cutlery, etc for Sunday best. I think this set could well have come into that category. Bowl diameters 26 cm and 14.6 cm. Density 2.4 g/cc, uranium 0.05% wt. Value for small bowls and one large one, $60 - $80.

Photos 300 and 301. The reader flicking through these pages will probably be surprised to find these items un-attributed. The bowl in Photo 300 and the green fruit dish on the left hand side of Photo 301 are a set. They look as if they should have come from Davidson or Bagley, however I can find nothing to match them to either of those factories. The dish on the right hand side of Photo 301 is from Davidson, see *BBVG* p 63. The two look similar in shape, but there are some slight differences. If these differences are not significant and the dish on the left hand side was also made by Davidson, then why does the bowl in Photo 300 not appear in the same Davidson catalogue as the fruit dish? I do not think these are from the depression years or from either of those firms. Perhaps more like the 1960-80 *period*. Fruit dish, 10.5 cm diameter, density 2.48 g/cc, uranium 0.06% wt. Value of bowl and set of six dishes $20 - $40.

Photo 302. Of these two sweets only the amber contains uranium. They are similar to those shown in Photo 337 *BBVG*, although smaller and without any pattern. Their density and uranium content surely indicate they came from the same factory. Height of both 8.25 cm, density of the amber 2.66 g/cc, density of the mauve 2.7 g/cc. Uranium in amber 0.43% wt, in mauve nil. Both show moderate wear on the base so I will date them *about* 1935. Value $6 - $20 each.

Chapter 41

Jugs

Photo 303. This little jug is much younger than its claw handle would suggest. The metal is of good quality and there is little sign of wear. Height 10 cm, density 2.38 g/cc, uranium (which is only in the white) 0.12%wt. Date probably *about* 1920. Value $50 - $75.

Photo 304. A water jug in the Jacobean style that originated in Czechoslovakia in the 1920s. After an import duty was levied in 1931, moulds were brought over to England and this type of glass was made by several English firms. It remained popular until post-World War II years. Most of the glass is clear, but some was made in uranium green. Height 17.5 cm, density 2.5 g/cc, uranium 0.14% wt. Value $10 - $30.

Photo 305. Water jug with a lid that I cannot attribute. Height 25 cm, density 2.46 g/cc, uranium 0.14% wt. Date period 1930-50. Value $30 - $40.

Photo 306. It is ddifficult to imagine that this jug would have appealed to anyone. It is heavy and the handle only allows two fingers to get cramped. It was made in a two-piece mould-and, surprisingly, the calibrations tell us something. They show a pint equal to 2 cups equal to 16 oz. This is a USA measure; a UK one would have had a pint equal to 20 oz. and a Continental one would have had litres. The density says it is not a boro-silicate glass. While the heat resistant properties of boro-silicate glass were discovered about 1912, it did not come into more general kitchen use until the early 1920s, and then Corning held the patent. Every housewife or househusband post-World War II would expect such a jug to be made of heat-resistanta glass, so I would date this in the 1930-45 era. Height 14.5 cm, density 2.49 g/cc, uranium 0.09% wt. Value, well, sosme collector of bad jugs or radioactive ones might be persuaded to part with $20 for it.

Chapter 42

Vases and Flower Holders

Photo 307. These "Jack in the Pulpit" vases are popular among collectors, but I am not at all sure how popular they were with the Victorians from whose era they came. The style and density of this example says it probably came from the English Midlands. While the top of the stem, with its precise milky white area is impressive, the crimpwork and feet are very basic. This piece was found in Australia and I speculate that, perhaps at the end of the nineteenth century, some glassblower, perhaps an apprentice, made it up as a friggers piece and presented it to his family as a keepsake when they emigrated. Height 19 cm, maximum diameter 11.7 cm, density 3.11 g/cc, uranium 0.24% wt. Value $80 - $120.

Photo 308. My feeling is that this could have come from the Greener Glass Works, however the density is a little high and the uranium does match my other data for that origin. Height 12.6 cm, density 2.68 g/cc, uranium 0.47% wt. Date *about* 1880, value $30 - $40.

Photo 309. Sold as a Victorian glass goblet. Well, I would not like to drink out of it with its uneven lip, so I am calling it a vase. But is it Victorian? It is in style and after due consideration I will give it the benefit of the doubt. What worries me is that it shows no sign of wear, either on the base or the body. If it is that old it must be one of those rare items that spend their lives in grannies attic! It has been made in a single four-piece mold and at the base the stem shows signs of twist suggesting it was fire polished. Height 19 cm, density 2.55 g/cc, uranium 0.3% wt. If it is English, the density suggests it *could be* Greener. Value $30 - $40.

Photo 310. The acanthus leaf was a popular decoration for the English Midlands glasshouses. Manley[1] tells us that it was used by both Stevens and Williams and Boulton and Mills. This piece has a hollow foot and the leaf is simple, more characteristics of continental glass. Date *about* 1900. Height 13.5 cm, density 2.38 g/cc, uranium 0.12% wt on the white. Value $40 - $60.

Photo 311. The blue acanthus leaf contrasts with the pale ivory of the vase. It looks as if it may have come from the English Midlands but it has not. The top has been cut and ground flat, Continental style, and the density is not what would be expected from that part of England. It is not repro, the wear and, in particular, the ingrained dirt that has worked its way behind the leaf, says it is older than I am. Height 10.5 cm, density 2.39 g/cc, uranium 0.29% wt. Date *about* 1910, value $20 - $30.

Photo 312. The pink trail round the edge of this piece of Victorian ivory opaline is unusual, so is its shape. I have not been able to find anything like it in my search through old pattern books. The deep ground pontil makes me wonder if it is English. Height 11.5 cm, density 2.5 g/cc, uranium 0.29% wt. Date *about* 1890, Value $50 - $80.

Photo 313. I am not sure what purpose, if any, this item was intended to fulfill. For the want of classifying it I will say it was to hold a flower. The delicate turquoise color is not common, the twisted trail work is also uncommon. The top is ground and there is no pontil mark. Probably blown in a mold, then the trailwork added while still on the blow tube. Typical of the Continental way of making glass. Height 11 cm, density 2.38 g/cc, uranium 0.22% wt. *Could be* French, *period* 1910. Value $20 - $30.

Photo 314. The vase has been made with three layers, blue on the outside, white in the sandwich and pink on the inside. It is by no means certain which contains the uranium but I suspect it is on the outside, although I would have expected a stronger response under uv light. It has a pontil dimple. Height 12 cm, density 2.46 g/cc, uranium 0.22% wt. *Best guess* is Continental, date *about* 1900. Value $30 - 325.

Photo 315. This is the item in Photo 314 under uv light. It is giving a weak response but the blue now has a green tinge. If it were not for the Geiger reading, I would have been doubtful about the presence of uranium.

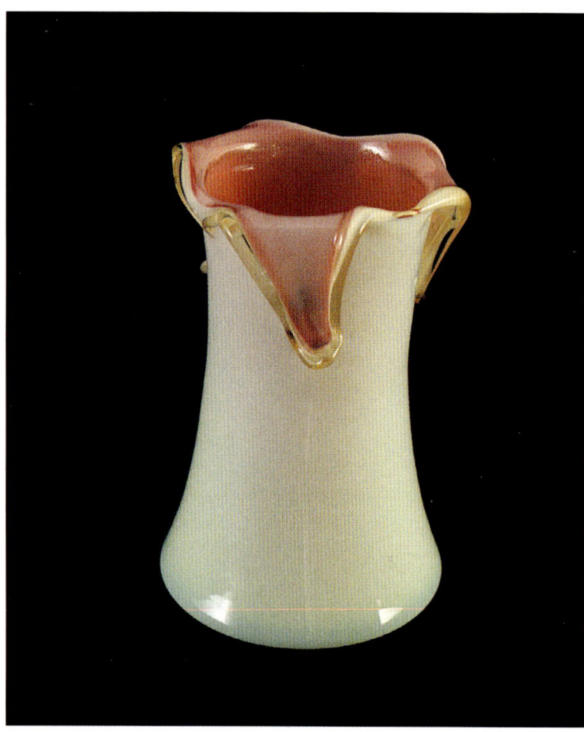

Photo 316. Pink on the inside has been overlaid with ivory, which appears to contain the uranium. Ground pontil dimple. Height 10.25 cm, density 2.47 g/cc, uranium 0.5% wt. *Best guess* is Continental, date *about* 1900, value $40 - $60.

Photo 317. Turquoise vase with hand painted decoration. The ground flat top and lack of a pontil indicates it was blown in a mold then finished on the blowing iron. Almost certainly Continental *about* 1900. Height 16.5 cm, density 2.47 g/cc, uranium 0.19% wt. Value $30 - $40.

Photo 318. Unusually the base of this vase is not glass but probably a hard plaster. The cut and polished top suggests a Continental origin. Turquoise does not seem to have been a popular color with British glasshouses. The décor is hand painted. Height 28 cm. Density as measured, 2.33 g/cc, (this is probably lower than the density of the glass because of the plaster base.) Uranium 0.3% wt. Date *about* 1900, value $60 - $80.

Photo 319. A simple but good example of a rich uranium glass vase as the color and technique gathered popularity. The foot has been hand-formed and the pontil is broken and rough. There is considerable wear on the base and the inside is heavily water stained. My gut feeling is that it is English and the density suggests it may have come from Tyneside. Height 11.5 cm, density 2.47 g/cc, uranium 0.8% wt. Date *about* 1870. Value $40 - $60.

Photo 320. The art work on this piece does not send me into raptures. It is hand painted but there is a trace of green in the outside metal, no doubt due to the not insignificant amount of uranium in the mix. It also has the hallmarks of coming from the Continent. Height 20 cm, density 2.46 g/cc, uranium 0.3% wt. Value $30 - $40.

Photo 321. Small hand painted spill vase has been blown in one operation and the top has been cut and ground flat. Typical of what we would expect from the Continent at the turn of the nineteenth century. Height 11.2 cm, density 2.48 g/cc, uranium 0.56%. Value $30 - $40.

Photo 322. Not exactly the most beautiful example of a hand painted vase, but I have included it as a good example of uranium in white opaque metal. The reason for its use in this mode is far from clear. The hollow base and cut top indicates a Continental origin from the early twentieth century. Height 20.5 cm, density 2.44 g/cc, uranium 0.9% wt. Value $30 - $40.

Photo 323. I suppose this must have been intended as a vase, I would hate to drink from it with its irregular top. One of the interesting things about glass collecting is trying to figure out the story that each piece has to tell. This is a good example. I have examined two of these vases, to the eye they appear identical although one is slightly smaller than the other, I will call them A and B.

A appears to have been much more heavily fire polished, it is badly twisted at the base of its stem and the edges of the pattern are rounded, not sharp. It is 16.5 cm high, density 2.53 g/cc, uranium 0.37% wt., wear slight.

B is 15.5 cm high, density 2.72 g/cc, uranium 0.37% wt. and moderate wear.

Why are the densities so different; what can we deduce? The wear suggests B is considerably older than A. The twisted stem and loss of sharpness may be due to bad fire polishing, a worn mold, or perhaps a change of metal quality. The density suggests a Lancashire glasshouse, the best fit from the information available being Derbyshire. Unfortunately little is known about the fate of this firm and its molds. My suspicion is that piece B was made by Derbyshire then later the mold was taken over by another glasshouse that made piece A, using a different mix for their metal. Can any reader tell me different? Value $30 - $50.

Photo 324. There are two sibling vases. A yellow one is illustrated in *BBVG* Photo 355, the green one is new to my study. For comparison purposes I quote for both. Yellow, density 2.56 g/cc, uranium 0.37% wt. Green, density 2.51 g/cc, uranium 0.28% wt. Date *about* 1880, value $40 - $60.

Photo 325. A large heavily water stained trumpet vase. This is not from hard water but from water attacking the glass. It could possibly be removed by acid polishing. There is no pontil mark, the foot is molded. The red trail work was probably applied before the top was shaped. It was too large to measure density but my fingernail ping test says it is non leaded. Height 31 cm, date *about* 1910. Value $50 - $70.

Photo 326. I suppose this is best described as a vase, but I am not at all sure for what it was intended. The interesting point is that the uranium in not in the white spattered yellow, which has been cased with clear glass, but in the green base. The top has been cut and ground. Dating and attribution is difficult but *best guess* is early 1900s and from Czechoslovakia. Height 18 cm, density 2.41 g/cc, uranium 0.12% wt. Value $10 - $20.

Photo 327. Although I bought this in Belgium I have a feeling it was made in England. Unlike so many similar specimen vases the top of this one has not been ground flat. The slight irregularity in height suggests it was cut by hand rather than on a turntable. There is little sign of wear so I am going to date it *about* 1950. Height 15 cm, density 2.46 g/cc, uranium 0.09% wt. Value $4 - $10.

Photo 328. The resemblance between this and the preserve jar in Photo 405 *BBVG* are so strong that it is likely they came from the same glasshouse. Their basic color has the same delicate green uranium tint. They each respond identically to both far and near uv light and both have the same uranium content. Even the hand painted red matches. For all that I still do not know who made them but my *best guess* is still French, this time *about* 1910. Height 12.5 cm, density 2.47 g/cc, uranium 0.25% wt. Value $20 - $30.

Photo 330. One of the fascinating aspects of glass collecting is to work out how an item was made. In most cases it is straightforward, but this one has me puzzled. The inside has 18 vertical ribs, while the outside has a multi spiral twist. The stem and foot have been applied separately. The teaser is "How do you get the straight ribs on the inside while the outside has been twisted?" I think the clue is that the internal ribs only extend down to the neck of the vase. My guess is that it was blown in a dip mold which had the outside threads cut in. The bowl of the vase was then blown, twisted and shaped, the top end of the bowl being shaped on a plug, which had been shaped to make the ribs. But I may be wrong. Height 18.5 cm, density 2.51 g/cc, uranium 0.16% wt. I don't know who made it but would date it *period* 1910. Value $20 -$30.

Photo 331. When I first saw this, I thought it might be an example of Stevens and Williams Alabaster glass. On closer examination I do not think it is. It shows only very slight signs of wear but the top has a small bead on its rim indicating that it has been hand cut using shears rather than cut on a turntable as is the more common modern practice. Of course it could be a studio piece but it is uncommon to find modern studios that use uranium. So it dating and origin defeat me. However it is a very attractive piece of glass with the uranium in the pale yellow. Even the density adds to the mystery, it is higher than I would expect from this type of translucent glass. Height 28 cm, density 2.59 g/cc, uranium 0.16% wt. Value $30 - $50.

Photo 332. Hyacinth vase of unknown origin, though the density suggests it may have come from the Continent or even the Lancashire area. Height 14.5 cm, density 2.98 g/cc, uranium 0.22% wt. Date *probably* somewhere between 1930 and 1950. Value $20 - $30.

Photo 333. A green vase with an iridised surface. It has 12 spiral ribs on the outside with corresponding depressions on the inside. It was probably formed in a dip mold, then blown and twisted. This has had the effect of making the ribs wider and shallower where there has been most expansion. It would then have been cut from the blow iron and polished. Height 26 cm, density 2.38 g/cc, uranium 0.6% wt. *Probably* Continental, *about* 1930. Value $20 - $30.

Chapter 43

Oil Lamps, Candlesticks, and Lampshades.

Photo 334. This lamp is in much the same style as that shown in *BBVG*, Photo 366. It has simple dual-wheel burner controls made of brass, which look old but may not be original. There is an interesting "X" pattern worked into the brass base. There is no design registration mark. Height (excluding the burner) 26.5 cm. Uranium 0.3% wt. Date *about* 1900, value $240. - $300.

Photo 335. I well remember at my Gran's house, before it was fitted with electric light, being given a candle in this style of holder, like a saucer with a handle, to light my way to bed. I reckon this must have been a little beauty, but alas age, as it does to us all, has taken its toll. It was made in three parts, the base, the candleholder stem, and the handle. The top of the stem has been cut and the whole piece liberally decorated with gold. It would be easy to attribute this green opaline piece to the Continent, maybe France or Bohemia, but I have a nagging doubt. The metal is heavily crizzled with the surface having the appearance of flaking. This may well account for why so little of the gold work has survived. Furthermore, the hole for the candle is a neat half-inch diameter. So I wonder, was this from some British glasshouse? Diameter of base 11 cm, density 2.36 g/cc, uranium 0.47% wt. Date *period* 1880, value in its present undamaged but worn condition, $30 - $50.

Photo 336. Another of these "take to bed" candlesticks. This one is fitted with what must surely be a brass chimney support. Although chimneys were standard on most oil lamps they are unusual on a candlestick. Height 8cm, density which is only approximate because of the presence of the brass, 2.6 g/cc, uranium 0.15% wt. Date *about* 1900. Value $40 - $60.

Photo 337. I have not been able to find anything like this shape in my researches. The only clue I have is its density, which makes me think in terms of Lancashire glass. It has a slight twist, which suggests fire polishing and a modest amount of wear on the base. Height 19 cm, density 2.77 g/cc, uranium 0.29% wt. Date *about* 1900. Value $30 - $50.

Photo 338. I have not been able to work out who made this piece, but everything about it says the date is *period* 1880. It is pressed in a three-piece mold and has a few air bubbles and a seed. Height 20.5 cm, density 2.55 g/cc, uranium 0.37% wt. Value $30 - $50.

Photo 339. Another "whodunit." The glass is heavily crizzled and brittle, so brittle that the top broke off when I was unpacking it. The density is that of a glass with about 15% lead. It has a modest amount of wear. The crizzling indicates a poor quality metal that has not stood the test of time. The style and wear suggests something like 1850 – 1900 period. The lead content suggests Lancashire, but I have no other evidence to link it to that area. Perhaps it was an experimental mix or a batch made in error. Maybe it is not British. I will just regard it as one of life's failures that has survived the years. Height 16 cm, density 2.78 g/cc, uranium 0.17% wt. Value $30 - $40.

Photo 341. The base of this candlestick looks as if it is from the late Victorian period. It has not. The metal candleholder is in two pieces, the lower part, glued to the glass, has been cast in a two-piece mold and then plated and lacquered. The glass is almost without wear. Diameter of the base, 10 cm, uranium 0.25% wt. Make, not British I hope, quite possibly Malaysian. Date I will guess at *about* 1970. Value $10 - $20.

Photo 340. How I wish I could attribute this beauty. The rich green has to been seen to be appreciated fully. My instinct says it was made in the North East of England but that is as far as I can get. It has been pressed in a four-piece mold and almost certainly fire polished. I date it *about* 1880. Height 23.5 cm, density 2.51 g/cc, uranium 0.47% wt. Value $40 - $60.

Photo 342. I debated with myself at some length whether this was a "curiosity" or a "candlestick." I decided the latter, for I can think of no other use for it. Basically a square block of uranium glass with three concentric rings and a pimple in the middle on each of four sides. A 2 cm diameter hole on one side and a 5 cm on the other. My guess is that the large hole would take a squat "night light" and the other a standard candle. My gut feeling is that it Scandinavian, but that is not an attribution. 6.75 cm cube, density 2.49 g/cc, uranium 0.28%. Value? Well, I was daft enough to pay $68 for it.

Photo 343. A simple design, similar to one shown in the Bagley Catalogue of 1938. However, that item has six sides whereas this one has eight, a difference which I think is significant. Height 12 cm, density 2.46 g/cc, uranium 0.19% wt. Date *about* 1940, *probably* Continental. Value $10 - $20.

Photo 344. An attractive leftover from the deco period. Height 18 cm, density 2.48 g/cc, uranium 0.12% wt. Date *about* 1935, value $20 - $30.

Photo 345. Several glasshouses make use of the Dolphin for the basis of their designs. I do not know which produced this one. However I would not be surprised if it had come from the USA. It has been made in a four-piece mold, shows only very modest wear on the base and the metal is of high quality. I reckon it is much younger than me so let's say *period* 1960. Height 22 cm, density 2.52 g/cc, uranium 0.2% wt. Value $20 - $40.

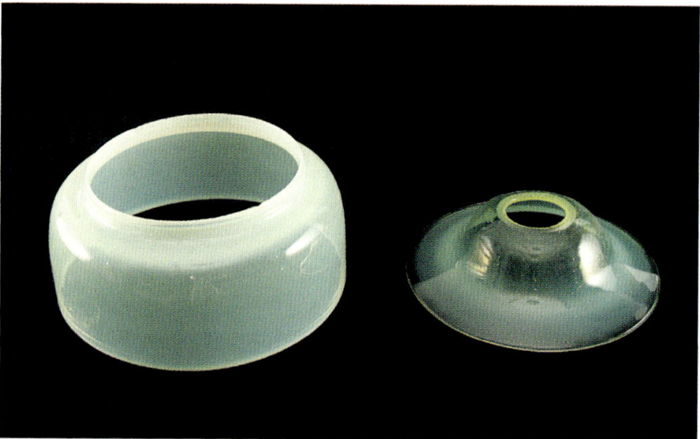

Photo 346. I have never seen another lampshade like this. In fact, when I first saw it I wondered what it was. The shallow disk on the right hand side takes a standard light bulb fitting and snugly fits inside the short cylindrical piece, thus forming a two- part shade. It would appear from density and uranium measurements that the two components were made from slightly different mixes. Almost certainly English, could be Whitefriars or English Midlands, *about* 1910. Diameter 14.5 cm, densities of cylinder and disc, 3.16 g/cc and 3.04 g/cc respectively. Uranium content, cylinder and disc, 0.12% wt and 0.19% wt, respectively. Value $80 - $100.

Chapter 44

Plates, Dishes, Compotes and Tazzas

Photo 347. When I first saw this plate, I thought there was a good chance it was Whitefriars. However I cannot find an exact match to the pattern, although there are similarities. It has a perfect pontil dimple, suggesting it came from a quality glasshouse but its density is not what I have found on other Whitefriars items. I am also having great difficulty in dating it. It shows moderate wear but the metal is of high quality. I will go for a *probably period* 1930. Diameter 22.8 cm, density 2.57 g/cc, uranium 0.09% wt. Value $20 - $30.

Photo 348. The plate has been press molded and the base ground and polished. Although it does not show up on the Photograph, there is a single joint line running through the pattern on the outer part of the plate. If it were a mold mark, there should be at least two. I can only assume that a metal disc, like a large circlip was placed in a standard mold to form the pattern. Diameter 20 cm, density 2.64 g/cc, uranium 0.9% wt. I have difficulty with dating, the plate shows considerable wear, so will say *period* 1930. Value $4 - $10.

Photo 349. All my instincts say this is English, but search as I have, I cannot find any basis for an attribution. Its density would be consistent with Greener, Derbyshire or Percival, Vickers but it could well have come from some glasshouse, which has now been lost in obscurity. It has been made in a single 3 part mold which is quite an achievement considering the narrow gap between the indented underside and the upper rim of the base. The odd rough patch of molding and the signs of wear over the whole item are good indicators of its age. Diameter 21 cm, overall height varies from 1.25 to 2 cm, density 2.62 g/cc, uranium 0.31% wt. Date *about* 1880 Value $30 - $50.

Photo 350. A satin-finished dish in a delicate pale lemon, produced from a four-piece press mold. Unfortunately it was just too large for a density measurement. Diameter 26 cm, uranium 0.17% wt. Date *about* 1935, maker unknown, value $10 - $30.

Photo 351. At first glance, I thought this bowl might have come from Tyneside, but now I don't think so. The daisy button and hobnail patterns were popular in the USA and I suspect that is where this piece came from. Close examination shows signs of wear on the hobnail feet and there are scratches on the inside. This makes me think it is not all that recent and I would date it *probably about* 1920. Diameter 22 cm, density 2.43 g/cc, uranium 0.18% wt. Value $30 - $40.

Photo 352. I do wonder if this dish should have had an EPNS lid. I cannot make any attribution, but I would not be surprised if it had come from the North of England. Its density and uranium content and slightly unusual shade of yellow are not dissimilar from the *probably* Sowerby salt shown in Photo 59 *BBVG*. Width 11.5 cm, density 2.55 g/cc, uranium 0.43% wt. Date *period* 1910. Value $16 - $24.

Photo 353. A superb, decorative plate in a delicate opaque metal. The uranium is used to give a very pale green tint without which I would probably have passed it by. The centre is hollow which forms the base. On the underside of this is the dimple where the pontil has been ground out. Clearly the product of a quality glasshouse, but which one? The underside carries the mark "R 709" with a crossed Continental style "7". (See Photo 354) It has a strong response to uv light, see Photo 355. I have not seen anything like this before so my dating and valuation needs to be treated with caution. Diameter 30 cm, density 2.7 g/cc, uranium 0.14% wt. Date *about* 1900, value $200 - $300.

Photo 354. The mark on the underside of the dish in Photo 353, clearly showing the Continental style crossed seven.

Photo 355. The dish in Photo 343 under uv light.

Photo 356. A mundane but attractive table bowl from the 1930-40 period. I cannot trace its maker, although it bears a close resemblance to Davidson's "Ripple" design of the 1940s. If it did come from that factory, then I would need to revise my theory that they did not use uranium in their green glass (see *BBVG* p56–57.) Diameter 20 cm, density 2.47 g/cc, uranium 0.14% wt. As for value, well, I was given it by a tired car-booter who could not sell it!

Photo 357. What a pity there was not a law that required glass-makers to identify themselves on their wares? This is so typical of the uranium ware at the turn of the 19th century, I only wish I could name its maker. The pattern is unusual in as much that the common diamond is broken in the middle with a band of squares. The density may give a clue to its origin. Height 15.5 cm, density 2.71 g/cc, uranium 0.43% wt. *Best guess* Manchester area, date *about* 1900. Value $40 - $60.

Photo 358. A beautifully made compote in green opaline. The edge has been skilfully trailed with a white thread. At first sight I thought this might be a relatively modern piece, but close examination of the amount and type of wear says it probably isn't. The inner surface of the bowl is crisscrossed with a mass of fine scratches, but the outside surface is largely unblemished. The base where it would contact the surface upon which it stands is also a mass of fine scratch marks. These are virtually impossible to fake and indicate the item has had a lot of use. So, if we exclude the possibility that it was used in a cafe, then I would date it *probably about* 1900. Height 14 cm, density 2.38 g/cc, uranium 0.43% wt. Value $60 - $100.

Photo 359. The color of this compor is very close to that of the one above, the uranium and densities are close enough for them to have come from the same glasshouse, but gut feeling advises caution. Taking a good look at it can tell us a lot. The foot is slightly ellipsoid, suggesting it was hand formed and not molded. The pontil dimple is perfect in shape. The lip of the bowl shows the trace of a "bud" and it has been cut with shears and rounded off. All this suggests a British make, in a quality glasshouse by a skilled worker. The bulbous shape finished by a turned-out lip is unusual and I have not been able to find a match in any of the records I have searched, although there is some resemblance to items shown in Stevens and Williams and Thomas Webb pattern books. In Chapter 29, Table 1, I quote my estimates of density and uranium in Webb's chrysoprase; the figures for this item are not the same, but they are close. *Pottery Gazette*, p 10, 1st March 1894, quotes an exchange of correspondence between Walsh and Webb, it seems both these glasshouses were about to introduce a new color - "chrysoprase". Is this what they were discussing, I wonder? Height 9 cm, diameter 9 cm, density 2.4 g/cc, uranium 0.56% wt. Value $30 - $50.

Photo 360. Before there are howls of "this is Davidson" let me explain. This is a piece from the "Chippendale Range." According to Dodsworth[1], Chippendale started in the USA about 1907 and large amounts were imported into the UK. About 1930, the National Glass Company purchased the molds and had items made from them in the UK. In 1933 Davidson purchased the molds. However Davidson was taken over by Brama in 1955 and then eventually the Company went into liquidation. The glassworks demolished, but what happened to those molds? There are three reasons for thinking that this piece did not come from Davidson. The density indicates a leaded glass, something we do not associate with Davidson. The green is obtained by use of uranium which, to say the least, was an uncommon practice for that company. Thirdly, the wear is very slight suggesting the item dated to the 1990s, rather than the 1930s. Height, including the handles, 10 cm, density 2.68 g/cc, uranium 0.14% wt. Value $30 - $50.

Photo 361. The interesting aspect of this deco compot is its graduated color. It is the same as the candlestick in Photo 373, *BBVG*. The density and uranium content also match. It must have come from the same factory but I still have no idea which. Diameter 11 cm, density 2.47 g/cc, uranium 0.11% wt. Value $6 - $10.

Photo 362. The fascinating thing about this little compote is that I cannot make up my mind whether it is green or yellow, it seems to depend upon the angle from which it is viewed and the type of incident light. It was produced in a three-piece mold, shows the slight distortion of fire polishing and has several seeds in the metal. There is moderate wear. The density indicates it is unlikely to have come from the English Midlands or Lancashire. Perhaps it is a product of Tyneside or perhaps it came from abroad. Height 9 cm, density 2.53 g/cc, uranium 0.4% wt. Date *about* 1880. Value $50-$70.

Photo 363. A simple but interesting piece of glass. It is opaque white, which has been cased with a uranium green. Cleverly the green has been made to cover the edge of the white. The basic shape would have been formed in a dip mold. It is mounted onto a spelter like metal casting. The underside of the dish, where it sits on the mount is hollowed and is filled with plaster, probably to cushion the seat and stop the glass from fracture. I suspect it may be French and would venture, with some hesitation, a date of *about* 1870. Diameter of dish, 21 cm; density 2.414; uranium (in casing) 0.28% wt. Value $60 - $80.

Chapter 45

Scent and Toilet Water Bottles

Photo 364. I am not a collector of scent bottles as such, but they interest me only in so far as they contain uranium. Having said that, this is one of the most unusual I have come across. The brass chain and ring must be associated with the means of carrying or storing, for it will not stand up unaided. It is surely too large and heavy to be disguised as an earring. Length 6 cm, uranium 0.38% wt. Date somewhere in the region of 1900. Value $60 - $80.

Photo 366. At first sight I thought this was a turn of the century toilet water bottle in the same ilk as Photos 267 and 397, *BBVG*, but on close examination I don't think it is. It appears to have a thin layer of uranium over clear glass and has been made in a four-piece mold in what looks like a one-stage operation. There is very little wear on the base. I could be wrong, but I am going to date it post-WW2. Height 17 cm, density 2.46 g/cc, uranium 3.8 cps. Value $30 - $40.

Photo 367. Everything about this scent says Art Deco, the shape and the aluminum top. The color is rather pale for the uranium content. Height 7.25 cm, density 2.49 g/cc, uranium 0.26% wt. Value $10 - $20.

Photo 368. I can only presume this vessel started life as a toilet water bottle. The dealer who sold it to me said it did have a stopper but she broke it. What is interesting is how it was made. The spirals get thinner and closer together at the top. The ring has been applied on top and melts into the spiral ribs. On the base there is a perfect dimple where the pontil has been ground out. I can only presume it was cast in a shallow pillar mold then blown, drawn and twisted, the top being held on the blow pipe until a pontil was attached for the finishing work. Undoubtedly produced by a skilled worker at some quality glasshouse, but which? The density says it is unlikely to be from the English Midlands or Lancashire. Height 15.5 cm, density 2.51 g/cc, uranium 0.68% wt. Date about 1900, value $30 - $50.

Photo 369. I am not sure for what purpose this little bottle was intended but, giving it the benefit of the doubt, I have included it in this section. For a yellow, it is very rich in uranium and it has been made in much the way I would have expected for a bottle in the early 1900s. It has been blown in a two-piece mold and the top of the neck finished separately with an add-on from another two-piece mold. The mold marks on the top and body of the bottle do not align. There is a seed in the metal, something we would also associate with age. I am going to date it *about* 2000 because there is no sign whatsoever of any wear. The base is free from scratches and the inside and outside of the body are pristine and shiny. Height 10.5 cm, density 2.52 g/cc, uranium 1.24% wt. Value $16 - $24.

Chapter 46

A Miscellany of Items

Nearing the end of the book this is a collection of items for which I have not found a home in my preceding chapters. Some pieces included here might have been more appropriately included in earlier chapters but arrived after they were finalized. However, the majority are here simply because, while I thought them to be of interest, they did not conveniently slot in elsewhere.

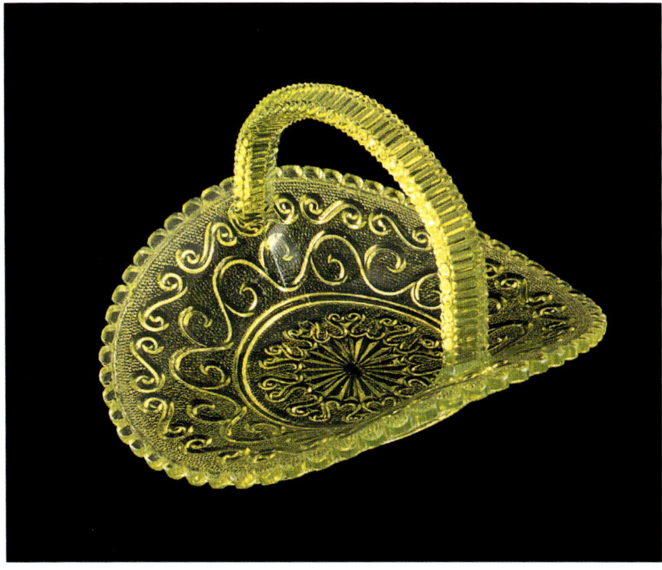

I will consider the bon-bon dishes in Photos 370 and 371 together. There are characteristics about these, which suggest they may have come from Greener, Sowerby or Ed. Moore, but they may have come from none of them. They have a line mark running across the middle of the dish and the handle, indicating only a two piece mold. Although identical in pattern they appear to have come from different molds.
Green dish, height 11 cm, density 2.47 g/cc, uranium 0.12% wt. Date about 1880. Value $40 - $60.
Yellow dish, height 11 cm, density 2.47 g/cc, uranium 0.43% wt. Date about 1880. Value $50 - $70.

Photo 372. I would like to have been able to identify which English Midlands firm made this piece of Victoriana. Unfortunately I am not even convinced it came from there, although it is in the style associated with that area. It has an uneven pontil dimple, the casing is not of the highest quality and neither is the applied glass decoration. All this suggests it did not come from one of the top glasshouses. The style, wear (including a little damage and cracking), and the dirt that has found its way behind the applied work all confirm its age. A lot of work went into its making. I surmise that the basket body would have been formed, probably in a mold, from two gathers. Then a pontil applied and the blow tube cut off. The top edge would have been worked and then the trail applied. After that, the decoration and handle. Finally, two red cherries attached by their stalks. All this time the piece would go back and forward to the furnace to keep the metal at working temperature. Finally it would be carefully annealed to prevent cracking as it cooled down. Width 20.5 cm, density 2.48 g/cc, uranium 0.25% wt. Date *about* 1880, value (in perfect condition) $200 - $400.

Photo 374. Seven items all subject to uv light (near). Reading from left to right, Bottom row: Burtles, Tate and Co., Burtles, Tate and Co., Davidson. Top row: Davidson, Burtles, Tate and Co., Item in Photo 373, Greener. The Davidson and Greener pieces respond more strongly than the others.

Photo 375. I have not much of a clue as to who made this basket but I include it because it is another example of white uranium glass. The amber handle and trim are uranium free. It has a ground pontil and a large seed in the opaque white. Height 22 cm, density 2.46 g/cc, uranium 0.16% wt. Date *about* 1900. Value $30 - $50.

Photo 373. I have discussed this piece with several collectors and the consensus of opinion was that it had some of the design characteristics of Greener. The density seemed to confirm this, then I subjected it to uv light, see Photo 374. Its response is not at all like that of the other Greener piece but similar to items from Burtles, Tate and Co. However the density says it did not come from there. Another of those interesting "don't know who made it" but date must be *about* 1895. Width 14.4 cm, density 2.51 g/cc, uranium 0.3% wt. Value $80 -$100.

Photo 376. Perhaps this was intended to hold pot-pourri, a common practice in Victorian times and the days before air conditioning, extractor fans and aerosol sprays? It has an irregular ground pontil mark. The turquoise is thinly layered on the outer dirty white. The uranium is probably only in this layer. I don't think the quality is good enough for the English Midlands, the density appears to agree. Date *period* 1900. Height 14.75 cm, density 2.5 g/cc, uranium 0.25% wt. Value $30 - $50.

Photo 377. A Victorian lustre in a pale ivory. This is not usually a candlestick, as some people may suppose, but simply a light catching device to create a sparkle in the room. On this piece, there are seven droppers and the decoration has been hand painted. The base is hollow and part of the main piece. It has not been cut and ground in the Continental tradition, instead it carries a rough pontil mark. I did not think it practical to measure the density but I think it likely it came from a British glasshouse. Height 24 cm, uranium 0.3% wt. Date *about* 1890. Value $160 - $200.

Photo 378. The opaline white has a distinct lemon tint no doubt due to the uranium. Although plain, the inside pink adds interest. Unfortunately it is another of those "I haven't a clue who made it." Height 12 cm, density 2.45 g/cc, uranium 0.22 g/cc. Date *about* 1890. Value $30 - $50.

Photo 379. There should have been three bottles in the stand, one was broken before I got to it, so I have only shown one as this gives a clearer view of the stand. The silver plate is on copper, it is badly worn and unmarked. This makes me think it is Continental, late nineteenth century. The bottle has a molded-in dimple and no pontil mark. It was too large for me to measure the density. The color is not the bright yellow (Topaz) but has an amber tint. Height of bottle without stopper, 30 cm, uranium 1.1% wt. Date *period* 1900. Value is difficult. I suspect that if each of three bottles were sold separately, they would fetch between $50 and $100 each.

Photo 380. I am convinced this small bottle was made in recent years solely for the benefit of the Vaseline glass collector. The body has been made in a two-piece mold. The top was also made in a two-piece mold and added separately. The mold marks do not line up. I would not have expected a bottle from the early twentieth century to be made in this way. The metal has small bubbles but no seeds. The real giveaway is the complete absence of wear, not only on the base but the body as well. Height 11.3 cm, density 2.48 g/cc, uranium 19% wt. Value depends on how much you want to add a piece of modern trash to your collection!

Photo 381. I guess that this little bottle would have been used for vinegar or a similar table condiment. The uranium is only in the stopper and handle. Height 13.7 cm, density (stopper) 2.46 g/cc, uranium (stopper) 0.19% wt. Difficult to date but I will say *period* 1950. Value $10 - $20.

Photo 382. It would surely be difficult to find a design that is more deco than this little clock. The chrome is in poor condition and the backing plate showing rust. I have no doubt the clock and glass are original. The hands and numbers on the dial lack the luminous paint of later years. I wonder if it saw service in an air raid shelter during WW2. Height 8.5 cm, density 2.44 g/cc, uranium 0.09% wt. Date *about* 1925. Value, if in good working condition, $80 - $120.

Photo 383. Very much in the style of a Victorian salt, this could easily be mistaken for a piece of Davidson's Pearline. I am convinced it is not. The density is too high, I have not been able to find the pattern, the finish is heavily acid polished and there is not the slightest blemish or scratch, which would be expected on an item a century old. Maximum width 8.5 cm, density 2.7 g/cc, uranium 0.25% wt. *Best guess* on date, 1980. Hunch tells me it came from the USA. Value $10 - $20.

Photo 384. No, I have not placed this little salt in the wrong chapter. The "broken" diamond pattern is certainly characteristic of George Davidson but this did not come from that factory. The metal is just too pristine for it to be more than a few decades old. Diameter 4.5 cm, density 2.49 g/cc, uranium 0.26% wt. Date *about* 1980, value $10 - $14.

Photo 385. A salt with an attractive uranium yellow. I have little idea who made it. Diameter 5.5 cm, density 2.5 g/cc, uranium 0.17% wt. Date *period* 1950, value $10 - $16.

Photo 387. This little pot (or is it a salt?) was sold on eBay as being Ed Moore. The vendor assured me that it had been attributed by a friend with access to some old Ed Moore catalogues. It is yet another example of a dubious attribution. I don't for one moment believe it came from that firm. The density, which I have checked twice just to be sure, says it did not. It is more likely to have come from one of the Lancashire glasshouses, but the information on these is scant and I have not been able to confirm this. It was made in a four-piece mold and I am dating it on the basis of wear and style. Diameter 8.5 cm, density 2.87 g/cc, uranium 0.2% wt. Date *about* 1910. Value $30 - $50.

Photo 388. I guess this must have been intended as a salt. It is the design that intrigues me, was it inspired by the contents of a car gearbox, I wonder? Diameter 3.5 cm, density 2.47 g/cc, uranium 0.15% wt. Date *period* 1950, value $4 - $8.

Photo 389. I often wonder why it was found necessary to have these double salts. Perhaps some reader will tell me. This duet has been made in a four-piece mold. Length 11.25 cm, density 2.46 g/cc, uranium 0.12 % wt. I bought this in Belgium but it could have been made anywhere. Date *about* 1900. Value $20 - $30.

Photo 390. Another double salt. This came from a Belgian dealer selling at an English antiques fair. It was probably made in a two piece mold but the density says it was not from the same factory. Length 14 cm, density 2.58 g/cc, uranium 0.12% wt. Date *about* 1900. Value $20 - $30.

Photo 391. This must be one of the smallest ashtrays. The four scallops in the rim, for taking a cigarette, say that it is not a salt. Diameter 6.5 cm, density 2.44 g/cc, uranium 0.43% wt. Difficult to date, but *probably about* 1920. Value $10 - $20.

Photo 392. Just what purpose this was intended for, I cannot say. There is no evidence that it ever had a lid and I doubt if the top was closed with a large cork because of its shape. There are 20 internal vertical ribs. They have a slight twist, which probably occurred when the clear band of crimpwork was applied. The ribs would have been formed in a small dip mold then the vessel formed in a blow mold. There is little clue to age, the wear being slight for its size. Height 13.5 cm, density 2.47 g/cc, uranium 0.53% wt. Date somewhere between 1930 and 1970. Value $20 - $30.

Photo 393. I am going to call this a "wine cooler," although it could well serve as a vase or even a wastepaper receptacle. It looks as though it could be Stevens and Williams dark amber, but it is not. It has a large dimple where the pontil has been ground out. The density casts doubt on the theory that it came from the English Midlands or Edinburgh Crystal. Height 20.5 cm, density 2.75 g/cc, uranium 0.6% wt. Date *about* 1920. Value $30 - $40.

Photo 394. It would be easy to attribute this toothpick holder to Sowerby. They used the weave pattern in the 1880s in a number of their basket products. The similarity extends to the rope twist rim, but I feel sure this is not from that factory. Close examination shows the patterns are not exactly the same, nor have I come across this type of metal from Sowerby. As far as dating, based mainly upon the wear on the base, I can only say somewhere between 1880 and 1930 which is not very helpful. Height (including handles) 7 cm, density 2.38 g/cc, uranium 0.19% wt. Value $10-$30.

Photo 395. One of a pair. The color of the glass suggests they are Georgian. They each have a nicely ground and polished pontil dimple suggesting a quality glasshouse but probably not quite up to the standard of Webb. They are well blessed with striations, confirming they were handmade. There is the odd imperfection. All this would support the Georgian dating. Two things say they are much later. The presence of uranium and the absence of substantial wear. They could be mid or late 1800s but I think not. We know there was a vogue for this type of repro in the 1920s and I am convinced they come from that period. The density and style of manufacture suggests the English Midlands or possibly Whitefriars or Edinburgh Crystal. My hunch says Stevens and Williams but that all it is. Height 5.3 cm, density 3.15 g/cc, uranium 0.62% wt. Value each $20 - $30.

Photo 396. The uranium is in the ivory lining of this little pot. Close examination shows the top has been cut and polished, while a narrow strip running just inside the top has been ground but not polished. I think that at one time it had a lid or possibly a cork. The simple but attractive transferred decoration is heavily worn. I would date it *period* 1890, with a best guess that it came from the Continent. Diameter 7.75 cm, density 2.48% wt, uranium 0.22% wt. Value $20 -$30.

Photo 397. Nearly everything about this decorative bowl says English Midlands or even Webb, but a chain is only as strong as its weakest link, which in this case is the density. The shape is typical of some Webb and Steven and Williams pieces, the decoration has a close resemblance to Webb's patterns 18658 and 18995, (1890). The pontil dimple is a perfect circle but its density is only 2.44 g/cc. The *BBVG* shows some examples of Stevens and Williams with low densities but I have not seen any evidence of this style of decoration in their pattern books. Perhaps I have missed it but until there is more evidence it must remain un-attributed. Height 9 cm, density 2.44 g/cc, uranium 0.25% wt. Date *about* 1890, value $60 - $100.

Photo 398. I puzzle over the purpose for which this item was intended. Perhaps it was meant to hold a candle, I cannot imagine it holding flowers. Even if I don't know why it was made, it is an attractive piece of uranium glass. Marks indicate it was formed in a two-piece mold. The top has been ground flat. I have been told by someone who claimed to understand such items, that it was made by Helena Tynell for Riihimaki Riihimaen of Finland. The density is consistent with a piece from that firm shown in *BBVG*, p 148, but the uranium is a little lower. I will not quote another collector's opinion as an attribution but it might give the interested reader a starting point for research. Height 7 cm, density 2.54 g/cc, uranium 0.3% wt. Value $10 - $20.

Photo 399. Two piano insulators, legend has it they were intended to go under the feet of pianos to spread the load on the flooring. They look identical and could be attributed to Davidson who produced this design. Closer inspection shows they are slightly different, the left hand side one has angular small pillars, on the right hand side one they are rounded. Only the left hand side has uranium and I do not believe this came from Davidson. the density is not what I have found in any Davidson metal I have examined. The right hand side could well be Davidson, it does not contain uranium. Left hand side diameter 8.5 cm, density 2.68 g/cc, uranium 0.93% wt. Value $10 - $20.

Photo 400. This is not likely to win any design award. If it is a salt, then it will surely not be very stable with its narrow base. Mundane though it be, it owes its place to the fact that it is radioactive. Height 5 cm, density 2.54 g/cc, uranium 0.22% wt. Date *probably about* 1940, value nominal.

Photo 401. The sharp-eyed reader will notice that the two sweet dishes in this picture are shown on page 177 in *BBVG*. I have repeated them here, but this time with a wine glass interposed between them. All three items would have started life in the same dip mold. They have the same ribbed pattern. The gather would first have been blown in a dip mold with a wavy vertical pattern. It would then have been re-blown into a plain surfaced mold to reverse the pattern and form the shape of the bowl, be it the sweet dish or the wine. From left to right: density 2.64 g/cc, 2.67 g/cc, 2.64 g/ cc; uranium 0.06% wt, 0.09% wt, 0.43% wt. Date *period* 1940.

Chapter 47
Jewelry

Despite the general view that uranium glass jewellery is little more than cheap artificial trash it still has a place in my collection of radioactive glass. Somewhat surprisingly it is probably more available than the other forms of uranium glass. Perhaps that is because few people collect it. Never the less it has a place in my research and I am adding a few more examples to those I have already shown in *BBVG*.

Photo 402. I hardly need to say the uranium is only in the "jade" green beads. The three dice-shaped ones have a gold triangle set into them. I don't know whether this is gold or just a gold-colored metal; it is not paint. I am no authority on dating jewelry, real or artificial, but I think this must be late nineteenth century. Extended length 70 cm and weighing in at 100 g I would not like to have had it hung round my neck! Geiger response 3.5 cps. Value $20 - $30.

Photo 403. The fastening on this necklace shows lots of wear, in fact the silver plate is almost completely worn away. The stringing is with what looks like a coiled copper wire with a thread running through it. The wire has broken and the inner thread looks like nylon! My gut feeling is that the clasp is original, the threading probably about 1950, so how old does that make the glass beads? I am going to guess at 1920. Length opened out 42 cm, density 2.42 g/cc, uranium about 0.3% wt. Value $20 - $30.

Photo 404. A sparkling necklace made from cut pieces of uranium glass. I wonder how many of the ladies who have worn this over the years and not realized it was radioactive! Although I have not been able to measure the uranium content with any confidence, it is in the region of 0.3% wt. Length of the extended necklace, 37 cm, diameter of the largest stone,8 mm. Date likely to be early twentieth century. Value $20 - $30.

Photo 405. The uranium is not always where you might expect it to be. In this necklace it is only in the elongated beads and the smaller spheres. It is not in the three larger spheres, not in the two tiny clear yellow spacers and not in the cylindrical spacers. *Probably* early twentieth century. Geiger response 5 cps. Value $10 - $20.

Photo 406. Oh, just another necklace. I never cease to wonder how such pieces were made. Each of these beads has many flat ground and polished faces. The edges of each are sharp and defined. Certainly not acid polished. How did they do this and also get the hole so exactly through the centre? I have to confess I do not know. The density suggests that the glass may well have come from the English Midlands. The amber is typical of that which appears to have come in during the early part of the twentieth century. The wear on the beads is considerable, but then we would expect this. Length, opened out, 43 cm, density 3.47 g/cc, uranium approximately 0.6% wt. Date *about* 1920. Value $30 – 20.

Photo 407. I found this small pendant difficult to photograph. The view is from above, looking down. It is attractive multi-faceted Topaz. The fastening is a metal triangle, which should have had four small diamonds, or imitation diamonds, on each of the visible two sides. Time has reduced this number by half. The density, 3.9 g/cc, is unusually high, this may be in part due to error in measuring such a small item but still indicates it has a high lead content. Length, including the metal fastener, 3.3 cm, width 2.2 cm. Uranium was difficult to measure because of the size and shape of the item but I estimate it to be 0.4% wt. I will not date it but gut feeling is that it hails from the middle of the nineteenth century. Value $20 - $30.

Photo 408. The uranium is in the yellow beads. As ear-rings they are modern, but as beads they are old. The dealer who sold them to me confirmed that she had taken the beads from an old necklace and mounted them in modern ear fittings. Be that as it may, they still have uranium in them. Length of the bead 1.1 cm. Uranium only very approximately estimated 1% wt. Date of the beads, *probably* late Victorian. Value $4 - $6.

Photo 409. A single "stone" broach set in a white metal ring. The uranium glass has been hand cut, the striations are visible under an eye glass. *Probably* from the late Victorian era. Length 2.75 cm , width 2.5 cm, density not measured. Uranium about 0.4% wt. Value $20 - $30.

Chapter 48
The Tail End

The problem with writing a book like this is that it takes a considerable time to put together, meanwhile more interesting items are coming along. Sometimes just a few arrive too late to be included in their appropriate chapter. Rather than let them escape publication I have included five of them here.

Photo 410. This candlestick is in the style of Walsh Pompeian glass. I have not found it illustrated in any of Walsh's designs but the uranium and density are within the range I would expect for this type of metal. Height 5 cm, density 2.9 g/cc, uranium 0.31% wt. *Almost certainly* Walsh, *about* 1930. Value $30 - $40.

Photo 411. This particular basket has a Design Registration lozenge mark that is unreadable. However I have identified the pattern from another, which identifies it as deposition number 238105 by Greener, dated 1870. Width 16 cm, density 2.62 g/cc, uranium 0.23% wt. Value $40 - $60.

Photo 412. Everything about this style says Art Deco style. The dropper on the end of the stopper is a nice touch of class. Height 9 cm, density 2.47 g/cc, uranium 0.12% wt. Date *about* 1935. Value $20 - $40.

Photo 413. A single trumpet epergne supported in a silver plated stand. Probably came from the English Midlands and I would put Walsh high on the list of the usual suspects for this one. The stand bears the inscription EPNS and 2626. Height 14 cm, density 3.17 g/cc, uranium 0.18% wt. Date *about* 1910. Value $40 - $80.

Photo 414. Similar to Photo 207, this item is in pale lemon. It carries the Fenton trademark. Height 7.8 cm, density 2.53 g/cc, uranium 0.08% wt. Date *about* 1975, value $10 - $30.

Chapter 49
Going Pottery

I have not changed my mind, I am still determined not to research the use of uranium to color pottery, but I have included the photos below to demonstrate that not all uranium glazes come out orange. I can only describe this as a dirty brown, but there are suspicious glimpses of orange peeping out from under. I can't imagine that uranium orange has been over coated but rather perhaps something has changed most of the uranium to brown. I just mention this in case someone else wants to undertake the research.

Readers wanting to learn more will be interested in a short article by Brian Bowley in *Ceramic Review*[1] or Maria Betti's paper published by the *Journal of Environmental Health*[2]. It seems that the uranium used in ceramic glazes is more prone to leaching out than when it is used in glass!

Photos 415, 416, and 417. Uranium doped glazes were also used extensively on pottery to give a characteristic orange color. Two examples are shown in *BBVG* p 204, and I show two more here in Photos 415 and 417. The Photo 416 item, hideous as it is to my eye, is also glazed with a uranium mix, but this time it is predominantly an unattractive brown, although it has traces of orange peeping through. Seems to me a waste of good uranium.

Notes

Chapter 2. Uranium, Radioactivity and Radiation Riosks

1. Mr S. Eveson. Private Communication.
2. Depleted Uranium: A Study of its Uses within the UK and Disposal Issues. R & D Technical Report P3-088/TR, J H Jackson, Environment Agency, ISBN 1 85705 524 1".
3. Dr David Wade, Book and software Reviews, Glass Circle No 97.
4. Nuclear Issues, Vol 26, No 12, December 2004.
5. Cardis et al. 2005 BMJ 331 77-80.
6. Journal of Radiation Protection, Editorial v 25, No 3 September 2005.
7. Dr P J D Snow, Letter to Glass Cone, (Glass Association UK) No 41 Spring 1996.

Chapter 3

1. UK Atomic Energy Authority Report, PG 403 (W).
2. Eveson S R , Sixty Years in Crystal Glass Industry.
3. Baker & Crowe, Guide to Jobling Glass.
4. Sheets, Southwest Missouri State University, Private Communication.
5. Murray Sheilagh & Haggith John, *Estimation of Uranium in Colored Glass* 1973.

Chapter 5. Density of Glass

1. Elvelle E M – *English Table Glass*, p257-259.
2. Slack R – *English Pressed Glass*, p 103.
3. Slack R – *English Pressed Glass*, p 113.
4. Westmoreland J – *The Glass Cone*, p 4-5, No. 65, Autumn, 2003

Chapter 6. Who Made it and When?

1. Correspondence, *Glass Cone, No 64*, Summer 2003, p 9-10. No 63, Spring 2003, p 12. No 62, Winter 2002, p 6. No 61, Autumn 2002, p 7.
2. Buckley, Francis, *Old English Glasshouses*, Society of Glass Technology, 2003. ISBN 0-900682-46-9
3. Slack, R. *English Pressed Glass*
4. Thompson, J. *Identification of English Pressed Glass.*
5. *Glass Association*, Registration Numbers 1908-1945.
6. Pullin, A. G. *Trademarks and Trade Names from Seventh to the Twentieth Century.*
7. E-mail: archives.centre@dudley.gov.uk
8. Pellatt A, *Curiosities of Glass Making*, p 84-85

Chapter 7. North East England

1. Ashurst, Denis, *The History of South Yorkshire Glass*, Alden press, ISBN 0 906090 46 6, 1992. p 73.

Chapter 8. Bagley & Company

1. Bowey, Angela and Derek and Betty Parsons. *Bagley Glass*, CD, OAR Publishing, PO Box 113, PA1 HIA, NZ. 2004.

Chapter 9. Davidson of Gateshead

1. Murray, Dr Sheilagh. *Peacock and the Lions*. Oriel Press, ISBN 0-85362.
2. Slack, Raymond. *English Pressed Glass, 1830 – 1900*. Barrie & Jenkins, ISBN 0-7126-1871-6.
3. Lattimore, Colin. *English 19th Century Press Moulded Glass*. Barrie & Jenkins ISBN 0-214-20598-3.
4. Thompson, Jenny. *Identification of English Pressed Glass, 1842 – 1908*. self-published. ISBN 0-9515491-0-3.
5. Stewart, Chris and Val. *Davidson Glass a History*, self-published. ISBN 0-9550363-0-5.
6. *George Davidson & Co. Catalogue No 1 & 2 with additional pages from 1903 & 1910*. Pressed Glass Collectors Club Publication. May, 2005.

Chapter 10. Edward Moore & Company

1. Edward Moore, Unregistered Glass C1870, Pressed Glass Collectors Club, UK.

Chapter 11. Greener and Jobling

1. Sue Davis, *Pictorial Guide to Vaseline Glass*, Schiffer Publishing, 2002, p 137.

Chapter 13. North West England

1. Francis Buckley, *Old English Glasshouses*, pp 213–235.

Chapter 14. Edward Bolton, Orford Lane Glassworks

1. Lattimore, C. R. *English 19th-Century Press Moulded Glass*, p 110-111.

Chapter 19. London

1. "Old English Glasshouses," *Society of Glass Technology*, 2003. p. 174 – 193.

Chapter 20. Nazzing Glass Works

1. "75 Years of Glassmaking to the World," *A Celebration of Nazing Glass Works 1928 - 2003*. Self-published, 2003.

Chapter 22. James Powel, Whitefriars

1. Evans W et al. *Whitefriars Glass*, p 240.
2. Jackson, *Whitefriars Glass*, Plate 83.
3. Jackson, *Whitefriars Glass*, Plate 23.

Chapter 23. English Midlands

1. Northwood J. *John Northwood, His Contribution to The Stourbridge Flint Glass Industry, 1850 – 1902*. Mark & Moody, 1958.

Chapter 24. Etna Fling Glass Works, Birmingham

1. Alex Werner, "The Wyllie Family of London," *Journal of the Glass Association*, Vol 7, 2004.

Chapter 25. Richardsons of Wordsley

1. Hajdamach C, *British Glass*, p 95–130
2. Manley, C, *Decorative Victorian Glass*, numerous pages.
3. Eveson, S., Chief Chemist, retired, Thomas Webb & Sons. Private communication.

Chapter 28 Walsh Glass (John Walsh Walsh)

1. Reynolds, Eric, *The Glass of John Walsh Walsh*, Richard Denis, England, TA19 OLE. ISBN 0903685744.
2. Reynolds Eric, private communication.
3. Reynolds Eric, P3, *The Glass of John Walsh Walsh Newsletter*, Spring/Summer, 2000.

Chapter 29. Thomas Webb & Sons

1. Eveson S R - Sixty years with the crystal glass industry. Society of Glass Technology, Glass technology, Vol 31, 1990.
2. Old English Fairy Night Light Advertisement, Marking Times, (Journal of the Pressed Glass Association), No. 38, Summer 2005, p 6.
3. Eveson, S. R. Private Communication.

Chapter 31. Edinburgh Crystal

1. Woodward, H. W.,*The Story of Edinburgh Crystal*, Dema Glass Ltd., 1984.

Chapter 32

1. David A Peterson, *Vaseline Glass*, p 44 Item 182.
2. Glickman, Jay *Yellow Green Vaseline*, p 54.
3. Glickman, Jay,*Yellow Green Vaseline*, Item 365
4. Pullin A G, *Glass Signatures, Trade Marks, and Trade Names*, p 228-9

Chapter 42 Vases and Flower Holders

Manley, C. *Decorative Victorian Glass*, p 24.

Chapter 44. Plates, Dishes, and Tazzas

1. Dodsworth, R. *Glass Between the Wars*, p 73.

Chapter 49

1. Brian Bowley, *Ceramic Review*, Issue 211, Jan/Feb 2005, p. 55.
2. Maria Bettis, *Journal of Environment*, Vol. 64 (2003), p. 113-119.

Bibliography and References

Angus-Butterworth L M. *British Table and Ornamental Glass.* Leonard Hill Books Ltd., London 1956.

Arnold, Ken. *Australian Glass, 1900 - 1950, Valuation Guide.* Crown Castleton Publishers, Australia. ISBN 0 9587953 6 3.

Ashurst, Denis. *The History of South Yorkshire Glass,* Alden Press. ISBN 0 906090 46 6, 1992.

Baker, J. and Crowe, K. *A Collector's Guide to Jobling 1930's Decorative Glass*, Tyne & Wear County Council Museums, 1985. ISBN 0 905974 25 5.

Bowey, Angela; Parsons, Derek & Betty. *Bagley Glass*, CD 2004, OAR Publishing, PO Box 113, PA1 HIA, NZ.

Billings, Sean & Johanna. *Peachblow Glass, Collector's Identification & Price Guide*. Krause Publications, USA, ISBN 0-87341-971-5.

Brill, Robert H; Fleischer, Robert L; Burford, Price P; Walker, Robert M. "The Fission Track Dating of Man-Made Glasses: Preliminary Results." *Journal of Glass Studies,* Vol. VI 1964.

Buckley, Francis. "Old English Glass Houses," (Series of Papers 1924-5) *Society Glass Technology,* 2003. ISBN 0-900682-46-9.

Cable, M, and Smedley, J W. "William Vernon Harcourt: Pioneer Glass Scientist and Founder of the British Association," *Glass Technology*, Vol 33 No 3 June 1992.

Caley, Earle R. *Analyses of Ancient Glasses 1790-1957. A Comprehensive and Critical Survey*, The Corning Glass Museum, Corning Glass Centre, Corning, New York, 1962.

Cardis et al. *British Medical Journal 331*, 9 July 2005, p 77 – 80.

Cottle, Simon. *Sowerby Gateshead Glass,* Tyne and Wear Museums Service, July 1986, ISBN 0 905974 27 1.

Davis, Sue. *Pictorial Guide to Vaseline Glass,* Schiffer 2002. ISBN 0-7643-1644-3.

Dearden, C P, Ex-Technical Director, Bagley & Co, Knottingly, Yorkshire.

Dodsworth, Roger, *British Glass Between the Wars*, Dudley Metro.olitan Borough Council. ISBN 0 900911 220.

Dodsworth, Roger. *The Royal Brierley Collection of English Glass*, Sotheby's, London 1998.

Dudley Public Records Office, West Midlands, E-mail address – archives.centre@dudley.gov.uk.

"Editorial Comment," *Journal of Radiation Protection,* V 25, N0 3, 2005. ISSN 0952-4746.

Elville E M. *English Table Glass*, London Country Life Ltd.

Evans, W. Ross C, Werner A, *Whitefriars Glass*, James Powell & Sons of London, Museum of London, 1995. ISBN 0 904818 56X.

Eveson, S R, retired Technical Director, Thomas Webb & Sons.

Eveson, S R, "Reflections, Sixty Years with the Crystal Glass Industry," *Glass Technology,* Vol 31 1990.

Fleischer, R L and Price, P B. "Uranium Contents of Ancient Man-Made Glass," *General Electric Research Laboratory Report No 64-RL-3634M*, March 1964, Schenectady, New York.

Fleischer, R L and Price, P B. "Uranium Contents of Ancient Man-Made Glass," *General Electric Research Laboratory Report,* Reprint 8479, Schenectady, New York.

Freestone, Dr Ian, "Romans & Uranium Glass - a Red Herring Question?" Letter to *Nuclear Europe Worldscan*, p 45, 1-2, 1998

Gilbert, C S. *An Historical Survey of the County of Cornwall*, Plymouth, 1817.

Glass Association, Registration Numbers 1908-1945, February 1996. Broadfield House Glass Museum, Dudley, England.

"Glass Cone," *The Glass Association, Correspondence*, p 7, No 61 Autumn 2002; p 12, No 62, Winter 2002: p12 No 63 Spring 2003; p 9-10, Summer 2003.

Glickman, Jay L. *Yellow-Green Vaseline. A Guide to the Magic Glass*, Antique Publications, Marietta, Ohio, 1991. ISBN #0-915410-76-1.

Graziano, J H and Blum, C. "Lead Exposure from Lead Crystal," pp141 -142, *Lancet 337*, 1991.

Greenwood, N N and Earnshaw, A. *Chemistry of the Elements*, Butterworth, ISBN 075628324.

Gulliver, Mervyn. *Victorian Decorative Glass, British Designs 1850-1914*, Schiffer 2002, ISBN 0-7643-1597-8.

Gunther, R T. "A Mural Glass Mosaic from the Imperial Roman Villa Near Naples," *Archaeologia*, pp99-105, Vol 63, 1912.

Hajamach, Charles R. *British Glass 1800-1914,* Antique Collectors Club. ISBN 1-85149-141-4.

Heacock, William. *Fenton Glass, The First Twenty-five Years.* O-Val Advertising Corp., Marietta, Ohio, 1978.

Heacock, William. *Fenton Glass, The Second Twenty-five Years.* O-Val Advertising Corp., Marietta, Ohio, 1980.

Heacock, William. *Fenton Glass, The Third Twenty-five Years.* O-Val Advertising Corp., Marietta, Ohio, 1989, ISBN 0-915410-36-2.

Jackson, J H. "Depleted Uranium: A Study of its Uses within the UK and Disposal Issues." *R & D Technical Report P3-088/TR*, Environment Agency. ISBN 1 85705 524 1.

Jackson, Lesley. *Whitefriars Glass, The Art of James Powell & Sons*, Richard Dennis, 1996. ISBN 0 903685.

James, A J L Frank. "The Military Context of Chemistry; The Case of Michael Faraday," *Bull. Hist. Chem.* 11 (1991).

Klein, Dan; Lloyd, Ward. *The History of Glass*, Macdonald & Co. (publishers) Ltd., 1989. ISBN 0-7481-0246-9.

Landa, Edward R. and Councell, Terry B. "Leaching of Uranium from Glass and Ceramic Foodware and Decorative Items," *Health Physics,* pp343-347, Vol 63, No 3, 1992.

Lattimore, Colin R. *English 19th Century Press-Moulded Glass*, Barrie & Jenkins. ISBN 0-214-20598-3.

Lesser, Richard. "Bref apercu de l'histoire non nucleaire de l'element uranium." *Revue Generale Nucleaire 1989*. pp453-454, No 6, Novembre-Decembre,

Manley, Cyril. *Decorative Victorian Glass*, Ward Lock Ltd., London. ISBN 0-7063-6644-1.

Marking Times, Journal of the Pressed Glass Collectors Club, Birmingham B35 6BB, UK.

McDonald, David, Former Director of Johnson Matthey, unpublished research into the history of the Cock family. Courtesy of Johnson Matthey & Co. Ltd.

McDonald, David, *Percival Norton Johnson, The Biography of a Pioneer Metallurgist*. Johnson Matthey & Co. Ltd., 1951.

McKearin, George and Helen. *American Glass*, Crown Publications, New York.

Molineaux Webb Trade Catalogue. Trade Catalogues, believed to be Molineaux Webb and without doubt about 1851 or later, in possession of Manchester City Art Galleries, Manchester, England.

Morey, George. *The Properties of Glass*, Second Edition, Reinhold Publishing Corp. New York.

Murray, Dr Sheilagh. *The Peacock and the Lions*, Oriel Press. ISBN 0 85362 1951.

Northwood, John. *John Northwood, His Contribution to The Stourbridge Flint Glass Industry 1850-1902*. Mark and Moody Ltd, Stourbridge, 1958.

Nuclear Issues, 12 Ruvigny Mansions, London SW15 1LE, Vol 26, No 12, December 2004 ISSN 1367 X.

Partington, Prof. J R. *General and Inorganic Chemistry,* 2nd Edition, Macmillian, 1951.

Pellatt, Apsley. *Curiosities of Glass Making.* Original publication David Bogue, London 1849. Reprinted 1968 by Ceramic Book Company, Newport, Mon. England. (the reference quoted applies to the reprint).

Percival Vickers & Co. Trade Catalogues.Manchester City Art Galleries, Manchester, England.

Peterson, David, *Vaseline Glass; Canary to Contemporary*, The Glass Press Inc. Marietta, 2002. ISBN 1-57080-088-X.

Pollock-Hill, S. Managing Director, Nazeing Glass Works Ltd., Broxbourne, Herts. EN10 6SU, England.

Pressed Glass Collectors Club, 4 Bowshot Close, Castle Bromwich, West Midlands, B36 9UH, England.

Pullin, Anne Geffken. T*rademarks and trade Names from the Seventeenth to the Twentieth Century*, Walace-Homestead book Company, Pennsylvania. ISBN 0-87069-462-6.

Revi, Albert Christian. *Nineteenth Century Glass.* Schiffer Publishing Ltd., ISBN 0-916838-43-9.

Reynolds, Eric. *The Glass of John Walsh Walsh, 1850 -1951.* Richard Dennis, England., TA19 OLE. ISBN 0 903685 744.

Sheets, Prof. Ralph and Thompson, CC. *Thorium in Collectible Glassware*, Chemistry Department, Southwest Missouri State University.

Slack, Raymond. *English Pressed Glass, 1830-1900*, Barrie & Jenkins, ISBN 0-7126-1871-6.

Snow, Dr P J D. "Letter to Editor," *Glass Cone,* Journal of Glass Association, UK, p8, No. 41, Spring, 1996.

Stewart, Chris & Val. *Davidson Glass a History*, self-published. ISBN 0-9550363-0-5.

Taylor J R. Senior Technical Manager, Cookson Minerals Ltd., Stoke-on-Trent. Personal Communication, May, 1990.

Thompson, Jenny, *The Identification of English Pressed Glass.* 1842-1908. by Mrs Jenny Thompson. ISBN 0-9515491-0-3 and Supplement ISBN 0-9515491-1-1.

Timberlake, Geof. "Researching Nazeing Glass," Unpublished Lecture to Glass Association, 29/10/99.

Timberlake, Geoffrey, "75 years of diverse Glass-making to the World, A celebration of Nazing Glass Works 1928 – 2003." Self-published 2003.

Tooley, Dr Fay. *Handbook of Glass Manufacture,* 3rd Edition, Vol. II. Ashlee Publishing Co., New York.

UKAEA United Kingdom Atomic Energy Authority, *Windscale Report* PG Report 403 (W). Unclassified 1962.

Wade, Dr D. "Book and Software Reviews," *Glass Circle News*, No 97, p 9.

Westmoreland, J. *The Glass Cone,* (The Glass Association), p4-5, No. 65, Autumn, 2003.

Werner, Alex, "The Wyllie Family of London," *Journal of the Glass Association,* V 7, 2004.

Weyl, Woldemar A. *Coloured Glass*, Society of Glass Technology, Sheffield. Reprinted by Dawson's of Pall Mall, London, 1959.

Whitefriars Stock Book 1836, Museum of London, Whitefriars Folio 2 ref. 2.

Whitefriars Recipe Book 1832, Museum of London, Archive 3118/10

Wilkson, R. *The Hallmarks of Antique Glass*, Richard Madley Ltd., London, 1968.

Wills, Geoffrey, *Antique Glass for Pleasure and Investment*, John Gifford Ltd., London. ISBN 70710222-7.

Woodward, H W. *Art, Feat, and Mystery. The Story of Thomas Webb & Sons*, Mark & Moody Ltd., Stourbridge. ISBN 0-9506439-04.

Woodward, H W. *The Story of Edinburgh Crystal,* Dema Glass Ltd, 1984.

Yates, Barbara. "The Glassware of Percival Vickers & Co. Ltd., Jersey Street, Manchester, 1844-1914." Journal of the Glass Association, pp29-40, Vol 2, 1987. ISBN 0 9510736 13. ISSN 0951-3108.

Index